I0415125

Zimbabwe my home my frustration: Articles of defiance

Elliot Pfebve

Copyright © 2012 Elliot Pfebve

All rights reserved.

2nd Edition

ISBN: 1460907620
ISBN-13: 978-1460907627

LCCN:

DEDICATION

I would like to start by dedicating this book to my brother Mathew who was murdered by the ZANU (PF) thugs in pursuit of true freedom for Zimbabwe. Great thanks go to my family whom without their support I would not have accomplished the task of writing this book, my son Gerald for the assistance in cover design. Great inspiration came from my parents, Sinoia and Serena who had over the decade bore the brunt of a brutal regime including being abducted and tortured several times yet remained focused and determined to support me in the quest to bring about real freedom and the rule of law in Zimbabwe.

Great Support also came from my party colleagues in the Movement for Democratic Change (MDC), who provided me with valuable resources and photographic evidence making this book a vivid living memory of a brutal regime bent on persecuting its own citizens.

CONTENTS

ACKNOWLEDGMENTS

My sincere acknowledgements go to MDC Zimbabwe for the access to a wealth of information archives regarding the brutality perpetrated by the Mugabe regime against innocent civilians. Nampa-Reuters for the information regarding coverage on the murder of my brother Mathew . The ABC archives regarding the information about the 1970s protected villages set up by the then Rhodesia government of Ian Smith, during the UDI, The Zimbabwe Daily News and Financial gazette for the wealth of resources in their articles, and many more who contributed to my resources for this book that I may have omitted.

1 ZIMBABWE THE HISTORICAL PERSPECTIVE

Zimbabwe is home to a Bantu group of South and Central Africa. The Black Zimbabweans are divided into two main tribes, the Shona people who constitute 75% of the total population and the Ndebele representing about 20%. The Shona people are further divided into fragmented into small dialects such as the Manyika, Vhitori, Kore Kore and the Tavara otherwise all collectively known as the Shona. The Shona has lived in the country the longest and are the majority language group. The Ndebele people speak a language known as Sindebele similar to Zulu and are believed to have arrived in Zimbabwe about 150 years ago as a breakaway tribe from Zulu of South Africa. The Ndebele a skilled warrior tribe, dominated over the Shona tribe until the occupation of Rhodesia by whites in 1890.

Zimbabwe was colonised by the British in September 1890 by Cecil John Rhodes who named it Rhodesia after his name. Zimbabwe became under the British South Africa Company administration. Zimbabwe was annexed by the United Kingdom in 1923 and thus became part of the British Empire. Through a series of land apportionment acts, white settlers reposed land from the black majority evicting them to region 5 with barren and non productive land. In September 1953, the Rhodesia federation was formed involving Southern Rhodesia (Zimbabwe), Northern Rhodesia (Zambia) and Nyasaland (Malawi) hence these three countries became one until the fall of the federation in 1963. Both Zambia and Malawi became independent in 1964.

The whites in Rhodesia had amassed so much wealth that they were not prepared to surrender the country to a black majority rule. In April 1964, Prime Minster Winston Field a moderate was replaced by Ian Smith with his Rhodesian Front Party. Despite the British's intervention for the white minority in Zimbabwe to share power with the black majority, the whites were not ready to relinquish their dominant position. On November 11, Ian Smith declared a Unilateral Declaration of Independence (UDI) from the United Kingdom. The British and the United Nations slapped the rebellious Rhodesia with sanctions in November 1965. On December 16, 1966, Rhodesia became the first state to be slapped with mandatory economic sanctions by UN Security Council. A nationalist movement grew in the 1960s opposed to the oppressive white rule. Zimbabwe African Peoples Union (ZAPU) was formed in 1963. After a series of arrests and power struggle the Zimbabwe African Union (ZANU) became a breakaway party in 1963.

ZAPU and ZANU became the main guerrilla movements fighting for the independence of Zimbabwe. ZAPU was based in Zambia and ZANU in Mozambique. The two parties eventually formed the Patriotic Front PF ZAPU and ZANU (PF). Zipla and Zanla became the guerrilla armies of the two parties. After a bitter struggle, the whites conceded to a settlement and in 1979 at the Lancaster House conference, an agreement was signed for a majority one man one vote election. The conference was facilitated by then Prime Minister Margaret Thatcher.

In the elections of April 1980, Robert Mugabe then the President of ZANU (PF) won the first democratic election with 57 seats. Smith's party won 20 and Nkomo of PF ZAPU 20, with Muzorewa's UANC getting 3. At the time of writing this book, Mugabe is still the President 27 years after independence. He has defied all pressure to pass the torch of leadership to the new generation regardless of the fact that he remains politically marooned with targeted sanctions by the European Union and the United States.

The dangers of a Zimbabwean politician the facts

The Zimbabwean political saga is a complex one, its casualties far much more than the pen can write and its social impact disastrous. The world will never fully understand it. It takes the soul within to understand it, yet it means to be tortured, murdered, raped and imprisoned to fully understand it. How many would be prepared to go through this ordeal for the sake of writing a story? This account is about a man who grew up in a bloody ring of politics in Zimbabwe, detained for confronting authority, arrested for his birthright, businesses ransacked, property destroyed and family members maimed and murdered. This account transverse the valleys of power struggle in the two most powerful political parties in Zimbabwe MDC and ZANU (PF). From the ruthless regime of Robert Mugabe to the struggle within struggles in both parties to control this rich Southern African country leaving a trail of destruction never to be seen in the history of the country. The economy in ruins and the infrastructure shattered. Man became the enemy of man forcing over 3 million people in exile, three times the population of neighbouring Botswana, and all but few the highly educated and skilled manpower. No sane nationalist would claim victory over such calamity for whatever reason. In trying to be makers of history we have become the enemy of history.

Zimbabwe, conflict analysis who is who?

Zimbabwe conflict might fast slip into a civil war if the International Community does not heed the numerous early warning reports widely publicised by conflict resolution watchdogs, then another Rwanda-like genocide is in the making. The violent seizure of farms, state sponsored terror by police, army, militia and war veterans, murders, rape, repressive laws, gross human rights violation, state inflicted poverty and the degeneration of the rule of law all are recipes for a bloody civil war in the making. There is a limit to human submission to oppression and Zimbabwe has long passed a conflict development phase, what remains is a trigger event. All this is targeted at opposition the MDC, the white farmers and the civic society.

The formation of a labour driven opposition party MDC was necessitated by poor governance, resulting in high inflation rate causing the economic meltdown. An unemployment rate of over 70% by 1999 and the poor government human rights record were a push factor for the launch of the MDC which almost unseated Robert Mugabe only 6 months after its launch. Mugabe responded with systematic state sponsored violence and indiscriminate arrests of opposition members and many continue to be murdered by security and ZANU (PF) supporters with impunity. While MDC was formed to gain power through democratic elections Mugabe continue to survive through election rigging, violence and persecution of perceived opponents which includes destruction of property like the ethnic cleansing in the Darfur region of Western Sudan by Janjaweed. This is not the first time Mugabe has used violence to silence dissent, in the 1980s, Mugabe pursued an ethnic cleansing against the Ndebele people in the South West of Zimbabwe who predominantly supported a rival party ZAPU, killed approximately 6,000 civilians according to a report by the Catholic Commission for Justice and Peace (CCJP). Some reports estimate the number murdered to more than 20,000, the International Community did not intervene.

This is an asymmetric conflict which means the state have all its military hardware at its disposal. Its military security is compounded by the use of partisan police and army against defenceless opposition members. More violent have been the use of the 1970s war veterans and a continuation of forcible inscription of youth into a militia brigade which has committed numerous atrocities. ZANU (PF) has been seen to use all government forces to eliminate its opponents. The MDC with no military hardware and institutions remain at the receiving end.

ZANU (PF) is physically secure, given the situation that it uses all its military resources to perpetuate an orgy of violence. The courts which have been militarised, now only serve the interest of ZAN (PF) and as a result thousands of people languish in prison accused of politically motivated crimes never committed. In fact, in Zimbabwe there is no distinction between ZANU (PF) party and government. All elections are marred by violence and each time the opposition are at the receiving end hence physically insecure.

While the country's economy has been in the free fall, ZANU (PF) uses state money & resources to finance its violence against the MDC. The government has passed a law, Political Funding Bill that banned any outside organizations from funding political parties in Zimbabwe leaving the MDC in serious financial crisis. Looking at these facts, ZANU (PF) is economically secure and MDC is not.

Ecologically, MDC is not secure, the ZANU (PF) government has used food as a political tool including even donor food, ensuring that only its supporters get the food. In some remote areas, MDC supporters have been denied access to health care and water facilities. The controversial Operation Murambatsvina, the government targeted opposition strongholds to destroy houses causing over 700 families homeless in Harare and Bulawayo.

ZANU (PF) enjoys societal security while MDC continues to be at the receiving end. The opposition support base has been targeted causing massive brain drain to all over the World. Freedom of association has been severely curtailed as many rural areas remained closed out to opposition supporters. The social values and culture has been severely disrupted as massive internal displacement continues unabated.

Neither the ZANU (PF) government nor the MDC are politically secure. The reason why the government is using violence to stay in power, is because it feels insecure against a popular MDC party which has muscled itself in politics with a massive support base. It is partially secure in the sense that through the use of force it is able to impose its will on people. MDC, with a minority seats in parliament, can only watch Mugabe enacting new harsh laws against it.

In contrast to other conflicts, Mugabe remains popular with African governments because of his ability to hoodwink them into believing that the conflict in Zimbabwe is racially motivated, between Tony Blair and Robert Mugabe over the land issue. The fact of the matter is that Mugabe is only using the land issue as an escape goat to obliterate the opposition from the political scene in

Zimbabwe. Many commentators have warned that all signs in Zimbabwe resemble that of humanitarian catastrophe like that of Darfur, Rwanda, Yugoslavia and Republic of Congo. With the World still blood bathing in Iraq and Afghanistan, can the World ignore Zimbabwe?

2 GROWING UP IN AFRICAN CONTEXT

My Childhood, an African perspective.

I was born in Nyakatondo, an impoverished village 250 km north of the capital Zimbabwe. This is a fertile agricultural land near the Mozambique border called Mukumbura, divided by the Mukumbura River. The inhabitants are peasant farmers. The land stretching along the river banks is a hive of agricultural activity all year round from gardening to small scale farming. This river for generations after generations has united the two nations together. Livestock and people from both countries draw their water from this river that eventually off load its water into the Zambezi River. Victoria Falls, one of the "Seven Wonders of the World" is found on the banks of the Zambezi River. Both Mozambicans and Zimbabweans regard the river as a symbol of their heritage and over the years have learned to mix freely without hindrance. Both governments accepted the need to waive any travel documents between the two sides up to today. This is the only border, without restriction in Zimbabwe and the Mozambican side. Intermarriages have occurred because of the symbolic importance of the river.

I was born 9 February 1969 of a Carpenter and a housewife, I am the 6th born in a family of 10 inclusive of a set of twins. My father Sinoia and mother Serena were respectable parents in the village. My father was a retired carpenter having worked in then Salisbury now Harare for his entire working life. Typical of workforce those years, we never grew up with him in town but he would come occasionally to see us and shower us with gifts and new clothes. The laws of the then Rhodesia did not allow non working people in the hostels or worker's lodges as they were called. Many children in rural areas grew up with their mothers and only seeing their fathers once a while. We grew up marvelling the hard work of my mother Serena; she was so hard working that she was highly respected by the whole village and beyond. My father born 1925 was the only of his age that could read and write. He had a good communication of English that no-one believed him that he taught himself to read and write. Even we the children find it hard to believe that he taught himself the language that we find ourselves difficult to master in full time education. Whatever the truth we were proud of his intelligence, after all he was a carpenter, a prestigious profession of those times. Many of those whom we knew were gardeners, wrongly addressed as "garden boys". He made sure that all his children went to school and those opposed to education were put to strict discipline. As a result no family in this village was as educated as the Pfebve family at the time of printing this book.

My elder brother Mathew was one of the first in the village to go to a boarding school, Mavhuradona Mission School, run by the Evangelical church along the Mavhuradona mountain range. After finishing his studies he enrolled for a diploma in Carpentry following the footsteps of my father. After a long career in the carpentry industry he left and joined the police force. He rose through the ranks to become an Inspector in the force. He retired in March 2000 after 22 years of service, only to be murdered exactly a month later by the same government he saved for 22 years, he died at the age of 50. He lived a wife and 5 children, unfortunately by then Mugabe has become obsessed with power and was determined to wipe out the Pfebve family whom he believed were opposed to his rule of terror. He knew the family had regional influence and indeed he was right, by then I was a National Executive Member (in the policy making body of the powerful newly formed MDC), shadow MP for Bindura and National Executive in charge of Mashonaland Central province (In charge of 10 constituencies). My second brother Ephraim Pfebve, a retired police officer was the shadow MP for MT. Darwin North, including our village Nyakatondo. My sister Ephurida was the chairwoman of the province. I was born in a family of 5 men and 5 women and at the time of writing this book 8 are surviving members of the family, 4 women and 4 men.

Like most children of my age those days, I grew up in love with football. We used to play football made of plastic papers. It was one of the universal sports of the time. We could call up names like

Pele and George Shaya, yet none of us knew the significance of those names. They were like types of football games to most of us. I enjoyed the social gatherings associated with it rather than the real game. I grew up a shy and naïve boy yet liked by many for being well mannered and tough looking. During those years all children would herd cattle before going to school, I mean it was not surprising to see a boy of 6 herding cattle. Some children were not even allowed to go to school by their parents but would move from one household to other herding cattle for a reward. The reward was in most cases a heifer after three years of active herding cattle. Parents would then confiscate the heifers for their own wealth, in this way they were using children to amass wealth. In so doing the more children you have the more wealthy you were likely to have. Not that it encouraged a baby boom but contraceptives were not available, so whichever way nature was left to take its course. They were many games played out in the forest herding cattle including fighting, by the way not boxing but blood fighting. I loved the sport but never participated, all I was interested in was to watch and applaud. Each time the fight ended in a blood defeat, the more I felt I could have done better if I was in the ring. I am sure I was not alone, it's humane to see defects from the bench rather than being physically in the ring. Names like Mohammad Ali would feature much during these fights although nobody could explain what the name stood for.

I grew up disliking my father who did not want his children to be associated with herding cattle not alone our own cattle. He wanted all his children to be groomed to go to school early and to pass. I remember being beaten for having sneaked to accompany the worker who was herding our cattle. I felt my father was a bit hash for I did not see the significance of education by then. Everybody was talking about hunting and games played in the forest herding cattle. I looked stupid to listen to stories I could not understand, nobody for whatever reason can be comfortable with ignorance of facts. I needed to be part and parcel of the heritage, to me it was like denying me of my childhood, after all I was not old enough to go to school, I was only 5. During those days school going age was 7 years and sometimes 8 to 10. It was not about birth certificates, it was about whether you will be able to hold your left ear with your right hand. This meant that if you had a short hand, you will never go to school. The nearest primary school was about 7 km away and not most children were comfortable with the distance, the only buses would leave early in the morning and arrive in the evening. None of their timetables were suitable for students' programmes. Even if the buses were available few could have afforded the fares. At that time education was not of any importance to me but the participation in social values was important to me, it was tangible and real. The rewards were immediate, you gained respect in society for being part of it and toughened by the harsh weather.

I remember one day I sneaked out of the house to follow my nephew who was the principal cattle herder of the family, his name was Claude. His father who is my mother's brother was a skilled hunter and well known in his trade. His children grew up knowing the trade more than other children of their age. I liked him because I learned quite a lot from him. During those days cattle rearing was the symbol of African wealth, the more herd of cattle one had the more you could afford anything. Herding cattle were done in groups of 5 households or even more. It was important for security reason because when communities met there were always fights for the control of grazing land and sometimes just for the fun of it. Claude was about 6 years older than me and I trusted him to defend me apart from being a bully he always moved with his pack of vicious dogs. It was early in the morning when we set off with a herd of cattle in the valleys beyond. We were joined by two other boys all with a herd of cattle and dogs. By the mid day we had killed a buck and a hare. We made a fire and roasted the beasts; there was always salt available, salt from the river banks. It was natural and taste. I enjoyed the meat and this part of the game was the one I cherished most, hunting and roasting the kill.

Later in the afternoon it started to rain, rain after rain and eventually it was raining cats and dogs. The rivers became valleys and valleys became fields it was frightening. Lightening was every way and I feared for my life since I have never seen such rain before. I was the youngest in the group and a young man whom I later learned was called Kamuchiriko Bande grabbed my hand and started running with me towards home. It was so fierce that we got lost and we were marooned by rivers. It was not easy to tell whether there was a river or not, all I can remember was that there was water everywhere. We climbed in trees to avoid sinking until the rain stopped. By the time the rain stopped nobody knew where we were, we started walking, I mean just walking. I learned later that we were going in the wrong direction and we ended being in Mozambique at a village called Muteresi. We were then accompanied by a well wisher half way, showing us the direction. I have no idea how we ended up in another country, although Mozambique is 5 km from our village, my surprise was in the direction rather than in the distance. When I got home, my family was looking for me everywhere and by then it was deep into the night. I knew I was going to be beaten so I decided not to go home straight but to go to my uncle first and ask him to accompany me. I knew that was the safest thing to do, not that I hatched the idea, no, but that the other boys' assistant me. My uncle accompanied me home and I temporarily gained my freedom only to be beaten after he had gone. I was warned never to go with the boys again. I regretted having gone in the first place but I was consoled by the fact that I enjoyed myself and learned quite a lot though the hard way.

Soon it was May 1975 and the rumours had it that the Smith regime was coming to arrest all men in the village for what reason nobody knew. The men were always sleeping in the bush to avoid the arrest. For weeks nothing happened and eventually it was dismissed as rumours. Only a week passed before trucks with armed soldiers surrounded the village. Everybody was forced in the trucks, some managed to run away. People were told to carry food for three days only, the reason why and where, we were being taken was never explained except to say that there was a meeting to be attended. Nobody believed them, what type of meeting would force kids and elderly to attend. I was sure something bad was about to happen. I had heard that there was war in the country during those days but I had never seen a gun myself. The sight of them this time terrified me. Yes I have heard gun fire before but that was in neighbouring Mozambique but not in Zimbabwe. The war in Mozambique was now over so we were told, not that it mattered to me because I was too young to understand it. Children of my age group all it mattered were playing street football and games like dunhu and goso. Eventually we were taken to Mukumbura protected village. It was like an open cast jail with high security fence right round and one gate. Robin Wright (January 5 1976) once wrote for the ABC Evening News;

Deeper into the fertile Zambesi Valley, less than two miles from the Rhodesia-Mozambique border, the richly wooded terrain suddenly breaks and a massive, barbwire-fenced village comes into view. Tightly guarded by Rhodesian soldiers, it could pass as a detention camp, army station or frontier outpost.

But it is none of these. The site is one of Rhodesia's now "protected villages" — the camps set up in the area of terrorist activity to guard the local population from assault — and one of the most controversial measures enacted by the government of Prime Minister Ian Smith in recent months.

There were other villagers in the *protected village*, which we did not know but learned later that they came from Rushinga 80 km from our village. We were told that this was going to be our new home. There were no houses and it was during winter, I could not bear the chilly weather but worse still I felt pity for my sister Fassy who was only 3 months old. There were only 3 blocks of toilets and bathrooms to a population of close 5,000 people. The gate was guarded and everybody was issued with an ID card bearing one's face. You would leave your pass at the gate each time you go out and nobody was allowed to be out after 6pm. Wright further wrote;

And the army presence is blatant. In the fields, armed black soldiers walk in front of and behind the workers as they till the land with hoes, directing action through a loudspeaker. Guards oversee all construction projects. And scattered around the camp are tents housing the soldiers who guard the villages at night...Government officials acknowledge there is a "slight departure from the normal regulation scheme" of the tribal trust lands, the rural black settlements throughout the country. Among the measures: a dusk to dawn curfew, registration of all people over thirteen years of age, and regulation of all people passing in or out of the camps. Thus at a young age I was caught in this web of cross fire between the Smith regime and the guerrilla giving rise to trauma, destruction of African lifestyle and inhuman degradation of the highest order. In 1975 my political life was born and every year from then on was a march to self determination crossing rivers of blood and tears. Today decades after, every molecule of my energy has been invested in fighting for global peace and justice. The knowledge that Robert Mugabe who knows much of what the people Zimbabwe went through to attain independence would revisit the use of torture, murder, rape and persecution against his own people for personal political expedience is profoundly beyond human disbelief.

The war intensified and the situation became desperate. Ian Smith then Prime Minster of Rhodesia (now Zimbabwe) was waging a war against the liberation movements, ZANU and ZAPU. The erection of the protected villages was a way of trying to isolate the freedom fighters. The government of the day made a big mistake because instead of silencing the war, they fuelled it. Gradually we got used to the lifestyle in the "Keep" as it was literally known. There were two *keeps* at Mukumbura and our one was *keep 2*, besides *keep 1*. People quickly built homes made of pole and dagger and did not matter whether you left a better house behind. Everybody lost property and was to start afresh. We became one big family united by the spirit of a raging war everybody was talking about war, war, war everywhere. I still remember, children making guns out of wood carvings and started shooting at each other in a mock battle. Eventually everybody knew why we were there but nobody knew how long we were going to be there. The security manning the gates were known as the DA (District Assistants) and wore khaki uniforms. Half of them could not read or write. This normally caused problem when one wanted to collect his or her pass, it meant that they had to do a facial comparison and most cases they got it wrong. It was common to hear somebody refusing a pass because it was somebody's. Sometimes they were so ruthless that they would beat people for no apparent reason or maybe because you refused a wrong pass. The most notorious of them all, I still remember was called Israel, people mocked him that, he was tall seated than standing, a fearsome man who could hardly write his own name. My father got a job with DDF (District Development Fund), this was under the ministry of roads. He was in charge of all carpentry work at the centre. We were all proud of him for few people from the keep were employed and if ever they were employed it was just for general work. Many continued as peasant farmers although the soils there were less fertile than that of our village where we came from.

Going to School the African way

It was January 1976 summer time in Zimbabwe, school term starts in January. This was my first year at School and I was eager to start although the school was 5 km away. In this area there were no pre- school and the primary school served both purposes. I was lucky enough to be able to write my name before going to school. Not that I taught myself like my father but that in our new founded home there were three students who set up a makeshift learning club. They were all doing grade 5 by that time and they were inspired by *the show off* rather than the need to help us the disadvantaged. The club was only run during weekends and it was always packed, not that all children wanted to learn but the competition to show off for these students was fascinating. Their names were Wilfred, Ofias and Medion. Whatever their motive some of us made the best use of the situation asking probing questions leading to being able to read and write basic language. These people were doing a great service to the society yet none of them so it that way. I enjoyed the sessions and credit my academic foundation to these people. I have not been able to get in touch with them at the time of writing this book except for Wilfred whom I still communicate with through emails. Wilfred is working for Windmill as a cost accountant. I am told Medion is now in Gweru doing pastoral work and Ofias is doing full time farming.

When I arrived at Katarira primary school 5 km way, it was like being born again to me. For the first time in my life I was to attend formal education. I have no idea what this meant in its greater sense but I was determined to be like the three students who gave us the initial training not because it was noble to do so but that I emulated the respect they got out of it. I was asked to hold my left ear and I did it with skill and confidence, the access examination was over in no time. I watched my fellow children failing to hold their ears and being refused enrolment. It was a sad story, I was lucky that I was born tall and tough. Some of those who failed to enroll were older than me but those days that was not important, the important thing was whether you were able to hold your left ear with your right hand. Many people went to school even after turning 10 years and there were so many of them in my class. I do not remember how much they were in our class for I could not count further than 10. The lady teacher was cheerful and we started by singing songs, she has not even had the courtesy of teaching us first but went straight into singing. Many of us were following her lips rather than producing any meaningful words, I could not tell whether she was singing in English or native language Shona. All the same the melody was enjoyable. There were many outdoor activities on that first day contrary to what I expected, I had come fully prepared with my pen and exercise books, ready to write. I got frustrated that we did not write anything, because I wanted to show the teacher that at least I could write my name and that of my surname before having started school. Finally the bell rang and it was time to go home.

My mother was waiting patiently to see if everything went well for the first day. She was happy to see me in uniform for her it was a sign that she had done part of her duty to look after me until school going age. It is every mother's pride who would deny that? I started rehearsing what we had done for the day although I had more blanks in between than real happenings. She seemed to take note of the blanks and fill them in, it really helped me and it showed that over the years she had mastered the trade after all there were 5 children who had been to school before me. When my father came it was like no event has occurred, he never asked about what happened in school. How much I wished he should not have asked me, for I was not sure how he would have reacted given the fact that he was very drunk and looked as if he had 2 too many. Knowing he was unpredictable when he was drunk I kept quiet hoping that tomorrow when I came back from school he would be available for me in his sober state?

The following day was more formal with registration of names and addresses. It was a big problem to the new teacher because we all had one address, *keep 2*. She had just come from the capital then Salisbury now Harare and it took her time to come to terms that the whole class of maybe 35 came from one address. I learned later that my teacher's name was Mrs. Gumbo ironically one of her leg was disabled although she could limp without the aid of clutches. Teachers those days were allowed to discipline children and the extent to which they could do it was left to their discretion hence mostly open to abuse. We were not sure whether the new teacher would be cruel like the others before her whom we learned earlier in our lives to have been obsessed with beating children. Not that the parents did mind, no, but would even come to school to tell the teachers to beat us hard as if beating would make us pass. Back home I saw both my mother and father waiting for me, I guessed my mother could have had a word with my father about his lack of interest in the small boy, it did work. We all spoke at length on various issues of the day from the name of my few friends in the school activities. It was like all of a sudden I was in control of the adult world.

By the time I reached grade 3 the war had intensified and the school had to close. There was 6 months of no school and it was a bad experience to us children who by then were in top gear of schooling. Ever since I started I was always top of the class. I cried and hated the war, I had no idea what this war meant in the first place. There were talks about guerrillas fighting for liberation or was it Rhodesians fighting for independence, the whole thing was confusing to us, nobody seemed to have the answers. After 6 months it was decided that a makeshift school was to be opened near the protected keeps under guard. We have started going to school again this time there were no benches or desks but we sat on rocks and wrote on our laps. In 1979 the war came to an end for the first time we saw the comrades as they were always referred to. People celebrated all over the country finally we were able to return to our villages of origin, again. I had a hazy idea of where we came from. All I needed was to continue with my education I did not understand the politics around my education, I did not care if they kept on fighting for as long as my school was not going to be disturbed. There was much campaign going on those days. I saw many people being forced to attend rallies and most ended up being beaten. The comrades had guns and the villagers were defenseless so they ended up attending pungwe (all night meetings) meetings they did not want. For the first time that is when I heard the name Robert Mugabe, Abel Muzorewa, Chief Chirau, Joshua Nkomo and others. They were always clashes between these parties and worse still the innocent villagers were caught in between. I was 11 years old I hated all the parties for being selfish and bully.

We then moved back to the Nyakatondo village in February 1980 and as expected there was no school to talk about. The school failed to withstand 7 years of isolation and bitter war. There were only heaps of bricks curios to see we went to the site. We did not know that there were landmines planted there. A cousin who was 2 years younger than me, Godfrey Pfudza had his leg ripped off by a landmine and we all scrambled for safety. It was scary, I ran as fast as I could towards our home, I told my parents who were devastated. I had nightmares for weeks that followed, to me the thought of going back to school was questionable. I could not understand that a human being could be as cruel as to plant landmines in a school targeting innocent children. I was not sure whether it was Mugabe or Smith but to me I hated the politicians all the same. Within a month my brother-in-law had his leg blown off by a land mine while ploughing, more incidences followed. Nobody was safe anymore you could not tell which area was safe it was a matter of being lucky to survive. After 6 Months people began to pick up a pattern in the manner the land mines were planted. This helped to avoid further casualties. People are a bit cautious about where to go and where not to even today. However as of today, the landmines continue to count down casualties 30 years after the end of the war, surely somebody must answer for this.

Finally the school was opened but it was decided that the original site was too dangerous so it was then moved elsewhere. On our first day at school we got lost not that we did not see the school but we passed the school several times not knowing that this was the school. There were three blocks made of pole and dagger, never had we seen such a school before. We did not know that this was our new school. There was only one teacher teaching grade one to five his name was Mr. Charlie. Everything did not make sense to me, I was by then in grade five the highest class at the school. I was not sure whether I was in grade five or grade four since all I knew was that I only was in grade four for three months and if I was to be in grade five I was going to be in that class only for 4 months before the year end. Mr. Charlie was keen to see me proceed to grade five. I took his advice and proceeded. There were limited facilities, no chairs, no desks, no books and no pens. There was nothing unusual of a school which has suffered a bitter civil war for more than 8 years. After two weeks, another teacher joined in, his name was Mr. Utseya, and this meant by default that Mr. Charlie became the Headmaster. More teachers followed the following year. I was now in grade six having taken the number one in grade five. Our new teacher was Mr. Chikuvire a young and talented teacher who had just finished his GCE O' Levels. I remember when asked what I wanted to be when I grow up, I bellowed "Politician", I had no idea what was involved to be a politician but after the ordeal that I went through during the war, I was determined that I could make a better politician, at least one who will never plant landmines at schools and villages. Little did I know that this was to be my political strength in life, I was only 12. I was surprised to note that after writing the final Grade Seven examinations, I was the best student with 4 units. The school was proud of me, I then went for Secondary education at Mavhuradona Boarding School. The school was still under construction after having been damaged during the war. All other facilities were ready for us, student halls, dining rooms and some classrooms.

I was surprised by the age group range which was between 14 and 35. Most of you would be surprised as to what the 35 year olds were doing in form one or two, you are justified but these were former freedom fighters returning to school. The government was encouraging and sponsoring those who wanted to proceed with their education. This brought problems to classroom environment they were some whose behaviour was disruptive to learning. It was very common to see students smoking "mbanje" in class and the teacher would just watch. Teachers were being bullied at and fellow students were fearful of this new generation of freedom fighters. At the dormitories things were not better either, the former fighters would involve themselves in all night drinking. Many never bothered to attend lessons after the drinking spree. I was luck in my class although we had 5 war veterans none were violent and where kin to learn. I quickly became their best friend because at least they could copy my homework after lessons and in return I would get protection from their fellow bad boys. The number of form one pupils was 88 and these were grouped in two classes of 44 each.

There have been so many strikes at the school always led by the so called the war veterans although some were justified some were not. Some complaints were to do with lack of classroom space and some for poor food offered to students. It was difficult to imagine that the veterans themselves failed to understand that the classroom shortage was because of the effects of war and the authorities were doing the best they could to repair the buildings. I am sure one of them was responsible for the destruction of the buildings anywhere. The principal Mr. L.J. Kavumbura had a bad time with the riotous behaviour of the war veteran students. He was a professional man of the cloth but at times he would mete out instant justice at these students, he was also quite a feared man.

The form one stream was academically competitive, they were many brilliant people some of them I still remember well, the likes of Vice Chingwena, Angus Zuze. The competition was so stiff that even after the generator lights were switched off at 9 pm students continued to study using candles deep into night although I do not remember using one. There was much to it than just passing, after each term exam, a minister or even better a governor would present some prizes to those who could have excelled in their particular subjects. There were 9 subjects at stake for 88 students. The first term I took number 2 out of 88 and collected 6 prizes out of 9, Vice took 2 prizes and was number one the margin difference was so small that I cried foul. I was a happy student after all this was the first time I had shaken hands with the governor the most powerful civil servant in the province. I remember vividly his words, "these are the leaders of tomorrow and today I take pride in presenting these prizes in recognition of their intelligence and wisdom, my government is delighted to have noted such an improvement in the quality of education barely 3 years after independence", said governor Joseph Kaparadza. I did not know whether to cry or to smile he had delivered his speech clearly, concise and precise, I was to be the leader of tomorrow. I was happy that the government was aware that leadership comes and goes but the nation continues generation after generation. I thought for one moment that the only position befitting me was that of a governor after all I have been brilliant enough to deserve it, what I was not sure though was whether the governor was as brilliant as I was during his school days. For the terms that followed although I was always getting more prizes than everybody else, I never took the first position, I was concerned. What made it more ironic was that I always took position two and none of those who took positions one repeated it, this meant either going as far back as number three or worse still like Angus Zuze who came from number one to number 12. For two years I was comfortably at number two and it did not matter how much you would study, you would not get number two at least you could get number one, how bizarre was that.

After writing my Junior Certificate, I was top of the school and decided to transfer to Harare to join my brother Ephraim who was a police officer at Glen Norah police station. The principal refused to give me a transfer, an important document those days if you were to be admitted to another school. I had no problem getting the place at Glen High because of my previous passes. I was now doing O' Level and within 3 months I was elected President of the school magazine. I enjoyed public speaking and I was instrumental in writing up an editorial that covered in-depth statistics of students being given pregnancies by teachers. The headmaster did not like the report, he summoned me and suspended me indefinitely. It was a difficult moment for me I did not know what to do, I thought I was only doing my duties as the president of the magazine club. For the first time I became politically mature, I was going to challenge the decision even if it meant in a court of law. As far as I was concerned it was my duty as a president to defend the defenseless and to put the office of the teachers under public scrutiny, I was not going to let it go, I was only 15. Many teachers were sympathetic to my cause and assisted me to appeal to the ministry of education. I did and the matter was swiftly put under investigation. I was acquitted of any wrong doing and the headmaster was found guilty of trying to cover up the sexual abuses of children by the teachers at his school. The teachers eventually were fired and the headmaster was transferred to another school, Victoria High. I became the darling of the students, they saw in me a true revolutionary leader who was committed to their cause. I tried to avoid being swallowed by the pride of victory but I was too young to swallow it, I accepted the challenge. By the time I finished my O'Level, I had mentally matured very fast. I had researched on the common law of Zimbabwe, a Roman Dutch Law and the bill of rights. I wanted to understand my rights and that of others around me, I didn't want to be taken for granted, and I wanted to shape my destiny. My brother being a police officer had all these books at hand and I had free access to them. I needed to challenge unprofessional fingers on me.

IT was 1987 and I was doing my A' Level at Allan Wilson. I felt proud that I had passed my GCE with frying colours despite the problems I had with the school authority, I was studying Sciences (Maths, Physics and Biology). I did not want to do sciences at A' Level, I wanted to do Arts with History being my major, I wanted to study law. My teacher didn't agree with me he thought it was going to be too dangerous for me given the social politics that I had already experienced. He wanted me to be an engineer, aware of the politics of the land and I had no option except to agree with him eventually. I accepted the challenge with vigour. Allan Wilson was a multi- racial School. During those days some schools were classified as B and these were in the majority blacks and the group A (multi- racial) dominated by whites. The group B school was cheaper than group A. This system was designed by the Smith regime when Ian Smith was Prime Minister of the then Rhodesia. The group A schools by then were a preserve of the whites but after Independence, the doors were opened for the blacks who could afford to attend. It was an honour for me to be at this school.

The composition of students was fascinating, I have never been on a multi-racial school before. For the first time I was in the same class with other races 7 years after independence. Within two months I was to be expelled by the then Asian Headmaster, Mr. Padyache for challenging the authority. I could not understand why? It was like I have to spend my whole life fighting authorities, I thought this was unfair to young student like me. I began a self assessed debate about my fate, I was not sure whether I was expecting too much from the authorities or maybe I saw problems where there were none. I was only questioning an irregularity which I felt it was in my right to do so. I had observed students being beaten for coming late not that there was anything wrong those days but those beatings were only being administered to black students only. Asians and whites were not being beaten even if they were late. To me this was not acceptable and I was convinced that either I fight for a change of policy or I quit the school totally. "I would rather be uneducated than to acquire education for oppression" the words I later become identified with at the school. One day I was late to school not that I wanted to test the powers of authority but it was a genuine problem not of my own making. The bus I used broke down, those days there were very old buses called Dakotas, too old and often broke down, there were no spare parts due to foreign currency shortages. I was stopped at the gate by a white head boy like any other black student. I watched whites and Asians passing by without being questioned or stopped. I recall it was about 20 of us and the prefects started writing the student names. When it was my turn to give them my name I refused and asked instead to see the Headmaster. They were not amused and promised to see me beaten thoroughly as an example for others. I was escorted with others to the deputy headmaster who was a black teacher. He was in charge of the everyday beatings for those who were late. I refused to queue to be beaten but instead asked to speak to the deputy head privately to which he refused as the head boy signaled that I be beaten thoroughly for disobeying him. It was a bombshell up to now, I don't know where I got the courage, and I called him a racist bend on oppressing his own people to please his white masters. I asked why he was beating the same black people day after day when they were as many whites coming late as blacks. I told the stunned deputy head that I would rather be uneducated than to acquire education for oppression. For the first time I was in charge of my life, I could hear the spirit of authority flowing into me and I had no idea where it was coming from. I explained to the pale faced deputy head that I had observed it for a very long time, black students being oppressed and tortured and him being used to beat his own people without questioning. What made it worse was that he was beating the same people every day, because these people had no alternative transport so they were always late. No sane person would enjoy being beaten every day for a system one cannot change. All the students were subsequently released without being beaten but I was ushered into the headmaster's office for a disciplinary action

I was subsequently suspended by the headmaster for rebelling against authority. I wrote a letter to The Herald Newspaper appealing to the highest authority to intervene. Contacts were made to then Minister of Education Dzingai Mutumbuka who intervened, ironically this was the second time in two years that the minister's office has intervened to serve me from expulsion. Drastic changes were introduced at the school including the introduction of a Student Union to which I became the President. The student union became so radical that I even feared that it was liberty taken too far. To the majority of the students it was a relief. I became so committed to the students' freedom that my academic life became secondary, a big mistake indeed.

The following year I became involved in the student movement against Apartheid in South Africa. I became the Harare Student Representative for Heal The Wounds Campaign, a civic group which was mobilized awareness against atrocities by the South African regime. I was particularly involved in the plight of children in a war torn South Africa. My political life had begun, I was deep into it, and I needed to know much about Nelson Mandela who became my hero and a symbol of the struggle in South Africa. I could sing the names like Walter Sizulu, Steve Bhiko, PAC and ANC. I wanted to change the suffering of the South African people with my bare hands I was so convinced that I could do it, I wanted to be the voice of the voiceless. I noticed that my family members were very worried that I was becoming more involved in the politics of the land worse still in the struggle beyond our borders at a tender age. They could understand school politics but taking on the mighty South Africa's P.W. Botha was a suicide never to be tried. I was prepared to ignore any advice for as long as Mandela and South Africa was not free. I participated in various forums throughout the country in my capacity as the Student Representative of the Heal The Wounds Campaign with the likes of James Maridadi who was in full time employment as the public relations officer at that time. James Maridadi then joined the Zimbabwe Broadcasting Cooperation (ZBC).

It was one morning I came to school to find a flat nearby, Earls Court, was blown off by a parcel bomb. The area was condoned, the police were busy investigating. This was the work of Apartheid I thought, nobody is at war with anybody except Apartheid. I felt the compassion to physically involve myself in the investigation. I needed to get to the bottom of the matter. I could not learn anything that day, I became restless and none attentive. To me it was pointless learning about the body anatomy when the very human beings I intend to serve are being blown apart by the greedy and the despot leaders. There was no reason to do mathematics neither nor to do physics knowing very well that the world await your destruction after finishing school. During break time I phoned Heal the Wounds Campaign and they confirmed that indeed it was the work of Apartheid. A middle aged woman by the name Tsitsi Chirisa died in the blast, a bomb which was placed in a Television set. The TV was sent from Maputo, Mozambique and when she switched it on it blew off killing her instantly. Here was a victim the victim that I was trying to protect was dead. I felt a hollow in my stomach at the thought that this could have been me. When I talked about the dangers of Apartheid, people thought that was a South African problem, here it was along Rotten Row in Harare, Zimbabwe. So I was right that nobody was safe for as long as Apartheid was in existence, Mandela was right, he was my hero, and he must never give up. Many incidences then followed, blasts in Bulawayo at PAC offices injuring many. I remember the arrest and trial of the accused like Kevin Woods, Phillip Conjwayo and many more. The whole episode gave me the zeal to face the real political life, suddenly human life meant more than education to me and that I could not be a spectator any more I have to fight the injustice even if it meant taking a gap year.

When a village boy becomes a politician!

The politics of the mind, a bread and butter issue

It was 1991 I was 19 and grown up now to be an adult. Some of you will remember Zimbabwe's 1991/1992 drought. While to me droughts are natural catastrophes, I felt then that the government has the duty to alleviate suffering of its citizens. The government of Robert Mugabe was selective in its approach giving food only to those who were ZANU (PF) members. Although many by then were ZANU (PF) members, my focus was on those who were not. In my earlier chapter I alluded that I had set myself as the voice of the voiceless, and to me watching these people die of preventable hunger was a negation of my bona fide principle. There were many small political parties those days, ZANU, DP, UANC, NDU etc. Although many had been contesting elections since 1980, only one party ZANU had ever won a parliamentary seat. I began to explore how I could contribute to the debate on food relief, I finally decided that the only way forward was to join the mainstream of politics. I officially joined the mainstream of Zimbabwe politics by becoming the provincial chairman of ZANU- NDONGA for Mashonaland Central in 1991. My official political enemy number one was Robert Mugabe, the President of Zimbabwe. Mugabe used to be my political idol, I would not miss his speech on the local TV. His speech characterised with wisdom, spoke English with such crescendo that even Tony Blair would find difficult to match. So what happened to this once admired leader? I was convinced power corrupts and absolute power absolutely corrupts.

I began a research on the political landscape of Zimbabwe. Reading books like Struggle within the struggle by Professor Masipula Sithole, the struggle for Zimbabwe among others. I travelled talking to people to get their personal experience and how they felt about their government. I was convinced that not only that Robert Mugabe had a case to answer but he could not be relied upon, he was capable of turning into a dictator any time, he did it in the liberation struggle so there was proof he could do it again. I was convinced I had a duty to pre-warn the people of Zimbabwe to breast for the worse if they did not change the leadership early. People like Timothy Mukwengwe and people in MT. Darwin agreed that I was the first opposition young politician to address on open rally criticising Mugabe's rule in 1991. Addressing a gathering at Dotito, Mukumbura and MT Darwin, I told them of a vision that I had, that of a country where everybody was free to be free, that every citizen was valued and politicians made accountable. I had a vision of a Zimbabwe where the rich are just and the poor protected. Mugabe was not that leader, the leader was yet to come, even today as I write Zimbabweans should be prepared for a protracted struggle that the president of my vision is not yet on site. Many were confused yet some supported me. In trying to speak up my mind I became the enemy of the state not surprising if you are a Zimbabwean where the government will try by all means to suppress opposing views.

The following day the papers carried no news of my address, not that I needed coverage but for the newspapers to ignore the voices of a multitude of people who demanded the resignation of Mugabe was irresponsible journalism. To me it was never here nor there, the daggers were drawn, the authority was now aware that the new blood in politics was speaking courageously against the ill fated regime. Many dismissed me as being too overzealous and a prodigal son. I have never been a ZANU (PF) supporter before, not because I saw no need to, but at the time ZANU (PF) appealed much to me, I was very young to actively participate in politics and when I was old enough to, the party had run out of steam and the leadership had become dictatorial outright. I became a target for CIO at 19 years and *I* knew I was going to be under surveillance for the rest of my life because I vowed I was never going to be silenced for as long as the masses were oppressed, I do not care who will be the future president, I shall not let the people, I shall speak and speaking I shall. I shall not accept the politics of patronage "nada".

What went wrong in ZANU? President of ZANU then known as ZANU (NDONGA) was in exile in the USA after he fled for his life against a background of political purging by Robert Mugabe. There was nothing new in that, the veteran nationalist Joshua Nkomo died a miserable man after having been under mental torture by Mugabe in the early 1980s which saw thousands of ZAPU supporters being massacred and maimed. Properties were seized and confiscated and this is still the same government that we pay allegiance to. Ndabaningi Sithole was to return to Zimbabwe to lead the masses. The structures were vibrant on the ground to usher the new political dispensation. The country was in turmoil and the people saw his coming as the coming of the political messier. His presence was being felt everywhere and the government knew about it. The government issued a statement that once he was going to land at the airport they would arrest him for treason charges. This was the mistake the government did. It became the talk of the day everywhere and more and more people joined the party. The people waited anxiously for his return and subsequently his arrest. It became a national, regional and international issue. Will Mugabe proceed with the arrest? Mugabe is one of the dubious leaders this world has ever seen. He is good at testing the waters and letting people play into his hands. The Harare International Airport was awash with people of all kinds and the police and CIO were equally forceful. But when Sithole finally landed he was allowed to give a press conference at the airport to local, regional and international journalists. He greeted the people with joy and he was surprised himself by the great numbers he met. No arrests were made. Sithole was allowed to go home a free man. I am sure you now know why I said Mugabe is dubious and good at testing the waters.

There is nothing wrong with African leaders but there is something wrong in African leaders. At the airport Sithole briefly had a meeting with his trusted few and with that went on to address the press outlining the party's policies. He was going to give everybody 600 acres of land (note where the land redistribution started), the unemployed would get each ZW$300. 00. Equal opportunities for education and a democratically elected government, transparent and accountable to its citizens. This was a mistake by Sithole, he should have consulted the greater public and structures first before going public with a foreign ideology which did not apply to Zimbabwean situation. Academics started calculating the land required for this ambitious drive and found that we needed twice the size of Zimbabwe to equally allocate 600 acres for every household. The economy was already on its knees and it was not feasible to generate such income per capita to be able to pay out the unemployed. It was a good borrowed idea but not workable to the developing world, people need jobs, schools, roads, hospitals, housing, better living conditions and above all security. Where did Sithole go wrong? He was guilty of politics of patronage, he trusted his few friends around him of cause they unanimously agreed that this was what the people wanted at that moment. I felt cheated, how could I have defended a policy which was unworkable and shallow. I wanted to be the voice of the voiceless not the political cheats of the time. I must be able to be accountable and be consistence but I was not going to tarnish my image in promising every Zimbabwean 600 acres the country could not afford or worse still paying ZW$300 to the unemployed which the country would never generate. I was convinced that the best thing for me was to meet Sithole and get to know his opinion on the matter and if that was his stand, voice my concern about it. I gathered a high powered delegation that included a well known traditional Chief who was once in Mugabe's Parliament. We were surprised that Sithole was convinced that the country had enough land and resources to support the said policies. He was rigid. We went home defeated. The following week I called Sithole at his Waterfalls Home/Office and he accepted the appointment. I made it clear to him that his policies were not feasible and that the party risk being sidelined by the very people it is suppose to serve. I also suggested that it was not too late to consult the electorate and let the electorate decide the course of action. He agreed it was a good idea but there was no going back on the land issue and economic issue. I left a defeated politician.

I met Sithole several times before I made a decision to quit the party. I wrote a letter in which I stated, "It is with regret that I announce my resignation as the Provincial Chairman of Mashonaland Central and as a member of the party. As you are aware I have voiced my concern on the new policies of the party which I feel contradicts with my political philosophy and that of many Zimbabweans. I have no ill feelings about you in person but I am convinced that maybe I am too young to be understood. I will come back into politics when I am old enough to be understood, and when I am old enough to be understood, not even a bulldozer can stop me. I am going back to pursue my education, I wish you and the party all the success."

3 MDC RISE AND RISE AGAIN

The rise of MDC

Contrary to national perception and belief, the birth of the Movement for Democratic Change (MDC) was a result of a series of people's emotions, political and social events preceding its formation. Its formation thus was seen as the climax of a political era waiting to happen. This puts MDC in a dilemma very few have been able to understand, that of transforming people's emotions into political democratic transformation. Such a challenge demands split second political decision and charismatic leadership, fearless and willing to take risks. Whether MDC has that leadership capacity to deliver the change remains debatable but in my own judgement, there have been leadership misfits and only when we swallow our pride and be prepared to change leadership shall victory be certain. We must change the MDC leadership periodically to give rise to leadership talent which Zimbabwe badly needs at the moment, however we seem to have been consumed by the African belief that calling for a change of leadership is seen as disrespectful to the elders and revolution values. In a country reeling from the rule of immense oppression, it is easy to replace one dictator with another and Zimbabweans must be warned.

The formation of MDC was a result of immense consultation forums among stakeholders which included labour movement, the civic society, churches, academics, student movements, business people and general public. Following a series of labour unrest in the late 90s for improved working conditions and wages, the government dealt with the labour movement with a heavy hand of oppression. This included arbitrary arrests and detention of leadership and demonstrators. This lead to the tripartite agreement involving the government represented by the Ministry of Labour, the labour movement represented by the Zimbabwe Congress of Trade Unions (ZCTU) and the employers represented by the

Employer Confederation of Zimbabwe (ECOZ). The tripartite agreement never worked as it always degenerated into a war of words rather than offering solutions to the social crisis it intended to arbitrate. The ZCTU turned militant under the Secretary General Morgan Tsvangirai and Gibson Sibanda as its President. Morgan Tsvangirai emerged as the government number one enemy culminating into numerous arrests and attempted murder by the Central Intelligence Organization. The more they tried to eliminate him the more he became popular with the struggling masses. Mugabe himself was forced to announce on the Zimbabwe Television (ZTV) that the labour movement was free to form its own party if it wanted to turn political accused its leadership of hiding behind the labour movement for its own political agenda. A series of political consultations started as early as 1997 culminating in concerted marathon meetings with stakeholders in 1998. The stakeholders then agreed to form a political pressure group in the name of MDC. The purpose was never political but a unified voice to force the government to arrest the imminent economic collapse, deal with high level of corruption in its ranks and move into a democratic dispensation for the benefit of all Zimbabweans. What this meant was that everything was left to the mercy of Mugabe, but knowing him, it was a waste of effort to expect a dialogue with a despotic leader of his stance. The formation of MDC in October 1999 as a political party was necessitated by the government's defiance that it will not yield to any demand from the imperialists by then Mugabe has already started labelling MDC a sell-out party bends on destabilizing the sovereignty of Zimbabwe. A stooge of British imperialist as he called it. In so doing Mugabe was drawing enemy lines very clearly in the sand which was going to be the beginning of a politically polarised nation.

Who became who at the interim congress to choose the leadership to spear head the preparatory launching of a new political party in the name of MDC? Gibson Sibanda became the President and Morgan Tsvangirai the Secretary General of the new party a simple transformation of positions in political leadership. Did this mean Sibanda and Tsvangirai were identified as the only candidates for the hot political seats or was it by coincidence?

Mugabe thus can be applauded for having visualised a labour movement being used for individual political gains, who can deny that now. But is it not only logical to aspire for a higher position once you have tested popularity, is it not exactly how Mugabe rose to be the president of this country, Zimbabwe. Mugabe is a teacher turned President.

The congress of February 2000 confirmed Tsvangirai (Manicaland) as the new President and Gibson Sibanda (Bulawayo) as his vice. Welshman Ncube (Midlands) became the Secretary General deputised by Gift Chimanikire (Mashonaland Central). Isaac Matongo (Masvingo) became the National Chairman. All the top six except Welshman Ncube were from the labour movement hence putting the ZCTU in total control of the new party. How then Tsvangirai did become the favoured candidate ahead of Gibson Sibanda? The answer was obvious, MDC was formed 6 months before a Zimbabwe general election which was earmarked for April 2000. There was no time to sell a new candidate and Tsvangirai's popularity during the labour unrest worn him the coveted seat for the MDC. We needed a candidate who was known by the general electorate, in fact at one point Tsvangirai was more popular than the new MDC party. As a result Tsvangirai became the natural choice not because of his charismatic leadership qualities but because of previous courage against the Mugabe regime. Was this a wise move by the MDC? Be it as it may, as a new party everything was out of political experiment and this choice was at that demonstration. Nobody will doubt that Tsvangirai rose to the challenges of his newly promoted post but critics believe he is one of the leadership misfits, lacking the combative stature required to confront Mugabe head on. Some cite his various blunders including his meeting with Ben Manasseh leading to the treason charge. In my own opinion, Tsvangirai has been a politician and a half leading a vanguard new political party against a might ZANU (PF). ZANU (PF) remains one of the richest political parties in Africa with unparalleled military machinery at its disposal, that MDC managed to survive up to this day should be applauded.

When did I become involved in the MDC and what has been my role? I remembered meeting Morgan Tsvangirai in 1998 at Chester House along Jason Moyo Avenue previously Stanley Avenue. I have to pass through a security barricade leading to his ZCTU office. He had been attacked by CIO before and almost left for dead in his office hence the security measures. After identifying myself he invited me in his office for a meeting. I had come without an appointment but he was ready to meet me and discuss political matters of interest. We talked about the political situation in Zimbabwe and the need for a movement that would bring about change in Zimbabwe. For the first time, I saw a future President of a new Zimbabwe, selfless and fearless. I saw a Tsvangirai full of defiance and energy, prepared to lose all in order to gain all. We all agreed that it was a surmountable task but we committed ourselves to be the conduit of change for a better Zimbabwe. I was given the mandate to organize and mobilise Mashonaland Central Province. Not that I was the first to organize in Mashonaland Central Province but there was already a labour activist by the name Chabayanzara based in Bindura. Mashonaland Central was one of the most dangerous places to campaign from by any opposition party given the fact that this was the province that bore the fierce war of liberation. By default it has the highest number of war veterans than any other province put together. It also was used as the crossing point by ZANLA forces from Mozambique into then Rhodesia. No opposition party before has succeeded to make any inroads into this province. All have been met by political hostility and Mugabe was aware of this and made sure he manipulated the people there. A mixture of poverty and illiteracy was to blame for the social and political vulnerability of the people in Mashonaland Central Province. Despite early advances in Education for all by the Mugabe regime in the 1980s, Mugabe soon was never comfortable with literate people because education world over have been the greatest weapon against injustice. Given this overview my task was never going to be easy but I embraced it with nationalism and pride. I was armed with nothing other than a personal car and a few personal resources to cover a province the size of Portugal.

I was strategically positioned in society, at the age of 28, I was a Director of a computer company, owned a Bottle Store at Gombe Business Centre in Seke, Pfebve General Dealer at Gomo Business Centre and Pfebve Distributors at Mkumbura Business Centre. The computer company, had business projects in Zimbabwe and Malawi, supporting government ministries like the Foreign Affairs, Local Government, Agriculture and District development Fund (DDF). The government froze all the payments for the company when it became apparent that I was one of the leadership of the MDC. The Bottle store suffered a series of looting by self styled war veterans with the full blessing of the government. The Mkumbura shop was petrol bombed in full view of the Police but suffered minor damages. The General Dealer Shop at Gomo Business Centre was looted by government militia (green bombers) accompanied by the then governor Border Gezi. I took a business decision to lease the shops and cease operation and concentrate on the politics of the country. To many this would be unthinkable but I was prepared to be the vehicle for change. I was prepared to lose all but my conscience has always been my master, to me the challenge was to remove Mugabe from power no matter the cost involved. In seeking peace and justice, I lost all and gained nothing and this is not new in African politics. I am still fighting and I will die a fighter for peace and justice, and such is my conviction.

I met Chabaya in Bindura to map out strategies for the formation of MDC in the region.C in the region. Mashonaland Central is a vast province coupled with poor communication infrastructure. Both Ian Smith and Robert Mugabe regimes left the province neglected and poverty stricken. We had no adequate finance to penetrate the vast remote area, I was forced to use my resources for the ambitious project. In Bindura there were more people disillusioned by the Mugabe regime, with no employment and livelihood, it was easy to recruit people into structures for the new party. The next move was to have an outreach programme to embrace the entire province. We travelled to areas like Dande Valley, where I come from, Rushinga, Mzarabani, Guruve, Centenary, Mazowe, Shamva, MT Darwin and Madziva. It was not easy to convince people that the time was ripe for a new political party to take over. Nobody had heard about the MDC by then although most of them had heard about Labour leader Tsvangirai. I have to confess that it was easier to use Tsvangiari's name than MDC to convince the electorate join the new party. Here was a classic example of an individual more popular than an organization. The initial stages of the campaign were not marred by violence at all because the government had dismissed MDC's formation as a joke of the year. We made use of the political climate venturing deep into the rural areas setting up structures. Sometimes we could set a structure of one man and move on. Once appointed people turned to set up their on structures and that is how MDC became so popular. We would identify an influential person in society and use him/her as a point of call for all official communications and political structures. The news then spread like veldt fire and we ended up with numerous calls from people who were eager to join the movement. We also proceeded with care knowing very much that Mugabe is well known for infiltration in newly formed political parties just like what he did for Tekere's Zimbabwe Unity Movement (ZUM). Tekere was left vulnerable after many senior posts were grabbed by Mugabe's loyalists who deserted him a day before the Election Day. ZANU (PF) then walked out victorious with a number of seats uncontested because the candidates had withdrawn a few days before the election.

I took unpaid leave from my company to give myself time to mobilise and campaign for the new party MDC. There were a lot of other activists who contributed immensely to the initial mobilisation. Some of the most prominent activists were, Tapera Macheka, Phillip Mabika, Mrs Violet Masawi, Trymore Midzi who was later murdered by ZANU (PF), Nixon Mabika (later had his eye smashed by MP Saviour Kasukuwere), Nzombe, Loice Mabande, Zure, Eckam Dandara, Kamusasa, Jack just to mention a few. We could go for days deep down the villains and valleys exposed to the bite of mosquitoes and the harsh weather. Some of us became victims to Malaria but we were determined to foster a formidable struggle for a new Zimbabwe, free of nepotism and corruption. While others were united by the lack of gainful employment, I was an employer on unpaid leave determined to fight a struggle for the majority of Zimbabweans unable to scratch a decent living because of a Mugabe regime which by then had become a liability to the people of Zimbabwe. I have to admit that those early days were free of violence. Not even Mugabe new that MDC would become a formidable political party. I remember Robert Mugabe calls us the joke of the year party. This was a perfect fit for us because it allowed us to concentrate on party structure building exercise without fear. This exercise was not unique to Mashonaland Central alone but was a nationwide endeavour, people sacrificing the best they could to implement structures of the new party. Thus a new Chimurenga for the emancipation of the people of Zimbabwe from the tyrant Mugabe had begun. Soon Mugabe was to awaken to a reality that this new party called MDC was here to stay and getting inroads to his trusted comrades who were leaving to join the party in a mass. It was not surprised to note that the political landscape of Zimbabwe was living on a time bomb, which at any time could manifest into ball of political fire. I was then the Interim Provincial Chairman of Mashonaland Central.

I left Zimbabwe December 1999 after having won a scholarship to study in Sweden a postgraduate in IT Management and Governance. MDC had its first Congress in February 2000 just before the Referendum which was held at the Chitungwiza Aquatic Stadium. Tsvangirai became the first elected President, Gibson Sibanda the Vice President, Isaac Matongo, the chairman, Welshman Ncube the Secretary with Gift Chimanikire the deputy secretary. Except for |Welshman a constitutional law lecturer at the University of Zimbabwe, all top posts went to labour activists. At the same congress, I was elected the National Executive member in absentia, the only National Executive to do so. While I was in Sweden I closely followed the elections and was surprised to see my name appearing among the top leadership of the newly launched party MDC. The people of Mashonaland Central had rewarded me for having steered through a dangerous mobilisation exercise during the formation of the party. Soon my fellow students from 22 countries and the Karlstad College staff hosted me a party as a celebration of my election. Suddenly I was home sick I needed to command the struggle in my newly elected capacity, I could feel Mugabe in my hands crumbling like a ball of clay. I did not need an election, I wanted a war, be it of words or gun fire, through me the people of Zimbabwe were going to be free. But how feasible was it that MDC would wedge a war against Mugabe if elections failed, probably nil.

I was soon to fly to Zimbabwe and monitor a government sponsored constitutional referendum. I was of the National Monitoring task force campaigning for a NO vote. Under pressure from the pressure groups and Civic society, the government hurriedly prepared a constitution in parallel to the National Constitutional Assembly (NCA). The NCA was the first to come up with a constitution sponsored by the Civic society with a wide based consultation framework. The government responded by hiring Jonathan Moyo former critic to the same government who was by then lecturing at a South African University. Jonathan Moyo became the Mugabe spin doctor, violating all norms of political reasoning. Jonathan Moyo became the government spokesperson for the referendum. He became more brutal than Mugabe such that even Mugabe could have been shocked by his turn around conviction.

The government wanted a constitution which would give the incumbent president much power over his subjects and opposition. One which gives him unchallenged powers over land seizure thus solves the land imbalance once and for all. Nobody would disagree that the land distribution in Zimbabwe favoured the white minority, 5000 of them occupying more than 2/3 of arable land in Zimbabwe. The difference was the methodology of the land redistribution, whether it was going to be based on a willing seller, willing buyer or through a radical constitutional reform. MDC had the best land policy in theory but whether that was implementable is another matter. It was based on land audit, documentation of who owns what and for what use. The second phase was to identify illicit land and landlordism, acquire it for resettlement based on skills and need. The third phase looked on governing the size of land to allow maximum agricultural production. A good example was farmers owning 10,000 hectares but utilising only 1,000 hectares of land. Once this was identified to be the case on a wider scale, a law can be passed to limit the size of farms and the specifics for its use taking into consideration the production levels. While the government wanted a radical seizure of farms without compensation and hurriedly resettle the black majority. How the government would identify the need was not clear and how it will deal with those who bought the land other than those whose forefathers forcibly dispossessed the land from the black majority during the 1890 British Occupation. Whatever the case neither MDC nor ZANU (PF) were prepared to listen to each other over the land issue.

The government lost the referendum, coming out of it a wounded and angry regime. This was the turnaround of what was by then a peaceful campaign. Mugabe unleashed the war veterans on defenceless innocent civilians. Rivers of blood flowed and property destroyed, a new form of war had begun, pitting the two political parties. The first star rally by Morgan Tsvangirai in Bindura catapult an orgy of violence throughout the country. Even Tsvangirai was surprised by the people's determination to change their own government. The first mark of a struggle has begun, this was my first major organization of a star rally.

Fighting the machinery of ZANU (PF) with bare knuckles:

Joining the opposition was not an easy choice, I was very well aware of the dangers that might befall me. ZANU (PF) had a history not only of violence but of orchestrating hit squads to eliminate opponents. I had a young family which needed caring a business which needed directing yet the decision to take ZANU (PF) head on was tempting to ignore, save your fellow

Zimbabweans from the jaws of a dictator. Selling the idea to my wife Dorothy was like asking for permission to marry a second wife, she was not comfortable with it and the thought of running battle with a brutal government for a period which can turn into years wasn't an option.

My parents who reside in the rural areas were more appreciating of my decision to fight the regime. To them just like many people in Mashonaland Central felt betrayed by ZANU (PF) which had promised them compensation after war and yet 20 years down the line nothing had happened. This was a region ravaged by the liberation war of the 1970s, then followed by the MNR raids from Mozambique. It's a region which never saw peace, never ruled itself and probably never, never! Unless we the sons and daughters of this vast impoverished region reclaim our destination, all subsequent governments will betray us, our rich history with Nyatsimba Mutota chieftainship, Mbuya Nehanda the national spirit medium and the Portuguese trade in the valley has been distorted by the power that be, for reasons best known to themselves. To me it's a history worth fighting for yet this is not about spilling blood this is about a peaceful fight to claim our right to be heard and to be respected as a person. MPs were imposed to locals from a top down approach and once they were elected that was the last time you could see them until the next election, which falls after every five years. Coming from the same area would give me an advantage both in terms of culture, language and terrain. Together with a team that included Kizito Macheka, Phillip Mabika, Mrs Violet Masawi, Loyce Mabandi, Nixon Mabika, Trymore Midzi and Tongai Jack ,just to mention a few. My brothers Ephraim, Fireson and sister Efurida were also part of the campaign team. Ours was a peaceful and purposeful campaign. We set on a mission to visit community leaders like chiefs, headmen and retired civil servants in the province. We needed to win their support after all these people were leaders by proxy in their respective communities. The strategy worked like veldt fire, soon the province was engulfed with Chinja Maitiro! The MDC slogan. Old and young all were ready to embrace change, after all it was easy to convince them for the time to change, and poverty was glaring into their eyes, over used and sentenced to scavenge from the none productive sun scotched peasantry land.

Soon it would be general elections and people would be free to elect their MPs and government, all seemed well as there was no slightest shrill of violence. But something was amiss, where ever we go, people with suits and dark glasses followed. They did not talk to us; neither did they greet us, a very un-African tradition indeed. We knew what they were but we underestimated what they were up to. There was a period when we could venture into the vast impoverished territories for days, but with no incidence or violence, ZANU (PF) was no way to be seen, as far as we were concerned, Mugabe was history. A new dawn has come to Zimbabwe, a crop of politicians, energetic and raring to turn the tape of fortune for Zimbabweans, will Robert Mugabe accept it? We knew it would come with a fight and indeed we seem not to run out of volunteers to fight for their country but at least in theory.

Campaigning for no vote:

Yes no vote! It was too late to explain to all voters, what no vote meant for some it did not matter for as long that means Mugabe will go. People were fed up, they had seen their life style invaded, unemployment rising and the economic meltdown had caused many companies to close. Yes the referendum was on the 8th and 9th February 2000, we needed people to vote unanimously NO to government sponsored constitution which meant Mugabe holding on to power forever, agriculture disruption and perpetual misery of Zimbabweans. Many people did not understand the significance of the no vote, but they were determined to show Mugabe the exit door at least faster than he came in. Voting was peaceful and when the results were announced, Mugabe was shocked, for the first time he had lost an election and it seemed too much for him to bear and he was bracing for a fight and we were going to be willing conscripts, let it be Sir Robert Mugabe.

Immediately after the referendum, while Mugabe was still licking his wounds we went on a ferocious outreach programme to remote areas. I remember on 13 March 2000, going to Mukumbura Shopping Centre where I had a retail business with my bodyguards and fellow MDC provincial executives. At the centre were off duty police officers and the dreaded CIO, Mugabe's security intelligence, of course they heard that I was coming to the centre. We had MDC T-Shirts, membership cards and pamphlets. Tapera Macheka, Phillip Mabika was busy handing out T- Shirts and pamphlets when a curious police officer off duty approached me and soon a CIO operative joined in. I began answering questions about the MDC's policies, founding principles and manifesto, as a one of the founding members, I always felt comfortable with explaining the MDC's philosophy and policies. To my surprise the police man whom I learned later was Sergeant Michael Langwani, asked for a T-Shirt. At a packed shopping centre the police officer wore the MDC T-Shirt on top of his civilian cloth, the cloud applauded and to the amusement of his fellow police officers. I knew the lines of engagement have been drawn and that his job and life was at risk. Soon there was commotion, the CIO operatives all vanished and nobody knew where they had gone, but he was prepared for his fate. He walked towards me and shook my hand firmly and assured me that he supported the MDC and he was prepared to die for it, and getting fired was his least worry.

I looked at him with admiration, only if all police officers would be so bold to stand up then Zimbabwe would take its rightful position in Africa, the jewel of Africa. It would be a mirror of democracy and citizen empowerment. I knew I was there to witness the extension of Mugabe's brutality, but the question was in what form? I waited for it with determination, I was prepared to support him with all the risks that went with it, only then can people respect MDC as a formidable party. But another question kept on hanging as to how I could defend a policeman when I am only a civilian exercising his right? Of course I was always legally armed both to defend myself and my property, but that did not mean I had the right to shoot defending another person. Soon a Defender truck came with two police officers who turned out to be the Police Member-in-Charge of the local station and his deputy. The crowd meanwhile had grown in number, in this sport starved part of the world, any incident that is likely to pass time is indeed received with amusement, even a death of a person is a crowd puller. I saw the two police officers approaching where sergeant Langwani and I were standing talking and he was still in his MDC T-Shirt enjoying his beer. In a commanding voice the Member-In-Charge ordered him to remove the T-Shirt as the law did not allow officers to be partisan or to wear any party regalia. Michael refused to obey the order from his superior, blaming them for hypocrisy as the same officer had openly boasted of being ZANU (PF) connected. Several orders were issued and he simply rebuffed them before the officers drove off in a heft, amid cheering crowd.

I knew that the law did not allow the police officers to be partisan but that has only been applied selectively to opposition parties, even Augustine Chihuri the Police Commissioner had earlier on went public on TV that he is a member of ZANU (PF). The way the Defender truck left leaving a grudging spiral of dust in the air was a sign that all was not well and worse things were yet to come. I feared for the Sergeant Langwani's life, this is Zimbabwe and anything can happen. I was his only hope, I had the press and publicity on my side which meant if anything happened to him I was his gateway to the outside world, he seemed to know that very well and at least he seemed least concerned with his fate, he was enjoying the support of the crowd and some of his fellow work mates. There were so many police officers who supported him, but to them wearing MDC regalia were taking risk too far.

After what seemed 30 minutes, 2 Defender trucks rumbled to a halt and off came about 8 officers from the Support Unit wilding guns and button sticks headed by the Officer-In-Charge. They immediately surrounded him and made an arrest handcuffing him amid ferocious resistance from Sergeant Langwani. He was quickly whisked away to one of the cars and off he melted into the world of the unknown. I quickly had to make a decision whether I had to pursue the cars to the Police station and fight alongside him or simply notify the press and the party HQ to take necessary action. I decided to take immediate action if Michael was to be saved. I gathered my bodyguards and the MDC team and ordered them to come with me to the Police and demand his release, not that it would stand any chance but it was the noble thing to do.

On arrival at the Police station Sergeant Langwani was already locked in a cell bleeding and bare footed but still proudly wearing his MDC T-Shirt. I asked to see the member -in -charge that was then said to be busy communicating with his superiors for the next action to be taken. When he finally appeared he smiled at me as if he wanted to deliver good news, only to say, "I am sorry Mr. Pfebve if we had caused you an inconvenience, but Michael should have known that he is not allowed to be partisan, how can I help?" I looked at him pensively with a deep chest full of bursting anger, "yes I demand to know where he is and what next", I demanded. "He is in custody as for what's next the bosses will decide", he replied, "Do you mean Mugabe will decide"? I asked. "No , no, no, the police" came the answer. I asked if I could see him and I was given an access to speak to him. He asked me to tell the member in charge that he needed a paper and a pen to write his resignation but

43

as he put it, "I am now a full member of MDC, I will have nothing to do with Mugabe force anymore" I let his wish be told, told him we will be watching his case closely and we left.

The following day he was transferred to Rushinga which was a bigger police base for detentions before being transferred to Chikurubi Maximum Prison. While in detention his wish to resign was granted. After 6 weeks in prison he was released and went straight to MDC HQ, Harvest House where he asked for my contacts and I was united with him. Meanwhile the whole country was awash with the story of a brave police officer who defied his superiors in support of the MDC, to many he was a hero. After his release I introduced him to the President Morgan Tsvangirai, and I was allowed to hire him as my security attaché. This book would not be complete without mentioning Michael Langwani, who went on to defend me against brutal attempt on my life by the regime. Michael suffered horrific knife attacks during the campaign in protecting me but kept his spirit alive until I left the country.

4 THE BINDURA FIASCO AND THE DEATH OF MY BROTHER

"I have degrees of violence", Robert Mugabe and the Bindura blood bath

Bindura the political blood bath

Bindura is capital of Mshonaland Central Province in rural Zimbabwe. It is surrounded by a rich belt of commercial farms, or should I say it used to be, because the same cannot be said of today. Mashonaland Central stretches from Harare the capital city to as far as the border with Mozambique, a stretch of over 300 kilometers north of the country. It is home to Kore Kore and Tavara people, Shona tribes of mainly subsistence farming. Bindura is their home town, where they rely on jobs and shopping.

The town is 90 kilometers from Harare overlooking a mountainous terrain. It is also home to the biggest Gold and Nickel mines. Trojan mine is the country's biggest producer of Nickel and ironically this is where Morgan Tsvangirai worked before leading the labour movement. Ashanti Gold mine is to the south of the city and is the biggest producer of gold in the country. Ashanti gold mine has changed hands previously and once owned by the British before being bought by Ashanti. There are other small gold claims surrounding the town. It is also home to Bindura Haulage one of the biggest haulage companies in the country jointly owned by the rich commercial farmers in the area. Mapunga Silos holds over 25 % of wheat supply in the country and boost the best hi-tech in the region. In all its essence, Bindura was the agricultural hub of the country. It boasted of tobacco, cotton, citrus fruits, maize, Soya beans and wheat production.

Looking at Bindura, a visitor would be forgiven to think that the people who live in this area are equally rich. The houses for labourers are in squalid condition, made of pole and dagger. The rural communities beyond are even worse off, most below the poverty datum line. The land barren and over used with high populations. A sad contrast to the white commercial farmers who owns vast tracks of fertile land however the two communities lived a symbiotic life. The farmers got seasonal cheap labour, while the locals worked for wages to supplement their harvest. The roads in the rural areas are both underdeveloped with no sight of any government care. Ironically, Mashonaland boasts the government's biggest support vote. It was home to government security agents left behind by the civil war in Mozambique in the 1980s which over spilled into Zimbabwe. It also had the highest number of war veterans of the 1970 war of liberation because of its proximity to Mozambique which was used as bases by the Zanla forces. With all its complexities and multiple stakeholder interests, Bindura was a time bomb waiting to explode.

The birth of MDC brought about a formidable opposition party that ZANU (PF) for the first time since independence panicked. From October 1999 running towards the general elections of 2000, Bindura like all other areas in Zimbabwe saw opposition activism. I was elected the MDC Provincial Chairman of Mashonaland Central. It was the biggest challenge in my life, to organize such vast impoverished area with poor communication network. I knew the job had to be done, and what better placed to do it than the people of Mashonaland Central themselves. In the middle of nowhere, political structures mushroomed. People volunteered collectively in mobilization without which MDC could not have succeeded. Such zeal and determination to change a seating government fuelled anger in the ZANU (PF) camp. Nowhere in Africa has such a concerted effort has been done successful than what Zimbabwe was experiencing. People of all walks of life, old and young were demanding what was rightful theirs. "Mugabe must go "was the campaign theme. Give Mugabe a red card was one particularly popular with the youth.

When the Minister and Governor turned thugs:

On 20 February 2000, a strong MDC provincial team headed for Shutu village near Nzvimbo growth point. This was under Mazowe East Constituency, a constituency under Chenhamo Chimutengwende, a ZANU (PF) stalwart and then minister of Information. Political violence by then hasn't irrupted as ZANU (PF) was just emerging from a referendum defeat, farm invasion however had then started. I was going to be the main speaker on the day.

In a village in the middle of no way attracting a crowd of about 350 was a sign of a wave of change sweeping Zimbabwe. I could not believe the enthusiasm and zeal from people of all ages, keen to shape their own destiny. They gave my team a rousing welcome, within my team included Tapera Macheka, Zule, Loice Mabande, Phillip and Nickson Mabhika.

I addressed the people and answering questions about MDC policies and the manifesto. People sang and ululated, MDC slogans and cards exchange hands with bravado never to be seen in the region. Old and young, people power was evident and tangible. During the meeting we noticed a vehicle passing slowly as if on surveillance and quickly sped off. We continued with our business as we were having local branch elections.

In the middle of the happiness and celebration 2 lorries full of ZANU (PF) supporters wearing Chenhamo Chimutengwende's campaign t-shirt written, *"wako ndewako Chen"* descended on the gathering with machetes, knob kerries, iron bars and guns. They started attacking indiscriminately to the unsuspecting crowd, even the police were surprised and caught unaware. I immediately pulled my pistol scare them and save the defenseless people under attack. The police unarmed asked me to fire in the air to scare them off and it worked. They all scattered and dived for cover before returning fire. They ran in all directions leaving a trail of destruction. Reflecting on the day today I am grateful that then the police were still professional, otherwise had they teamed up with the ZANU (PF) thugs, very few would have survived. Using my only B16 truck in sight I ferried the injured to the nearest Howard Hospital for treatment. My team was in the area until late ferrying people to their respective homes as ZANU (PF) thugs and the CIO were seen looking for all those coming from the meeting. It was then that we heard that Chenhamo Chimutengwende had given the youth Z$7, 000 the previous day with instruction to attack MDC at the rally.

We pressed for the arrest of those involved as these were well known ZANU (PF) men and youth campaigning for the Minister of Information, Chenhamo. Border Gezi and Chenhamo Chimutengwende tried to interfere with the police work but we came so forcefully that the police had no option except to arrest the perpetrators. ZANU (PF) Stalwarts, Benard Nyangoni (47), Thomson Shambare, Tendeai Musiyiwa (41), Tapera Marambanyika (23), Elijah Mpofu (38) Lytton Machokoto (18), Pearson Mugambiwa (27) and Zhuwawo Katore were arrested and hauled to Bindura court on Tuesday 23 February 2000. Border Gezi, Chenhamo Chimutengwende and the then MP for Bindura Kanisios Dengu were seen frantically talking to court officials with the hope of influencing the court proceedings. On that day ZANU (PF)'s dirty tricks of marauding the streets targeting the opposition had began, committing crimes with impunity. The 8 arrested were released on Z$800. 00 bails each and that was the last time we saw them in court. They were never prosecuted and that became the trend in all provinces of Zimbabwe.

This first encounter with violence and corrupt court officials being arm twisted by Mugabe regime became the norm rather than an exception, with it the rule of law suddenly vanished from the face of Zimbabwe. Other incidences to follow were a matter of flipping the pages of misery.

What the media said and forgot to follow up

At the height of Zimbabwean land invasions, the press from all over the world covered Zimbabwean mayhem. As Mugabe dug in so did the press vanishes. There are all indications that Zimbabwe with no oil reserves is of no significance to the international community anymore. Below I present some of the global reports which by design and intend to become the forgotten cause.

AFRICA

Taking on the Big Man

In New York five Zimbabweans sue Mugabe for millions. Win or lose, they've sent a strong message.

BY JILLIAN REILLY

ELLIOT PFEBVE WAS the one meant to die. A parliamentary candidate of Zimbabwe's nascent opposition party, the Movement for Democratic Change (MDC), Pfebve was challenging the status quo in ways government backers didn't like. But when 300 pro-government thugs stormed his rural home on April 29, he wasn't there. Instead they attacked his brother Matthew, mistaking him for Pfebve and carrying him off. He was found

ernment ministers to MDC members and supporters. For example, according to the complaint, Moven Mahachi, the minister of Defense, told a crowd on June 2 that "we will move door to door, killing like we did Chiminya." (A reference to MDC leader Tapfuma Chiminya, whose wife Adella is a plaintiff.) The complaint also alleges ZANU-PF named its campaign of intimidation Operation Tsuro, and Mugabe told Tsuro henchmen, "We are at war again... If one of you is asked why you are killing, you say, it is not us, it is the president."

Mugabe and the other defendants have not responded to the charges. The government denies orchestrating the political violence. But in October Mugabe issued an amnesty order for all perpetrators of pre-election violence, making it impossible to prosecute them. Harare also claims the lawsuit doesn't exist—despite the fact Mugabe was served with the papers while in New York attending the United Nation's Millennium Summit last September.

At an Oct. 24 hearing Judge Victor Marrero declared the defendants had defaulted by failing to answer the charges against

Plaintiffs: *Pfebve (center) with Chiminya and lawyer, Mugabe*

An article which was published by Newsweek in USA after the US law suit, December 11, 2000 edition.

Police quiz Pfebve

Staff Writer

Elliot Pfebve

LAST week, police quizzed Elliot Pfebve, the MDC's losing candidate in last month's Bindura by-election, on the violence which rocked the constituency during the poll. They also confiscated his pistol.

Pfebve, who lost to Zanu PF's Elliot Manyika, confirmed to *The Standard* that he was asked to report to the Harare Central Police Station on Tuesday morning and was told to bring his pistol along with him. He was later quizzed by police officers from the Law and Order section and ordered to hand over his Tokarev pistol which is licensed until 2004.

"Yes, I can confirm that I was questioned by officers from Harare Central. But I believe it was just part of a plot to intimidate the opposition.

grabbed my gun, about seven rounds, because I'm afraid they might use it to frame me," added Pfebve.

Police spokesman, assistant commissioner Wayne Bvudziena, confirmed that the police had confiscated Pfebve's pistol.

"We told him to bring his pistol. We are investigating incidents of violence in Bindura and we need bullets, evidence. We didn't question him on any other issues," said Bvudziena.

This was not the first time that the police had taken Pfebve in for questioning. On the first day of voting in the Bindura poll, Pfebve was briefly arrested for allegedly moving around in a convoy.

The Bindura by-election which was held on 29 and 30 July to fill the parliamentary seat left vacant by the death

An article which was published in the Daily News after my release from custody on drums up charges which later were dropped.

50

THE DAILY NEWS WEDNESDAY 5 SEPTEMBER 2001

Pfebve alleges CIO broke into his office

Staff Reporter

UNKNOWN people have broken into the Harare business offices of Elliot Pfebve, the MDC candidate for Bindura in the recent parliamentary by-election, for the second time in less than a month.

Pfebve on Monday said he suspected that members of the government's Central Intelligence Organisation (CIO) were responsible.

Describing the break-in as a professional job, Pfebve said: "I just found all my doors wide open and papers scattered all over the office,

said Pfebve. "Initially I thought it was a mere burglary, but after receiving the anonymous call, I now strongly suspect that this could be the work of the CIO." said Pfebve.

Pfebve said the caller told him that all his movements were being monitored and proceeded to narrate how he spent

'A cash box with more than $7000 and a cellphone were also stolen'

State security continued to use all types of tactics to silence and dispose me of the source of revenue which was a source of MDC funding.

Telephone: 263-4-733707
 263-4-737641
Fax: 263-4-733707
ESC Reference No.:
Your Reference No.:

ELECTORAL SUPERVISORY COMMISSION
First Floor, Mapondera Building
Samora Machel Avenue
ZIMBABWE   P.O. Box 722
Harare, Zimbabwe

10 February 2000

The Provincial Registrar

RE :   REFERENDUM : ELECTORAL SUPERVISORY COMMISSION OBSERVER

This is to certify that Elliot Pfebve (MDC), has been
accredited by the Electoral Supervisory Commission as an

*A letter issued by the Electoral Supervisory Commission for the February
referendum elections, which ZANU (PF) ended up losing.*

NATIONAL NEWS THE OBSERVER 24 FEBRUARY - 2 MARCH 2

Minister and Governor accused of inciting political violence

By Staff Writer

The Minister of Information, Mr. Chen Chimutengwende and the provincial Governor for Mashonaland Central, Mr. Border Gezi have been accused of allegedly inciting politically motivated violence which erupted last week in Chiweshe area with fierce fights between Zanu PF and Movement for Democratic Change(MDC) supporters.

Irate MDC supporters said Chimutengwende who is also Zanu PF's deputy secretary for information have no chance with MDC", said an MDC national executive member, Mr. Elliot Pfebve.

Pfebve said more than ten MDC supporters were severely injured last week on Sunday at Shutu in Chiweshe when Zanu PF youths allegedly wielding iron bars and chain whips attacked them after a peaceful and well attended meeting at the business centre.

"We had already dispersed and we were on our way to Nyvimbo Growth Point at about 2 p.m when some Zanu PF youths in

"The two police details from Chombira Police station who were unarmed were overpowered by the youths. Sensing danger I pulled out my gun to frighten them away,"said Pfebve.

An MDC chairman at Nzvimbo Mr. Matthew Macharaga alleged that Chimutengwende had given some Zanu PF youths the previous day (February 19) about $ 7 000 "to go and cause chaos" at MDC meetings the following day (February 20).

"Some of the money was used to hire vehicles to ferry the youths from Glendale, Bare and Bindura to come and disrupt our peaceful meeting. The lorry in question belongs to a prominent businessman(name supplied) operating at Nzvimbo. Some of our supporters were severely assaulted with iron bars and chain whips and had to be treated for head injuries at Howard hospital," alleged Macharaga adding that MDC supporters were now living in constant fear for their lives because of political violence which has engulfed the area.

"To make matters worse some of our supporters were followed to their homes and were severely assaulted and we no longer feel safe at all. There is no doubt that Chimutengwende is behind these attacks because he has been moving around in his Cherokee Jeep telling Zanu PF supporters to deal with anyone who wants to contest against him. Akanyatsoti vanhu ngavarohwe nokuti handidi zvokukwikwidzwa.(people must be beaten because I do not want anyone to contest,"said Macharaga.

Arrests have already been ...

were anxious to hear the verdict. Earlier on in the morning, some placard-waving MDC supporters demonstrated outside the Bindura magistrate's courts accusing some court officials of corruption.

"We were not happy at all with the way the court and the police handled this case. In the morning some Zanu PF councillors, and MP Kenisios Denga held a meeting at the court and we have a feeling that they were influential in the decision made by the courts,"said Pfebve.

The Observer has it on good authority that Gezi and Chimutengwende tried by all means to have the suspects acquitted. They allegedly mad[e] frantic calls to the police and courts to have the suspects released.

The suspects first appeared in court on Tuesday. It alleged that Gezi and Chimutengwende were not ha[ppy] that the case was later handle[d] by a junior magistrate only sworn in two weeks ago.

Chimutengwende and Gezi could not be reached for comment by the time of going [to] press.

Bvudzijena defends the police force

By Tawanda Tafirenyika

The Zimbabwe Republic Police (ZRP) superintendent Wayne Bvudzijena has defended the police force who are under a barrage of criticism from opposition political parties and civic organisations for not stamping their authority on the perpetrators of violence which has seen numerous people seriously injured in politically motivated clashes as the campaign for the 2000 parliamentary elections gathers momentum.

Speaking in an interview with this paper this week, Bvudzijena said the police was doing its job in accordance with their policy without being partial." I don't understand these accusations against us. Our policy is very clear; we do not condone violence and we bring anyone to book who is found guilty of assault but the truth is that we have not received reports of

ter accusations between Zanu PF an[d] labour backed Movement for De[mo]cratic change (MDC) with the latte[r al]leging that its supporters are being [as]saulted by Zanu PF members and the police is showing a " lukewarm [atti]tude" towards its assaulted memb[ers]. Zanu PF is also saying (MDC)members are the perpetrators [of] violence.

However what still baffles [...] is that only last week (MDC) mem[bers] at a press conference paraded seve[rely] injured men and women with deep [cuts] on their torn heads and fractured [...] and the victims say they reported [the] matter to the police but nothing [has] been done.

Tsvangirai further says that [Zanu] PF had hired a South African c[om]pany that was responsible for [...] ling clashes between the African ...

Article published in the Observer, 24 February 2000 in which Chenhamo Chimutengwende then Minister of Information hired ZANU (PF) thugs to attack MDC Supporters and leadership.

Pfebve suspects political motive in office break-in

Staff Reporter

THE Harare business offices of Elliot Pfebve, the MDC candidate for Bindura in recent parliamentary elections, were broken into on Sunday night.

Pfebve said yesterday the break-in was politically motivated because nothing was stolen from his company Computer Africa.

"I suspect that the incident is politically motivated because," he said, "if they were thieves I would expect to find some items missing. But nothing was stolen. I hope that nothing was planted in the offices."

The main door to the offices was destroyed.

Pfebve said the people who broke into his offices were probably looking for party documents.

He said he reported the matter at the Harare Central police station.

"The police visited the premises and advised me they would send detectives to dust for fingerprints," he said.

Pfebve is one of three citizens suing President Mugabe in the United States for human rights abuses. His brother, Matthew, was murdered by suspected war veterans and Zanu PF supporters in the run-up to last year's parliamentary election.

The others are Adella Chiminya, the wife of the slain MDC activist Tichaona Chiminya, brutally murdered in a petrol bomb attack at Murambinda growth point in Buhera, together with Talent Mabika, while they campaigned for MDC president Morgan Tsvangirai in last year's parliamentary election.

Maria, the wife of farmer David Stevens, also brutally murdered, is the third person suing Mugabe for the murder of her husband by alleged war veterans last year.

The High Court heard allegations that Chiminya and Mabika were killed by war veteran Kainos Tom "Kitsiyatota" Zimunya and Joseph Mwale, an officer of the Central Intelligence Organisation.

The two have not bee[n] arrested despite a High Cou[rt] directive ordering Andr[ew] Chigovera, the Attorne[y] General, to investigate a[nd] prosecute them.

SKF for SEALS, VEE AND WEDGE BELTS COUNTRYWIDE

Elliot Pfebve

Offices continued to be broken and documents missing as this article by Daily news before it was bombed indicate.

Plot to rig Bindura vote

From Page 1

The secret plan was put into full swing after ZANU PF's Joseph Chademana lost the mayoral election in Masvingo to the MDC's Alois Chaimiti, the sources said.

In Bulawayo, where a mayoral election initially set for last month is due to take place on September 8 and 9, thousands of ZANU PF activists mostly from Bubi-Umguza and Nyamandlovu have allegedly been added onto the Bulawayo voters' roll to beef up support for party candidate George Mlilo.

In Makoni West constituency, where another parliamentary by-election is going to be held, the governing party has registered its followers residing in neighbouring constituencies such as Mutare and Makoni East on the Makoni West voters' roll.

Gezi last year.

An examination of the new voters' roll for Bindura though shows names of some people now residing in that constituency but known to reside in neighbouring constituencies. Some names also appear to have been entered twice on the roll.

For example, one Karira Mukwari with ID number 45-061090V45 is entered on the roll as a resident of Chiwaridzo Farm which is in Bindura, although she is also listed as living at Dick Farm in the Mount Darwin South constituency.

Another voter, Charles Chihuri, is a resident of Madziwa in Shamva, although his name now appears on the Bindura voters' roll. The name of another voter, Front Mabika, appears on the new roll twice.

Manyika was reportedly

Rigging of elections in Bindura was well documented and the press also played a role in pre-empting it but this did not deter ZANU (PF) from stealing the elections, Financial Gazette, July 26- August 1, 20001.

violence carries the day for Zanu PF

Elliot Pfebve: "Zanu PF knew that given a free and fair election the result would have been a telling blow."

Chenjerai Hove: "It's a pilot project where Zanu PF has planned to unleash violence on the people and measure its effect."

Chenjerai Hove a well respected Zimbabwean author did an analysis of the results amid a wave of violence that swerved the results for the July By- Election in Bindura.

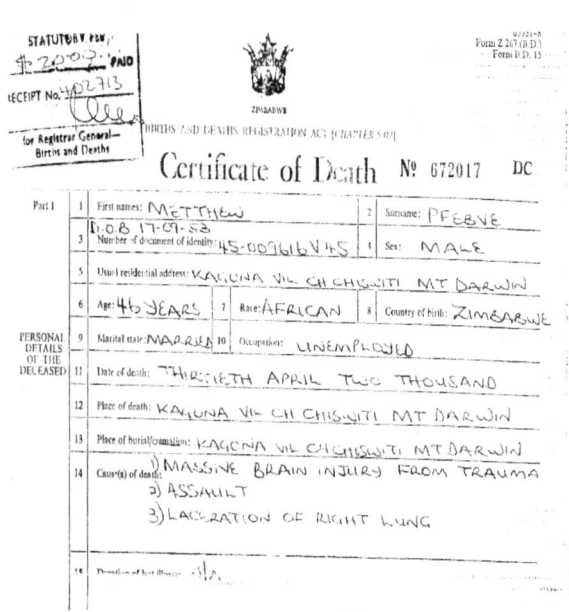

55

An extract of the death certificate of my murdered brother Matthew indicating how they murdered him in cold blood.

THE DAILY NEWS WEDNESDAY 10 OCTOBER 2001   N A T I O N

Judge orders release of three MDC supporters

By Pedzisai Ruhanya

HIGH Court judge, Justice Charles Hungwe, yesterday ordered the release of three MDC supporters in Shamva wrongly convicted and imprisoned for over three years by a Bindura Magistrate last December after the Attorney-General (AG)'s office, and the "prisoners" lawyer agreed that the ruling was a miscarriage of justice.

Hungwe said he would hand down the full judgment on Friday.

He said: "I intend to make an order to release the three accused but the full judgment will be ready on Friday."

Martha Muronzi, Fanuel Muronzi and Nickson Murari were convicted and sentenced to 40 months in prison with hard labour by Bindura magistrate, Simon Kachambwa.

The magistrate suspended 15 months of the sentence on condition of good behaviour.

They were sentenced and convicted together with five Zanu

He said the three submitted a simple story which was corroborated by the State witnesses.

"It is submitted that the State did not establish any case against the three," he told the court.

Mushimgwe said: "The nature of the State evidence gives a picture of the three being the unfortunate victims of political violence perpetrated by members of Zanu PF If this court is in agreement with the above submissions, the conviction must be quashed and the sentence set aside."

He said public violence of a political nature was on the increase in the country and said the courts must be seen to be imposing deterrent sentences because if inadequately punished it would spread throughout the country like a void fire.

"In the particular circumstances of this case, public violence which is politically motivated is on the increase in Mashonaland Central province and the courts must pass a clear warning that the perpetrators

Before Mugabe replaced most judges with his partisan ones, court after court were acquitting MDC supporters arrested by partisan police in liaison with the CIO and partisan war veterans. I stood for the voiceless and the weak.

Mr. Mathew Pfebve murdered by ZANU (PF) 30 April 2000

Brother and hero, its 7 years since your brutal murder by Mugabe regime yet we still languish in bondage, people continue to die, many lie in argon with broken limbs. The struggle that you died for being yet to be worn. We remain adamant that you did not die in vain as we enter a new phase in the struggle drawing parallel lines with the enemy that you know better which has no respect for human life. Guide us to victory knowing very well that you have a befitting place in our Zimbabwean history. We continue to be guided by your spirit and those who had fallen too many to mention, until victory.

Aluta continua, victoria aceta, victory is certain

The News Report:

NYAKATONDO, MT. DARWIN - Grief and fear gripped a village on Zimbabwe's border with Mozambique on Thursday as relatives prepared to bury an opposition supporter, the latest victim of political violence sweeping the country.... Pfebve a member of the opposition Movement for Democratic Change (MDC) was battered to death on Sunday by supporters of President Robert Mugabe's ruling ZANU (PF) party, villagers said.

Pfebve was among five kidnapped on Sunday in the latest act in a campaign of political intimidation that has terrorised this rural community, about 250 km (150miles) North East of Harare. Police and army soldiers watched the gathering, but Pfebve's family said they had little faith in the security forces. No one has been arrested for the attack, which injured four others including Pfebve's father.

Villagers pointed out to other houses that had been attacked in the area and one man, now virtually unable to walk, described how he was seriously beaten by thugs last weekend. Nampa-Reuters — 5 May 2000 14:26:54 GMT

How the death of my brother Matthew affected me

When I joined the politics of Zimbabwe, I knew what was in store for me but never fully understood the extent of violence that was to come with it. Some people joined politics because they were disgruntled with no prospects of employment and social injustice, while I had a job and a business my motivation was to make Zimbabwe a better and fairer for all. In Zimbabwe just like other African countries extended family is an integral part of our heritage. Any social injustice to one can have a ripple effect to many hence the problem in Zimbabwe was being felt at every level of society.

Zimbabwe politics is rough and dangerous but I chose it with zeal and determination, while I reflect the murder of my brother with a pinch of salt, I don't not for a minute regret joining politics to liberate my people from the yokes of Mugabe's bondage.

It was afternoon of 1 May 2000 when I received a call from Officer in-charge Mukumbura Police station, Daniel Makaure. The connection was very poor and all I could hear was a cracking sound and punctuations of inaudible shootings'. I have never had a call from this police station before, yes I knew the police office since he was based at a local police station and I had a business by the centre as well. The fact that I couldn't hear anything aggravated my curiosity to know what had happened. I felt uneasy and began to sweat and suddenly I feared for the worst, what could have happened. Getting information from such a remote area was not easy and yet I knew that was not an ordinary message it had to be treated with the urgency it deserved.

After several attempts my fear was confirmed, in a typical police language he could neither deny nor confirm that any one of my family was murdered but hinted that all was not well. What he confirmed was that ZANU (PF) supporters descended on our home armed with instruments to cause maximum harm and that they feared worse news although they could not elaborate. I knew either my parents, brothers or sisters could have been murdered, I knew ZANU (PF) was capable of doing that. They had tried several times to assassinate me and if this was true then finally they got my brother or sister, the bond inseparable. Before I could ponder on where to get full information, there was a knock at the door, my younger brother with a pale face ushered in. Then the bad news my look-alike brother Mathew Pfebve was murdered by the ZANU (PF) war veterans and militia. He related the events of 30 April 2000 when an army of ZANU (PF) thugs numbering almost 400 armed with iron bars, chains, axes, guns and hoes came to the house looking for me and took my family hostage. My father was knocked unconscious and my mother was able to hide in an outside toilet. The other family members scattered in all directions and my brother were abducted. They beat him with iron bars, chains and rocks until he fell to the ground. Each time he was pleading with them that it was not him and that he was not the MDC candidate, his pleas fell on deaf ears as they all shouted for him to die. They smashed his skull, limbs and smashed his rib cage. They even took his clothes and left him dead and naked in the middle of the road.

The narration was too vivid and too striking. Suddenly I was receiving calls checking on me as the news had been spread by ZANU (PF) that Elliot Pfebve has been killed and therefore they will be a no contest in Bindura. I phoned President Morgan Tsvangirai and told him of the incident and the party was alerted. Within a few hours so many people had come to pay their condolences with many volunteering to accompany me to Nyakatondo village, by then ZANU (PF) had sealed all rural roads and even my home was a no go area for me. I didn't even think twice, the fact that ZANU (PF) had sealed all roads leading to my home was never an issue as I was determined to get there at all costs. Strapping my Russian madeTokorova pistol, I put my jacket on and I was determined to die than ever before. I was prepared to fight any war to the last drop of my blood, I was not going to cower away from my family, I had caused them the fate and I was not going to forsake them. I was in a fighting mood and ZANU (PF) knew that if I was determined to do something I would do it and this is the reason that they awaited me knowing very much that I would come. My wife and others tried to persuade me not to go but I was not going to take a no for an answer, as far as I was concerned the war had started and so be it.

They might have been about 50 people who accompanied me in a convoy of vehicles, most of them MDC activists. I remember well activists like Tafadzwa Musekiwa, Job Sikala, Dr Zimudzi, Bigg Chigonero, Tapera Macheka, the 2 Mabika brothers Phillip and Giant, among others. There were numerous police road blocks (checkpoints) and at almost all of them we were told to go back as it was too dangerous for us to continue. This was the police who were paid to protect us and they also feared for their lives from ZANU (PF). I told them off and they could see death in my eyes no police post managed to turn us away. Then there were ZANU (PF) road blocks and we fought our way through until we reached our destination. We were surprised to see two armoured vehicles and tens of security officers, soldiers, support units and police officers. I have never seen such a big number of soldiers let alone the armoured vehicles in this remote village. The questions that many people were asking were whether they were there to protect us or to kill us? We were so much preoccupied with bereavement that we didn't even bother about their presents. Our presents changed the mood of the soldiers who intensified their patrols. We learned later that ZANU (PF) had asked the soldiers to patrol the area and beef up because they suspected that since I was armed I was likely to avenge the death of my brother.

The following morning we arrange for the body to be picked from MT Darwin Hospital 80 kilometers from the village towards Harare. Little did we know that the CIO had conveyed the news that we were on our way so that ZANU (PF) would way lay us and assassinate the MDC delegation. They allowed us to pass the roadblocks and to collect the body. Immediately after leaving the hospital they ambushed us attacking the vehicles including the vehicle carrying the deceased body. I have never been so angry, I could not believe that Mugabe was prepared to even finish me and my dead brother, what type of a leader is he? In a moment I thought of fighting a sole war calling it may be a 3rd Chimurenga. I thought at that time whether there was any reason to live when everybody around me was dead. Even after the burial of my brother under heavy army patrols, ZANU (PF) was sealing off the exit routes waiting to assassinate us. We were aware of it but we were determined to fight on.

Several years after my brother was murdered, the people who murdered him are known but no legal proceedings have been taken. The following names are known to have been directly involved in the murder of my brother and this is known to the police and authorities; The leaders were; Karikoga Janhi, Shepherd Kararira, Machemedzi and Wilfred Mapundu (brothers), Clemence Kavanji, Lemason Ghatsi, Camias Mafunga and a war veteran by the name Tobo. More than 9 years after the death of my brother I still await justice to be done.

Brother Mathew rest in peace! The struggle continues, Mugabe is still the president and I am still in opposition fighting injustice. I will continue the fight and give me the powers to change this regime once and for all so that we can save the future generations.

Mathew Pfebve is spirit lives on

Every April 29, I wake up to the reality that my eldest brother is no more. More striking is the fact that he died at the hands of the Mugabe regime, desperate to cling to power against all norms and odds.

Mugabe might have retained his job after murdering my brother, but my brother was never given the slightest breathing chance. Not only was he murdered but the ZANU (PF) thugs robbed him of his clothes – leaving him naked. Zanu (PF) had sent a clear message that it is a blood-thirsty party and made up of *bona fide* of robbers.

The long arm of justice shall surely catch up with them. What goes around comes around.

The events leading to the fateful day:

March 2000: A torture camp is established at Kamutsenzere Primary School. The School is forced to close. A war veteran and Zanu (PF) councillor by the name Karikoga Jani is appointed to head the torture camp. Government vehicles are being used to ferry more ZANU (PF) supporters and militia. By April the camp became the biggest in Mashonaland Central, supplies and logistics are being delivered by army trucks and DDF vehicles.

April 15 2000: The camp has become so big that Government supplies cannot support the army of ZANU (PF) militia in preparation to attack MDC supporters.

Villagers are being coerced to contribute $20.00 each for the upkeep of the camp. Non-ZANU (PF) supporters' cattle are being grabbed taken to feed the militia as punishment, later to include goats and any domesticated animal. MDC supporters are taken prisoner and held at the Kamutsenzere torture camp. Women are being raped every day, a police post is overlooking the camp, but no action is taken.

April 21 2000: MDC receives intelligence that about 200 ZANU (PF) militia was on their way from the torture camp in Nyakatondo Village, a stronghold of MDC and home to Pfebve family.

About 100 MDC youth is on high alert. ZANU (PF) abandons the plan upon receiving CIO intelligence that they are outnumbered. Councillor/war veteran Karikoga Janhi meets CIO and Lemason Ghatsi, another ZANU (PF) councillor, to map out strategies.

Border Gezi is contacted and more reinforcements from other parts of Mashonaland Central are called in.

April 26 2000: The camp's population is now estimated to be 400. The villagers live in fear around the area. MDC youths relax after no news of the impending invasion.

April 29 2000: A directive is given by ZANU (PF) for the attack. About 300 leave camp on a journey of 12km on foot to the North, forcing villagers' captive along the way to avoid information intelligence being leaked to MDC. By the time the terrorists reached Nyakatondo village the group numbered about 600.

April 29 2000 Night: ZANU (PF) takes the father of Hamu Chidzumo, my bodyguard who lives five kms away. He is shackled and asked to lead the way to the Pfebve family while being assaulted with chains. The group arrives and encircles the Nyakatondo village in a cow's horn format.

Their Leaders: Karikoga Janhi, Shepherd Kararira, Machemedzi and Wilfred Mapundu (brothers), Clemence Kavanji, Lemason Ghatsi, Camias Mafunga and a war veteran by the name Tobo storms the house with a group of 250 other unidentified men.

My brother Matthew and father are taken hostage and my mother flees. Both are beaten with iron bars. My father, an elderly man is knocked unconscious and left presumed dead.

My brother tries to plead his innocence but nobody listens. He is led away, beaten with iron bars, chains, and stones, presumably intending to take him to the torture camp, 12 miles away.

He collapses and they finished him off with iron bars, smashing his skull and internal organs. They robbed him of his clothes and left him naked, 3 miles away from the family home.

Eight years later

March 29 2008: Karikoga Janhi is still a ZANU (PF) councillor; Lemason Ghatsi is still a ZANU (PF) councillor. Shepherd Kararira, Machemedzi Mapundu, Wilfred Mapundu, Clemence Kavanji, Tobo and Camias Mafunga are still terrorising opposition supporters in Mt. Darwin for voting for Morgan Tsvangirai on 29 March 2008.

April 29 2008: Another wave of violence has been unleashed by the same ZANU (PF). After 30 days, still no news about the Presidential election results. Hospitals are littered with victims of political violence who voted in an election whose results are still not yet known.

Is it a sign that ZANU (PF) is aware that its era is over? How long shall we continue burying our dead and nursing wounds? How long is the string of our patience? The pain of the wounds on our souls will not heal, especially as it is now exactly one month since Zimbabwean people voted, and still no results have been released. Does Robert Mugabe think he can withstand the power of the people whose time has come? The struggle continues!

Summary of events: Elliot Pfebve, MDC MP Candidate in Bindura — June 2000

Some of our members were beaten by Zanu (PF) supporters who were sent there by Border Gezi to flush out MDC supporters. According to people in Manenga, Gezi arrived at that scene, dropped off the youth in his truck and then left them to unleash the violence. Our MDC supporters phoned us to say 'we are being beaten', so we sent our own youth to rescue them. We sent a lot of them, but when they got there they went amok and started beating Zanu (PF) in retaliation. There was a serious battle and Zanu (PF) was outnumbered. Some of our MDC youth were arrested; 11 of them are still on remand. But after that incident ZANU (PF) realised how strong MDC was and they became afraid to attack in Bindura area.

I had a rally at Musiwa business centre at the end of February. That used to be in my constituency, but has now been cut out. Gezi knows me well. We are both businessmen and both from Mashonaland Central. We used to interact. But before that rally, Gezi hired youth from Mashonaland East uses vehicles supplied by Paddy Zhanda (the provincial chairman of Zanu (PF) Mashonaland East).F) Mashonaland East). These people came earlier. There were about 150 of them. They were armed, including with a gun. Some of our youth came early to put up posters. They beat six of them before I arrived. When I got there I saw this truck and a pick-up. There were people with iron bars, axes and hoes and I realised they couldn't be our supporters as no one would come armed like that to a rally. This time I was driving a Mazda 626. I stopped in front of them. At first they didn't attack me. The Zanu (PF) supporters were from another province and they didn't know me. At least they knew the name, but not my face. But then they saw our supporters who were running towards me for help. They realised who I was and began coming to me with weapons saying, "Burn the car". I got out of my car and drew my firearm. They all rushed back and got into their truck. The driver wanted to speed off. I stopped the vehicle. They were farm labourers from Zhanda's farm. Some were women. I managed to hold them until the police arrived and escorted them to the Shamva police station. There were twelve people identified as having been trouble causers. They were arrested, but were released the same day. Apparently Zhanda and Border Gezi went to Shamva and got them out. There were some police officers who were sympathetic and they told me what happened. The member in charge just said he had instructions from above to release them and there were no docket and no charges. I have come through hell on earth.

In April, we had booked a rally through the police in Mount Darwin. I was the national co-ordinator for Mashonaland Central so I did rallies in other constituencies to beef up support. We travelled to Mount Darwin the day before the rally which we wanted to put up in town. There were about 300 of us. We were stopped just before we reached there by the police and told to wait until their bosses would come and tell us why it was not safe to proceed. These people were supposed to come from the police station about 10 kms away. After waiting 40 minutes or so we decided to go to the police station to check why we were being told to wait. When we got to the police station we were told by the member in charge that ZANU (PF) didn't want us to have a rally; that Mount Darwin is a no-go area for MDC. We protested that it was unlawful; that the police had given the go-ahead for the rally and we wanted them to cover it. We were not allowed to leave the police camp and we slept there overnight. At 5:30 am, the ZANU (PF) youths came to the camp. We discovered that the member in charge had notified Kasukuwere that MDC were at the police camp. There were about 40 youths toyi toying and chanting slogans and more were said to be behind.

In the morning, the police told us to give them time. They said they needed more manpower so we decided to go to Rushinga for breakfast. We arrived in Rushinga and had food there. The police from Mount Darwin must have been telling ZANU (PF) to bring more people as they had seen our numbers. The member in charge in Rushinga was professional. He called me and told me that ZANU (PF) had mounted an ambush about 20 km from Mount Darwin and he was right. We decided to proceed as there was no other route to get to Mount Darwin. When we were approaching the spot we saw lots of police officers in Santana and Defender police vehicles. There must have been about 11 AM. They had been sent from Bindura, Rushinga, Shamva and Dotito. They were there for reinforcements that had been called from all over. The police ordered us to stop and we did. There were ZANU (PF) youths by the roadside throwing stones at us. There must have been about 600. Later the police told us that they had been taken from other constituencies. There were running battles between ZANU (PF) and MDC. The police fired tear gas and live bullets in the air. ZANU (PF) was also firing guns. Eventually the ZANU (PF) youths ran away. Little did we know that there had been two CIOs sent from the President's Office to assassinate me. I was in my car at first, but then got out and was on foot with the police forming a buffer. Then as we moved a distance away from the ambush a Nissan pickup came out of the bushes and hit my car.

They had been waiting for the confusion so that they could force an accident and assassinate me in the confusion. They had planned to hit my vehicle and both of them would in turn fire at the car and in fact that is exactly what happened. They hit my car but it didn't overturn. It was being driven by my driver, Timothy Mukwengwe. There was a period when the two cars were spinning and hitting each other like in a horror movie. The front bumper and headlights were damaged. When they realised that I wasn't in my car they sped off. The CIOs must have called for more reinforcements.

As we went towards Mount Darwin, there were four pickups and a maroon Mercedes which belongs to ZANU (PF) MP candidate Kasukuwere waiting for us. There was another truck with ZANU (PF) supporters in it, about 80 of them armed with iron bars and other weapons. They were coming from the direction of Mount Darwin town. They sped past us and made a U turn near the Mount Darwin-Rushinga turn off. I was now driving my car again. Then the same car that smashed my car earlier on smashed into my other car a Toyota Hilux pickup, which was being driven by Nixon Mabika aka Giant. Then they blocked the road and four of them pulled their pistols, including MP candidate Saviour Kasukuwere. They began smashing the windscreens of vehicles. Nixon Mabika had his eye smashed by Saviour Kasukuwere and his team. Nixon went through a surgery to save his sight but lost sight of the other eye. Another man was beating people in a truck. Kasukuwere personally joined in the assault, tried to open the doors to beat the driver and his assistant, but the door was locked from inside and he couldn't get in. Kasukuwere stared at me with his hand on the trigger of his pistol ready to fire, I also had my hand on the trigger of my gun, and it was like two bulls charging at each other. I could smell death and a blink of a second it would be all over, the first to press the trigger would survive. Instantaneously, there was a helicopter hovering above us shouting for everybody to surrender by putting hands up. The army started firing and we all scrambled to safety, taking cover and many of MDC supporters run away fearing that the army could have been sent to massacre the MDC.

An army helicopter was hovering and then it landed. Three army officers jumped out. They ordered everyone to lie down and everyone complied except Kasukuwere. He was asked to identify himself and he said he was a candidate for ZANU (PF). They told him that they don't belong to ZANU (PF) and he must lie down and he finally obeyed. They beat him and disarmed him. They were shouting to Kasukuwere, "We were watching you and you are the main culprit". The army beat three ZANU (PF) members, but no one from MDC. Another truck then arrived full of ZANU (PF) and they were stopped and asked to disembark and lie down on the ground. We were then allowed to proceed and the army instructed the police to escort us to Bindura. Kasukuwere was ordered to be locked up in the cells, but he was set free at the police station. Many of our guys had run away when the army arrived fearing for their lives. I was still there until dark calling people with a loudhailer to come out from the bush. Some heeded the call, but some thought it was ZANU (PF). Some were missing for two days, as they didn't trust anything or anyone. They travelled about 60 kms to Bindura on foot. It all happened near to Mr. Chihuri's house [the Commissioner of Police]. Some of our members ran to his house, but there were kidnapped by war veterans guarding the house and further tortured.

After failing to kill me in this incident, they decided to unleash the terror on my family. They attacked our house (April 29,2000) in Mukumbura and beat my father. He now has two broken fingers. They kidnapped my brother and murdered him. The police arrested six and I realised that they were trying to cover up and I went to protest at the provincial commissioner in Bindura. Many attacks and torture of our supporters in Dande Valley happened 500 metres from a police post. ZANU (PF) supporters who set up numerous torture camps in the valley and especially those at Kamutsenzere the base of those who murdered my brother were bussed from all over Muzarabani, Centenary, Shamva and Mount Darwin in government vehicles. The police were also involved in the logistics of running the torture camp, providing the food and providing cover for those who were looting cattle and goats from villagers accused of being MDC sympathisers. Police were sharing the proceeds of crime with the militias. When I quizzed the provincial commissioner on why he was unable to arrest his own police forces involved in the torture, the militia camped at

Kamutsenzere School turning it into a torture camp, all he had to say was that he was doing his best to arrest those who murdered my brother and others. It was clear that the biased police was never going to get to the bottom of the case as this was top down directive from the President Mugabe himself.

When I got to Mukumbura for the funeral I wanted to hunt for those I knew who had done it. The police knew about this. I wanted to hand them over to the police. I caught two and they were also arrested. Among those put on remand was Pindirire a ZANU (PF) activist, a local war veteran Karikoga and all of them were released and no follow up to the case was done. Terry Marodza remained free although he was the campaign manager for the violence, the person in charge of all the atrocities with Saviour Kasukuwere now a minister in the government. As if this was not enough in the middle of the investigations, Mugabe declared a presidential pardon to all those facing politically motivated cases.

Border Gezi and others had plotted to kill me. There was a meeting at Tendai Hall in Bindura which lasted two hours in early April. There they were drawing up a hit squad and making a list of priorities. They didn't agree at that meeting so they had another one at the Kimberly Reef Hotel. This was a four-hour meeting. Comrade Sarudzai was present at both meetings of the ZANU (PF) apologetic war veterans and CIO. Apparently they finally agreed and high on the list was my head and whoever killed me was to get $300 000. Sarudzai was on that committee, but he refused. Also on that committee were other war veterans, John, a councillor in Bindura, John Chiteve who is a councillor in Bindura and has been implicated in other acts of violence, Mugarapanyama, a guard at Bindura primary school, John Karikoga who led the attack that killed my brother and who never was charged, and Comrade Satan, a notorious war veteran.

Comrade Sarudzai was a very powerful commander during the liberation war. After this meeting he sent word that he wanted to see me and he told me what had happened and who were the members of the committee. He once commented to me, "We went to war because we had a reason to fight as we would lead a better life. But now I am in poverty, my children are not working. I didn't fight the war so that Mugabe and his henchmen would enrich themselves. I fought so that all Zimbabweans would have a better and prosperous life. Now I want to join MDC as change is what we need." About two weeks after my brother's death, Governor Border Gezi had a rally in Dande in which he addressed the militia and ZANU (PF) urging them to unleash violence to all those who supported MDC, on the same day my general dealer shop at Gomo business centre was destroyed and looted. The goods were loaded in government vehicles.

On 10 May the CIO and militia started hunting for Sarudzai blaming him for warning me of their intention to kill me. Sarudzai was abducted and brutally attacked and left in a pool of blood to die. He gained consciousness and staggered out in the bush where he was rescued by a Good Samaritan. Sarudzai later crossed to Mozambique where he was rearrested after the government had issued a warrant of arrest in Mozambique. He was later released after he was identified as a former commander in the liberation struggle. He received treatment in Mozambique until he was good enough to return to Zimbabwe. He went through Machipanda border post and made his way to Harare. I met him in Harare and he offered to be my personal security attaché. He was to prove a pillar of my security and through him I owe my survival as we transverse through dangerous corridors of violence in both rural and urban areas.

Then three weeks later, when I was coming from Bindura there was another incident. There was a policeman, Michael Langweni, whom I had given a T-shirt to and they arrested him for wearing it. Since then he has resigned saying he couldn't work for the present government and would rather not be employed. So I employed him and now he was my personal security. We were all coming from Bindura, that day we decided to pass through Glendale in Mazowe East. Unknown to us was the fact that at the Glendale town centre there were youth militia permanently stationed at the rank. They were using the council beer hall and the Cocktail bar as a torture camp. The youth chairman from Bindura, Tongai, was wearing an MDC T-shirt. Michael and Tongai went to get drinks. Tongai was attacked by these ZANU (PF) youths who were armed with knives and iron bars. Michael was trying to assist him when he also was attacked. By then Langwani was stabbed in the thigh and Tongai was stabbed in the thigh and stomach and he was lying unconscious. His clothes were in a pool of blood and I rushed him to hospital for treatment. My bodyguard was arrested by the police for firing the gun and taken to Concession police station. After the hospital I went there and lodged a complaint with the member in charge who was pro-ZANU (PF). After diplomatic manoeuvres, I demanded the release of the bodyguard. Eventually he was released but the police refused to hand over my gun. It was only until the following day that I got back my gun.

An account by Sarudzai Chinoto [Chimurenga name: Cde Zulu] Elliot Pfebve's head of security — 10 May 2000

Last month I began to mobilise people. I am a former war veteran for ZANLA. I am well known. I was the security and intelligence officer for ZANLA for Nehanda sector during the Chimurenga. I was also working under the Presidential Guard since independence and I retired in 1997. The first incident happened on 13 or 14 April. I was on a bus getting home with John Zvenyika, my relative from Buhera. We got off in Mt Darwin around 6-7:00 pm. The youngsters they have hired were at the ZANU (PF) office. We were having drinks when I was seen by Marodza. We got back in the bus, but the bus was stopped by ZANU (PF) youths and we were pulled out. We were pushed into the ZANU (PF) office. I was holding a gas canister which they thought may be a bomb so they pushed us out again. Fortunately at that moment some soldiers were driving by. They saw us and took us into their armoured vehicle, and then the bus was told to follow them. At a certain point they stopped and we got back on the bus and went home. The case was reported at Dotito, but Marodza was never picked up. They have been trying to kidnap me because they know I have all the information about ZANU (PF) since I used to be once an aspiring candidate for that party in my area. But I gave the seat to someone called Patel. They know I am popular. I was organising well and I went as far as Kaitano. In one month MDC support boomed. There was no ZANU (PF) in my area. When they realised it that is when I began to have serious problems. I could not travel on any bus. There were people waiting for me everywhere. On 10 May I was beaten. There was a rally by Border Gezi at the Dande shops. I was outside. I wanted to come to town to Harare to draw money. I was talking with some MDC supporters as I waited for the bus. There were about seven of us. Then when someone from the rally saw me, they left the rally with the intention of kidnapping and killing me. There were two trucks of ZANU (PF) supporters – more than 40 of them. I was beaten badly. They had axes, spears and sticks. They attacked us and I was injured in the eye, leg, head and chest. I fought until they left me for dead. If there is a tense situation here, we cross into Mozambique since we are near the border. It's about 4 kms to the border from my house. I was trying to escape, but was wounded. There is a land mine company called Minetec, which found me and the doctor treated me. They are doing mine clearance near the border and because no one can come through those areas where they took me for treatment; that is how I survived. Then I decided to look for my relative Kagogoda who is Mozambican. I fought alongside Frelimo (Mozambican guerrilla movement) in 1971 so I know the area. My relative John had already heard of the fighting at Dande and he gapped into Mozambique to find Kagogoda. He reached Kagogoda's home and I came later. Then John went out to look for cigarettes and he was captured by the Frelimo police. Kagogoda was also caught and he was told to go and find me. Joyce Mujuru had given them the order to kill me. They were told they would be paid $25,000. John was held for four days, but Kagogoda came and told me to run. I went from there to Dzete, then Nyamapanda and then to Harare. The people who are organising this violence in my area are Gezi, Mujuru and Marodza. The youths are said to be paid $500 a day. They were staying at the Kamsenzere school camp under Marodza, but one of the leaders there, Karikoga, was arrested after the Pfebve's brother was killed. I was there at that time of the battle in Mukumbura when they came to kill him. I am sure I saw Marodza in a car even today in Harare. I suspect he has been sent to look for me and I even have to hide here. I cannot stay in one place for long. [Note: John Zvenyika was present during the interview and confirmed this statement also adding that, " When I was imprisoned by those Frelimo, they showed me that letter from Mujuru saying that Zulu must be caught with $25 000 for his head. They were thinking of telling Mujuru that I was the one. Then they decided they would release me for $4000, which Kagogoda managed to raise from Zulu. After I gave them the money I was released."]

An account by Nixon Mabika-Pfebve's driver now made blind— 13 April 2000

We had gone to a rally in Mount Darwin on 13 April. When we reached Mount Darwin, the police took us to the police camp and said 'You can't do your rally here because the ZANU (PF) candidate for Mt Darwin, Saviour Kasukuwere, doesn't want to see you here'. He's an ex-CIO. We said we have booked for the rally and if they want to kill us they can do so here. Our national coordinator said we should go to Rushinga as the situation was not so tense there and we could eat freely, and then come back for the rally later. After coming from Rushinga, we passed Kasukuwere's house along the road. He had hired about 1000 youths. They were by the roadside. He was not there and had gone to fetch more people in a lorry. There were also two vehicles belonging to CIOs. The youths on the road started throwing stones and the police fired tear gas at us instead of those who were attacking. There were two men in police uniforms, but they were not really police. I know those guys from Bindura. I worked at Kelly's restaurant which was beside the CIO office and I used to see them all the time. They were CIOs. There were also two CIOs in soldier's uniform. They were armed with sub-machine guns and pistols. I was driving a Toyota Hilux and I had hired a Kombi. We had a lorry, and a Nissan diesel which belongs to Elliot Pfebve, the aspiring candidate for Bindura. All the boys from the cars got down to take stones and throw them back so that we could pass through. We succeeded in fighting back and managed to move forward. Among the attackers were ex-combatants and some of them were armed with guns. Then we drove forward towards Mt Darwin. When we reached the junction of the road, Kasukuwere was there in his Benz with more than 500 youths in a lorry. He pointed a gun and fired shots from a pistol. He fired about seven, but they didn't hit anyone. The first one nearly hit me as I was at the front, but I ducked down. I was at the front of the delegation driving. He must have aimed at me because then I would crash and he could have attacked the others on the back. They youths were throwing stones at us. We managed again to keep on driving through them. There were policemen standing on the corners. They shouted we should turn towards Bindura. We did so, but we went about 500 metres, before he overtook in his Mercedes and with the Mazda's belonging to the CIO. They blocked the road and we were forced to stop. Kasukuwere and the others were pointing their guns at us. Then the police drove up just next to my car. It was the Officer-in-Charge for Mt Darwin. He must have heard something was going on and he came with six other police cars. But Kasukuwere went to the policeman and said: "We told you we don't want to see these MDC people here. This is a no-go area for MDC." He hit him across the face with his hand, and the police cars pulled over to the side to watch from a distance, like it was a football match. Then Kasukuwere took an iron bar and started hitting my windscreen. He broke through the window and then the bar hit me in the face and when I got out of the car he hit me in the eye. I have now lost that eye. He then went to the next car and with the others they were hitting them. The windscreens and all the lights were all broken. Then there was a helicopter above and when I heard it I began to run and I managed to run into the bushes. But although I escaped, he made others lie down in a circle, like they did during the war and they were beating them with sticks. The other ZANU (PF) supporters had by now arrived in their trucks and were helping them and some were pointing their guns. We couldn't fight back because of these guns. It was past 4 pm when we ran away. [The incident happened around 3 pm]. I went running through the bush, with about six others. I was in terror. My eye was bleeding. I just kept running. All night we kept going towards Madziwa. In the morning we reached there and went straight to the police station. The police wrote letters and we were given a car to go to the clinic and given some Panadols and sent to Bindura. I haven't yet had a chance to make a full report to the police, but will do when I get to Bindura. At the hospital in Bindura, he sent four CIOs to see if I was there. I saw them and told a nurse and they transferred me to Parirenyatwa. I got out of hospital two days ago and will try to go back to Bindura tomorrow. There is another guy who was with me whose name I remember. He was also from Bindura. He had an injury to his left shoulder, but mostly bruises. His name is Phillip Mabika. These ZANU (PF) people are burning everything. They have destroyed everything in Mukumbura. They have destroyed everything in Dotito, where Border Gezi has his shop. They are burning MDC houses. People are just running away. They killed someone in Mt Darwin four days ago. He was an attendant at the service station. It was Kasukuwere who did it. Border Gezi is paying people and he is taking ex-combatants to Nicholas Goche [Vice-minister]. He's one of the people who are doing these killings. Chen Chimutengwende has a farm near Glendale on the Bindura road and he's organising the burning of houses there.

Bindura By-Election Report 28-29 July 2001

Report Summary

The Bindura Constituency by-election held on 27-28 July 2001 was necessitated by the death in late April of Border Gezi, the popular and flamboyant ZANU-PF Parliamentarian. Gezi who rose through the party ranks of ZANU-PF to Governor, elected Member of Parliament and Cabinet Minister played a large role in the ZANU – PF campaign for the Year 2000 Parliamentary Election and was credited with retaining the rural vote for his party.

Gezi was the third Member of Parliament to die since the landmark June 2000 Parliamentary Election when the newly formed opposition Movement for Democratic Change won an unprecedented number of seats in Parliament. For the first time since Independence, ZANU-PF did not have an absolute majority of elected seats. The election results also exposed ZANU-PF's poor urban support base and the subsequent violence in rural areas resulted in MDC'S poor rural support base leading to the prevailing misconception that ZANU-PF has more support in rural areas than in urban areas and that the MDC is an urban party.

Border Gezi narrowly won the election in June 2000 amidst allegations of orchestrated campaign violence and rigging perpetrated by his supporters with his knowledge and encouragement. These allegations included the murder of my brother Mathew Pfebve.

Background Introduction

Bindura constituency is one of the most unique constituencies in the country. It encompasses rural, urban, peri-urban, communal, commercial farming and resettlement areas. This in itself raised the interest as people wanted to see how the vote would be divided amongst the rural and urban areas and how this would affect the final result. Heightening the interest is the fact that Bindura Town is the provincial capital of Mashonaland Central arguably one of the ruling party's strongholds. In the previous election, the winning margin of ZANU-PF had been relatively small. This all added to the interest surrounding the Bindura by-election.

Pre-Election Period

Pre-Election Violence

The pre-election period was characterized by reports of widespread violence between the two parties. Media reports detailing at least ten incidents of serious election related violence added on to the intimidation which was alleged to be going on a daily basis. Both parties accused each other of training and deployment of armed supporters to terrorize residents and potential voters in the constituency. But evidence to contrary showed that many MDC supporters were forced away from the constituency and were unable to vote due to widespread violence from ZANU (PF) militia and supporters. State sponsored violence was rampant.

Inspection of voter's roll and registration of voters

The voters' roll was opened for inspection and those not registered were given the opportunity to vote. By the time that the election was held, the total number of registered had increased by almost 4000 to 56 000. Although observers questioned the accuracy of the figure, and the authenticity of the alleged voters, the Voter's Roll remained the same.

Nomination Court

The nomination court was held at the Bindura Magistrates Court on 6th July 2001. Only two candidates presented themselves for nomination. Their papers were accepted and they were duly nominated. These were:

Elliot Pfebve of the Movement for Democratic Change (MDC), and Elliot Manyika of the Zimbabwe African National Union (Patriotic Front) (ZANU-PF).

Campaigning

Both parties campaigned vigorously in the run-up to the election. These took the form of rallies, night-time meetings, door-to-door campaigns and posters as well as the use of hailers and loudspeakers. There were periodic flare-ups in the constituency when supporters of both parties met. Both parties held star rallies addressed by prominent party members, the MDC President Morgan Tsvangirai addressed a rally in Chiwaridzo Bindura and at Mupandira Shopping Centre. This however turned tragic as our MDC team in 13-vehicle convoy, was attacked by about 400 hundred alleged ZANU-PF supporters resulting in injuries and damage to all vehicles.

Pre-Election Violence

There were reports of violence in all the areas of the constituency. It is clear from media in both the public and private press that violence certainly featured in the election. Several people were hospitalized as a result of the violence. Violence was initiated by supporters of ZANU (PF) supported by government agencies and took the form of

a) Assault with deadly weapons such as chains, axes and sticks,
b) Looting of property including foodstuff and household property
c) Arson and burning of houses, vehicles and foodstuffs.

Violence was mostly targeted at MDC supporters including disrupting rallies and meetings. More than forty people, the majority of them supporters of the MDC were arrested in connection with the violence, as the police targeted the victims of crime rather than the perpetrators. In one incident the police also seized my vehicles and that of my campaign team and arrested sixteen MDC supporters. We complained that the large number of our supporters who had been arrested was less a reflection of their party's involvement in violence than the results of an organized police crackdown on the opposition.

However the violence escalated to the point where a convoy of MDC vehicles was attacked, allegedly by ZANU-PF supporters.

Voter Education

The situation in the constituency became tense earlier on and it was decided that rather than holding only one meeting in the constituency, it would be better to distribute materials.

Media

The Bindura by-election received considerable media coverage before, during and after, mainly due to the politically related violence before the elections while excluding the contesting candidate's campaign policies. This limited the coverage to events rather than critical election issues like profiling the candidates. Campaign manifesto's dealt more with party policies rather than what the individual candidates had to offer for their constituency.

Media coverage preceding the election was characterized by biased reporting depending on the media. The Daily News provided horrifying evidence of what appeared to be a concerted campaign of violence against opposition MDC supporters around the country and in Bindura while Zimpapers reported attacks on ZANU PF supporters by MDC youths. The Independent press had difficulty in accessing information from the Zimbabwe Republic Police leading to the failure to get a response on the MDC' candidate's allegation that the *"application of the law by the police is selective because MDC and Zanu PF members are treated differently."*

The Zimbabwe Broadcasting Corporation through both radio and television covered campaigns for Elliot Manyika and his ruling party without giving the same coverage to MDC and my candidature. This would seem to violate the new Broadcasting Services Act, which stipulates an equal opportunity for air time for all political parties regardless of political affiliation. In many instances the MDC was accused of several acts including acts of violence but was not given an opportunity to respond to these allegations.

The Zimbabwe Mirror acknowledged the occurrence of political violence, but did not blame either party. The paper simply sought opinions from political commentators. On the first polling day only *The Daily News* profiled the credentials of both candidates, acknowledging the problem of political violence in passing.

One notable discrepancy of the media's Bindura by-election coverage was the lack of investigation into the use of the mechanisms employed in conducting the election. The *Financial Gazette* however detailed an alleged plot by ZANU PF to rig the presidential poll by relocating half a million extra voters from urban areas under the fast track resettlement exercise to bolster its rural support base. The Registrar General refuted the allegations. None of the media seem to have asked the Registrar General's office to account for the extra 4000 or so voters nor did they interview a single monitor or their supervising organizations in their reports on the conduct of the by-election. Only one presiding officer was reported in *The Financial Gazette* as saying that, *"...roll-calls of resettled farmers were being taken by ZANU PF officials at night to check whether they had voted."* If such serious allegations of the abuse of the instruments in the democratic process existed, they deserve to be subjected to diligent inquiry.

The state media provided no space to the opposition in its reports and follow-up stories on the election results, and ZBC carried no analysis beyond the comments of government officials.

Polling
Deployment of polling monitors

The election was monitored by over 90 monitors, deployed at the 69 locations, where polling took place. Five supervisors and one co-coordinator were also in the field to supervise the monitors and deal with any problems faced by the monitors.

The monitors were deployed on Friday 27 July 2001 from Kimberley Reef Hotel in Bindura.

There was a small presence of international observers. They were not accredited hence they were denied access into the polling stations. They however went along with their operations without any complications.

The polling days 28-29 July 2001

The most notable aspect of the polling days was that they were generally more peaceful than the pre-election days. The activities in the polling stations were managed by polling officers under the supervision of the presiding officers. These officers operated under the close eye of the party agents and monitors.

There were no major anomalies reported in terms of the voting process itself except incidences where voters attempted to vote twice. Confusion was caused by the arrest of a well-known MDC supporter, which was only cleared when it emerged that the arrest was not election –related. There was further confusion when as an MDC candidate, was arrested and detained when I was touring the polling stations. This could only be construed as having been done to allow ZANU (PF) a space for rigging the elections.

Voter turnout was high although a significant number of voters were turned away because their names did not appear on the voters' roll. The Constituency Registrar confiscated Voter's Rolls, which had been brought by the MDC into the polling stations. The MDC wanted to use the voters' rolls to verify if those who had been turned away did not appear on the Voter's Roll. Allegations of vote rigging were very rampant.

Polling Stations

In the by-election, there were 29 permanent and 16 mobile polling stations. A static polling station remains in the same location for the duration of the election and usually opens from 0700hrs and 1900hrs for the two polling days. Static stations are usually found in densely populated areas such as rural and urban areas. Mobile polling stations are those stations, which move from one location to another usually in sparsely populated areas such as commercial farming areas and peri-urban areas. Mobile stations open at 0700hrs and close at 1700hrs normally. The same Presiding Officer and polling officers officiate at all locations. These locations are usually not more than four. Depending on how many locations a mobile polling station is covering, it can spend a section of each of the two polling days covering one of the polling locations.

Generally there were enough polling stations providing coverage for all potential voters. Most polling stations in Bindura town were busy from the start to the end of polling with long queues being observed at these polling stations. Queues started forming as early as 0500hrs.

Voting Process

The Presiding officers and polling officers were generally in control of the polling station and these were appointed by Mugabe's government and their impartiality was questionable. The polling officers were knowledgeable about their roles and responsibilities and discharged these roles well. Most Presiding Officers were in good control of their stations. They assisted all voters that could not exercise their vote on their own. The presence of the police was pivotal in securing peace and tranquility during the voting process.

Despite reports of violence and the high levels of political intolerance preceding the election, the manner in which the party agents conducted their business was quite commendable. There were no reports of incidences between party agent and they worked well together in ensuring the smooth flow of the elections while assisting the Presiding Officer, polling officers and monitors.

Summaries of report of polling stations

1 Bindura Polling Centre

The polling station opened at 0700 hrs and closed at 1900 hrs. There were 6 political party agents divided equally between ZANU-PF 3 and MDC 3. The voting procedure went on well with no reported incidences. Fifty-nine (59) people were turned away. They were said not to have been registered in the voters' roll and not to have identity cards.

2 Tendai Hall

The station opened at 0700hrs and closed at 1900 hrs. There were 6 political party agents, 3 from each party. The election officials had a clear understanding of the voting procedures. Voting materials and equipment were available. Sixty-two (62) people were turned away either because they did not have identity cards or were not registered in the voters' roll.

3 Chiwaridzo Clinic

The polling station opened at 0700hrs. There were 3 party agents from ZANU-PF and 2 from MDC. Ballot equipment and materials were secure. Forty-five (45) people were turned away because they were not registered. The station closed at 1900hrs.

4 Open Space District Administrator's Office

The station opened at 0700 hrs and closed at 1900hrs. The ballot boxes were opened and verified. There were 5 political party agents, 3 from ZANU-PF and 2 from MDC. The election officials had a clear understanding of voting procedures. The voters also appeared to know what to do.

5 Dengu Primary School

The station opened at 0700hrs and closed at 1900hrs. There were 2 party agents each from ZANU-PF and MDC. There were no reports of incidences or irregularities.

6 Wayerera Primary School

There were 3 party agents each from both political parties. There were no incidences or irregularities that were reported. People voted peacefully. Ten people were turned away since they did not have national identity cards. The stationed opened at 0700hrs and closed at 1900hrs.

7 Manhenga Council Offices

The ballot box was opened and verified in the presence of party agents and monitors. The polling station was close to a previously established torture camp and this had an effect of intimidating the voters. There were no irregularities observed during the voting period. MDC had 3 party agents while ZANU PF had 2. People voted peacefully. At one point, Commissioner Chihuri visited this polling station to see the police force that was maintaining peace. There were enough voting materials, equipment or records. The voting began and ended at the specified times.

8 Maravanyika Primary School

The polling station opened at 0700 hrs and closed at 1900 hrs. ZANU PF had 3 party agents while MDC had 2. The election officials had clear understanding of the voting procedures. There were 10 people who were turned away because they were not registered in the voters' roll.

9 Masembura Primary School

The station opened at and closed at the specified times. Ballot boxes were opened and verified in the presence of party agents and monitors. There were 6 party agents evenly shared by the two political parties. The officials had a clear understanding of all the voting procedures. The ballot boxes were closed and sealed in the correct manner. Voting was peaceful at this station.

10 Jingo Primary School

Unlike other polling stations, this station started operating at 0630hrs and closed its doors at 1930hrs. The ballot boxes were opened and verified in the presence of party agents. There were 3 party agents from each political party. The voting process was peaceful. There were 41 people who were returned. Most of them were not registered and some did not have identity cards. The station received one thousand ballot papers, and there were 233 invalid ballot papers.

11 Chiriseri Primary School

The station opened at 0645 hrs and closed at 1900 hrs. There were 3 party agents from ZANU PF and 2 from MDC. The whole voting process was in order. No one attempted to temper with voting materials, equipment or records. Twenty-one people were turned away because their names did not appear in the voters' roll and some of them did not have identity cards.

12 Jigiji Primary School

There were 2 party agents from MDC and 3 from ZANU PF. The polling officers had a clear understanding of the voting process. Twenty-eight people were turned away. People voted peacefully at this station. The polling station opened at 0630 hrs and closed at the specified times.

13 Chireka Primary School

The station opened at 0700 hrs and closed at 1900 hrs. 5 party agents also observed the voting process, 3 from ZANU PF and 2 from MDC. There was no report of any irregularities. People voted peacefully.

14 Murembe Secondary School

The station opened and closed at the specified times. There were 2 party agents each from ZANU PF and MDC. There was no reported incidence of violence.

15 Musana Primary School

The polling station opened at 0700 hrs and closed at 1900hrs. All the party agents were present. There were enough material and equipment available from the start throughout the voting period.

There were 46 people who were turned away. Most of them were not registered in the voters' roll. A total of 19 people were helped to vote at this station mainly due to disability. The voting itself was very peaceful.

16 Muchapondwa Primary School

The station opened at 0701 hrs and closed at 1900hrs. There were 3 party agents from ZANU PF and 3 from MDC. The election officials had a clear understanding of the voting procedure.

Voting was peaceful at this polling station. There were fifty-three people who were turned away because their names did not appear on the voters' roll.

17 Chakanyemba Primary School

The station opened and closed at the specified times. There were 2 party agents from MDC and 3 from ZANU PF. The election officials had an understanding of all the voting procedures. Voting was peaceful throughout the elections.

18 Mupandira Primary School

The station opened and closed at the specified times. There were 5 party agents, 3 from ZANU PF and 2 from MDC. The election officials had a clear understanding of the voting procedures. There were no reported incidences or irregularities as people voted peacefully.

19 Mashambanhaka Primary School

The station opened at 0700 hrs and closed at 1900 hrs in the presence of 2 party agents from ZANU PF and 3 from MDC. The election officials understood all the voting procedures. No one tampered with voting materials. The voters appeared to know what they were doing. Sixty people were turned away. This was mainly because most of them did not have their names registered on the voters' roll. People waited and voted peacefully at the station.

20 Gorwa Primary School

The station opened and closed at the specified times. There were 3 party agents each from MDC and ZANU PF. The voting procedure was carried out in a transparent and peaceful manner. There were 9 people who were turned away.

21 Nyava Secondary School

The station opened at 0700 hrs and closed at 1900 hrs. There were 5 political party agents, 3 from ZANU PF and 2 from MDC. The election officials had a clear understanding of all the voting procedures. No one tampered with voting materials, equipment or records. The voters appeared to know what to do. All the voting materials were available.

22 Rosetta Rust Primary School

The station opened at 0700 hrs and closed at 1900 hrs. There were 2 party agents each from MDC and ZANU PF. The voting procedure went on quite well in peaceful circumstance. There were no reported irregularities. There was an incident of people who were wearing ZANU PF T-shirts, and this was one of the invaded farms.

23 Craigside Farm

The station opened and closed at the specified times. There were 6 political party agents, 3 from MDC and 3 from ZANU PF. There were no reported incidences of violence but presence of War veterans was noticed which had an effect of swerving potential voters' choices.

24 Cowley Farm Pre-School

The station opened at 0700 hrs and closed at 1900hrs. There were 2 party agents from MDC and 2 from ZANU PF. The election officials had a clear understanding of all the voting procedures. The voting procedure went on peacefully. There were no reported incidences or irregularities at this station, war veterans gave a watchful eye and this was another invaded farm. The siting of the polling stations near war veterans was strategic for ZANU(PF). This also supports the earlier press reports of a plot to rig using war veterans.

25 Trojan Primary School

The station opened and closed at the specified times. There were 4 political party agents, 2 from MDC and 2 from ZANU PF. There were 81 people who were turned away. The reasons could not be verified.

26 Chiumbere Primary School

The station opened at 0700hrs and closed at 1900 hrs. MDC had 2 party agents while ZANU PF had 3 party agents present. There were no reports of incidences or irregularities. The election officials had a clear understanding of what they were doing.

27 Nziwara Shopping Centre Open Space

The station opened and closed at the specified times. There were 5 political party agents, 2 from MDC and 3 from ZANU PF. The election officials had a clear understanding of the voting procedures. There were eleven people who were turned away mainly because they did not have identity cards. Voting was peaceful at this station.

28 Foothills Primary School

There were 61 people who registered. The polling station opened at 0700hrs and closed at 1900hrs. There were 5 political party agents, 3 from MDC and 2 from ZANU PF. 16 people were turned away because their names did not appear on the voters' roll. An MDC vehicle was attacked on its way to monitor the polling station.

29 Chipadze Farm Community Center

The station opened and closed at the specified times. There were 3 party agents each from MDC and ZANU PF. Voting at this station was calm.

30 Mobile 1

On both days the station opened at 0700hrs and closed at 1700hrs. Voting was peaceful at the mobile stations namely, Zvakwana Primary School, Avoca Primary School and Melfort Farm. There were 17 people who were turned away at Zvakwana Primary school and 14 at Avoca. This was due to them not being registered. There were no reports of incidences or irregularities at the mobile stations. The election officials had a clear understanding of what they were doing about voting procedures.

31 Mobile 2

On both days, the station opened and closed at the specified times. There were no reports of incidences or irregularities at both stations. Voting was peaceful at both stations. The polling officers understood their roles and responsibilities and discharged them well.

32 Mobile 3

There were 4 party agents at the 2 stations, Cheviri Farm and Tarlington Farm, 2 from MDC and 2 from ZANU PF. The station opened at 0700hrs and closed at 1700hrs on both days. The election officials had a clear understanding of the voting procedures. There were 14 people who were turned away. Most of those turned away were not registered and a few did not have identity cards.

33 Mobile 4

There were 3 stations under this mobile, namely, Bermerside Farm, Duiker Flats Estates and Batanai Hall. The polling stations opened at 0700hrs, 1400hrs and 0700hrs the following day respectively. Burmerside closed at 1230hrs and the other stations closed at 1700hrs. At Burmerside and Duiker farm, 324 people voted. There were 33 people who were turned away. The main reason is that their names did not appear on the voters' roll. At Duiker flats, voting delayed by about 20 minutes. The reason being that the election officials took time in changing the voting room. At Batanai Hall, 86 people cast their votes.

34 Mobile 5

The 2 polling stations under this mobile were Katanya Farm and Terragwai Farm. The polling stations opened at 0700hrs. There were 4 polling agents at this station 2 from MDC and 2 from ZANU PF. The voting was very peaceful on both days. The stations closed at 1900hrs. The polling officials had a clear understanding of the voting procedures. There were 157 people who were turned away.

35 Mobile 6

There were 2 stations under this mobile, namely, Butcombe farm (day 1) and Gatumba clinic (day 2). On day 1, the station opened at 0700hrs and on day 2 the station opened at 0645hrs. On both days the polling stations closed at 1700hrs. There were 2 party agents each from MDC and ZANU PF. The election officials had a clear understanding of all the voting procedures. The voters appeared to know what they were doing. There were no reported incidences of irregularities.

36 Mobile 7

Bemberero Farm, Vale Farm and SOS Maizelands School were the polling station under mobile 7. The polling stations opened at 0700hrs and closed at 1700hrs. There were no reported incidences or irregularities. Voting was peaceful.

37 Mobile 8

There were 2 polling stations under this mobile namely, Chelvery farm and Chomukuti farm. Both stations opened and closed at the specified times. MDC had 2 party agents and ZANU PF also had 2 party agents. The voting process was very peaceful. There were no reports of incidences or irregularities.

38 Mobile 9

The 2 polling stations where Manga resettlement and Ashcott School. Both stations were opened at 0700hrs and closed at 1700hrs. There were 4 political party agents 2 from MDC and 2 from ZANU PF. 44 people were turned away at this station. The Voting process was carried out well in a free and peaceful manner. Thirty-eight people were turned away either because they were not on the voters' roll or they did not have identity cards.

39 Mobile 10

Butleigh farm and St Basils primary school where the 2 polling stations for mobile 10. On both days the station opened at 0700hrs and closed at 1700hrs. Voting was peaceful.

40 Mobile 11

The mobile station comprised of Burton farm, Uronga South Farm and Dawmill farm. The polling stations opened and closed at the specified times. There were 5 political party agents, 3 from ZANU PF and 2 from MDC. The polling officials had a clear understanding of the voting procedures. There were no reported incidences or irregularities.

41 Mobile 12

On day 1, voting took place at 2 polling stations namely, Gosforth farm and Thrums farm. The polling stations opened at 0700hrs and closed at 1700hrs. On day 2, voting took place at Woodbroke South and Woodbroke North. There were no reported incidences or irregularities as people voted peacefully.

42 Mobile 13

The polling station under mobile 13 was Irenedale farm, Fox farm on day 1 and Kingstone farm on day 2. All stations opened and closed at the specified times. There were 3 party agents, 1 from MDC and 2 from ZANU PF. It has been reported that many people were turned away, but the actual figure is not provided.

43 Mobile 14

Both Benridge farm and Pednor School opened at 0700hrs and closed at 1700hrs. There were no reported incidences or irregularities as people voted peacefully.

44 Mobile 15

On day one, voting took place at Simoona Estates polling station and Pimento polling station. The stations opened at 0700hrs and closed at 1230hrs then at 1400hrs and closed at 1700 hrs respectively on day two. Mapunga primary school was the second polling station and it opened at 0700hrs and closed at 1900hrs. MDC had 2 party agents while ZANU PF had 3 on the first day. Twenty-one voters were turned away. The main reason being that either they were registered elsewhere or did not register at all. On the second day at the Mapunga polling station there were 4 party agents, 2 from MDC and 2 from ZANU PF 2. Forty-nine people were turned away mainly because they did not appear on the voters' roll.

45 Mobile 16

Hinton Estates and Lagnaha farm where the polling stations for day 1 and day 2 respectively. The stations opened and closed at the specified times. There were no irregularities observed. Voting was peaceful. Forty-five people were turned away. The main reason is that their names did not appear on the voters' roll.

Miscellaneous

There were no significant voting patterns observed. Voters queued in an orderly fashion and were allowed to vote peacefully. At the more congested polling stations voters complained that voting was taking a long time. There were no distinct voting patterns along gender or age lines.

There was a visible presence of party supporters at all polling stations. The supporters, the majority of them ZANU-PF supporters congregated in groups which were singing and dancing. Most of this activity took place beyond the 100m radius so there was little that the law enforcement officers were required to do.

At Tendayi Hall on Sunday 29 July 2001 prominent members of the ruling party were observed within the 100m radius of the polling station. This is a contravention of the Electoral Act. However the police did not take any action.

Overview

It has been observed that polling stations opened at 0700hrs and closed at 1900hrs generally and the mobile stations at 0700hrs and closed at 1700hrs. At each polling station, there were political party agents representing either party. Most of the people were turned away for various reasons. The main reason being that, most of them were not registered. Some did not have identity cards. Voting was peaceful in most of the polling stations. There had been enough materials, equipment, records, which were used at various polling stations. The general observation from the reports provided, it revealed that it was a fair and free election.

Counting and announcement of results

Counting

Counting took place at Tendayi Hall in Chipadze Township in Bindura Town. Ballot boxes began arriving at the counting centre on the night of Sunday 28th July. 2001 and were all delivered by 0800hrs on the morning of Monday 30th July 2001. The counting began at 0800hrs and finished at 2000hrs in the evening. This was due to the fact that some of the boxes had to be recounted in order for the ballot papers to tally.

The situation at the counting centre was relatively calm. Supporters began congregating at the counting centre as early as 0800hrs. Rival groups of supporters were seen singing and dancing outside the counting centre and were separated by the police. The police maintained a presence outside the counting centre from the early morning and increased this presence as the crowd grew larger during the course of the day.

Announcement of results

The results were announced to the shock of many people as follows;
Elliot Manyika of ZANU-PF polled 15864 votes.
Elliot Pfebve of MDC polled 9456 votes.

	July 2001 Bindura by-election	June 2000 Parliamentary
Registered Voters		53191
Total votes cast	25849	25589
Spoilt Papers	529	669
Percentage Poll	45.6%	48.11%
MDC	9456	11257
ZANU-PF	15864	13328
UP	-	335

Comparison of 2000 and 2001 election results.

Post- Elections

The situation in the constituency remains tense following the elections. Incidences of MDC supporters being targeted after returning to the constituency were reported. Many people were unable to vote because of violence and became IDPs, still returned to homes and property destroyed.

Voters turned away

As has become the case, a significant number of voters were turned away, most of them because their names did not appear on the voters' roll. This again exposed the fact that there is little voter-education taking place. Those who were turned away either did not register at all or had not transferred their registration from their previous constituency. Most people did not bother to inspect the voters' roll when it was opened for inspection. This was because they did not know and also because most did not give the exercise the importance that it deserves.

Mobile polling stations

There were a large number of mobile polling stations used in this election, in light of the fact that the constituency has a large number of commercial farms which are sparsely populated. One of the major challenges of mobile polling stations is to make sure that all the residents in the surrounding area are fully informed of the presence of the mobile. Where a mobile station is going to be in one area for a morning only once it moves, it does not return and those who have not taken the opportunity to vote will not get a second chance.

Recommendations

Voter Education

There is need to carry out voter education before any by-election to ensure that all voters have enough information to participate in elections and to inspect and re-register if necessary.

Violence

A more concerted effort needs to be taken to deal with the violence, which has continued to bedevil elections in Zimbabwe since the 2000 Parliamentary Election.

Code of conduct

Some of the political party supporters show no regard for the law and willingly break the election laws. This is especially so in the case of rank and file supporters who attack rival supporters and even high-profile party members who campaigned and shouted party slogans within the 100 m radius.

All stakeholders should sign a code of conduct, which they or their organizations have participated in drafting.

Location of polling stations

Polling Stations should not be placed near shopping centres and or bottle stores as this makes them difficult to control particularly where there is a degree of rowdiness.

Deployment of monitors

Deployment of national and international Monitors should take place a week or two before the election.

Conclusion

The results of the Bindura Bye-Election can not be said to be a reflection of the people's will for the following reasons;

1. State sponsored violence meant that it was difficult to have a free and fair campaign by MDC.

2. The monitoring and managing of elections was being done by partisan civil servants and times war veterans and militia of the ruling party ZANU (PF)

3. The high number of Internally Displace Persons (IDPs) meant that many people did not vote because they were still in hiding or had sought refuge to far away constituencies and were unable to cast their votes.

4. Unfair resource access as ZANU (PF) candidate was using state resources including a monopoly on state media both print and TV.

5. Most of the farming and rural parts of the constituency had become a no go area for the MDC as ZANU (PF) thugs had set up torture camps which they prefer to call re-education centres at every shopping centres.

Arrested and incarcerated 20 September 2001

It's almost a month since the Bindura By-Election on the 29 and 30 august 2001. The dust has settled the argon of losing yet another election on rigging is still vivid and real. I reflected upon the destruction of property, people maimed and I have also lost close colleagues during the campaigns. Trymore Midzi my provincial youth chairman who spearheaded the Bindura campaign was abducted and murdered. Scores were wounded, property destroyed and many have still not returned to their burnt houses. 12 youths are still in remand prison under drummed up charges of being suspected of found in possession of fuel likely to be used to make petrol bombs. In a country where fuel reserves are erratic it's common to find people with gallons of petrol and even selling it by the roadside, but if you are known MDC activist the penalty can be severe. I have visited these youth periodically at the Harare remand prison and they were all upbeat that one day they will look back to a country they have liberated. Tafadzwa Pfebve the only son of my late murdered brother Mathew Pfebve was one of those who were languishing in remand prison, what a double tragedy. He was arrested during my campaign trail and was still in remand together with others.

When I thought I had suffered enough then came a call from Law and Order department from an Inspector Dowa. Dowa was a notorious inspector who was more CIO than police officer in charge of Law and Order dealing with political arrests and detentions. Most MDC leaders have been arrested, detained and sometimes sent to remand prison by Inspector Dowa. His message was very clear that I was required at Central police station, Law and Order section for questioning regarding a shooting the month before. I was to bring my Tokorova pistol and any ammunition with it. I knew what that meant and I was not shocked by the charge but by the method of arrest which came through my mobile phone. Normally they would just arrest you in the middle of the night when you are enjoying a good night's sleep, this type of arrest was unusual. Never the less I was prepared for any eventuality.

The allegation related to the 27 August 2001 ambush in which a convoy carrying the MDC leadership including Morgan Tsvangirai was attacked in Chiveso village en route to a legal rally. The MDC leadership was supporting me in the Bindura Bye-Election a week before the election. Ironically we had applied for the 2 rallies as required by the law and the government had given us an approval letter. We had the first rally in Bindura, Chiwaridzo Township which was well attended and successful. The next rally was in the Musana rural area at the Mupandira shopping centre which was part of Bindura constituency. We were in a convoy of 13 vehicles when we noticed that the road ahead was closed. When we stopped immediately we were under a barrage of all sorts of missiles, stones, gun fire and any sharp objects which could make a maximum lethal impact. It was so calculated that we quickly discovered that we were encircled and we could see other cars in the convoy burning. I came out of the vehicle and briefed the President that we needed to move forward as there was anarchy behind us. I started returning fire albeit in the air to scare them while commanding the vehicles to move on. Other MDC activists with guns also returned fire in the air. By the time we came out of the ambush all 13 vehicles were damaged and scores of MDC activists injured. We continued, took stock of our colleagues but discovered that we were missing more than 20 people. We took a decision to continue with the rally while the security would check on the missing activists.

Little did we know that another ambush was waiting for us 5 km from where had the first one. There was even an army officer with an AK 47 pointing at us when we arrived. We were ordered to stop and we complied. The president Morgan Tsvangirai then embarked to confront the soldier who was encircled with ZANU (PF) supporters with all sorts of weapons. After some negotiations with the army the army convinced the ZANU (PF) thugs not to attack us, the soldier even jumped on one of our trucks to ensure our safety. We could not believe our luck on the day but little did we know that our colleagues, Dr Mudzingwa included were now in police custody charged with burning a ZANU (PF) car although it was his own car burnt by ZANU (PF) thugs. 3 days later he even appeared before a magistrate for remand in prison but they were all acquitted when the trial started because there were no complainants and it was proved beyond doubt that the car burnt was an MDC car. The late MDC spokesperson, Learnmore Jongwe was quoted in the Daily news on the day of my arrest as saying, "interestingly there is no complainant... this is ZANU (PF)'s view of justice, but we are prepared to fill their jails. The harassment will not halt the people's resolve to complete the change they started in June 2000"

The allegations by police were that I fired a gun towards ZANU (PF) armed militia who were firing at us. I was not going to deny that I fired a gun, after all this was a legally acquired gun to which the state had records. If Zimbabwe was still a democratic country then firing in self defence was within the law of the land but bravo this is Mugabe land. However Zimbabwe has changed, there was no rule of law any more the president was the law and indeed a law unto himself. I knew ZANU (PF) have been waiting for so long to find a reason to arrest me so that they could torture me to death after all their effort to have me killed has not been successful. I knew this was it, they got me and I had a one way ticket to prison. I contacted the President, Morgan Tsvangirai and the party HQ. I was advised to delay to report at the police station while the party was organized legal representation, and I complied. As a national executive member of the MDC I was entitled to a national representative lawyer, Innocent Chagonda was assigned to my case. The Mashonaland Central province also hired a lawyer, Shephered

Mushonga of Mushonga and company. I took my gun as instructed and the magazines and ammunition strapped the gun over my shoulder and kissed my wife and children goodbye. I knew I might not come back as many people who had been arrested and detained for even less cases like mine had disappeared without trace, was my popularity going to serve me I wonder?

I asked my driver to take me to the police station and also in the company of my 2 body guards who by now have been increased to 5. When I arrived at the police station and asked to see inspector Dowa of Law and Order, they all looked at me with a smile as if they knew my fate. They tried to contact him but came back to me that he was not in which later turned out to be a lie. When Dowa asked me to report to the police station, he expected me to try to run away so they could announce on national TV and radio and embark on a national manhunt. Once caught they would arrest me and put me on remand and possible jail for many years. It was a shock that I came to hand myself over and because this was not expected, he needed advise from the top as what was he going to do next I waited for about 1 ½ hours before he emerged at the main reception with anger and vengeance. He saw me charting and making jokes with the police on duty, after all they all knew who I was. The first thing he did was to disarm me and shouted at the police on duty as to why they were entertaining a dangerous person with a gun? I protested at his behaviour, reminding him that I was not a criminal but a politician fighting for his right. By then the lawyers had arrived and I was whisked to an underground dudgeon guns and grenades wall to wall. Although there was light it was dark, damp and smelling of blood. There were blood marks indicating that it had been used as a torture chamber for some time. Then came the shock, Inspector Dowa read the allegations against me that the state was charging me with attempted murder, arising from the use of a firearm a month before. He further alleged that forensic tests have concluded that the cartridges found at the scene were fired from my gun. I accepted that I fired the gun on the day in question and only in self defence, after I had applied to have the meeting that area and ZANU (PF) who ambushed our convoy had no legal reason to be there. I knew that the fact that I saved the MDC leadership was not going to be mitigating factor but I was prepared to prove beyond doubt that I acted in self defence. I then quickly asked to know the complainant whom I tried to murder, again no information was forthcoming except intimidation and none cooperation.

Finally he started taking statement, I made it very clear that I fired the gun and that MDC is at war with ZANU (PF) and I told him that I was prepared to do it again both in the name of the party and the people of Zimbabwe. I also made it very clear that whatever I did I did for the people of Zimbabwe and including Dowa and that I was prepared to go to jail for that noble cause. Suddenly my fear disappeared and I was prying my eyes to all corners of the room reminding him that I smell death here and I am no precious to the multitudes of people you killed in this room. He reminded me that anything I was going to say would be used against me in the court of law. I told him I will do it again and again with or without a gun. I would fight Mugabe and his stooges and that I was prepared to go to jail to save the people of Zimbabwe from the bondage. I reminded him that Mugabe himself went to jail for 6 years under Smith regime and that all the allegations labeled against me were drummed up charges to destroy MDC momentum. After he had written the statement he asked me to read it and the sign, I chose the easy way, I just signed it and say I am ready to die now what next?

The lawyers asked Dowa to prepare his papers as they wanted me tried the same day regardless of the fact by then it was 4:00 PM Zimbabwe time. Business close at 4:30 in Zimbabwe. He took us to a CID reception and told us that he was going to have the papers signed and then he disappeared for good. After 10 minutes a junior CID came to tell me that he had instructions that I must be locked up for the night. It did not come as a surprise, I knew in a country with no rule of law anybody is law more so if you support the Mugabe regime. After discussions with lawyers they left and I was then taken to the cell reception for detention. The sergeant who was in charge refused to lock me in the cells, he recognized me and was sympathetic to the cause. One thing was certain in his mind were that he would not lock me up for as long as he was still in charge of the shift, however there was going to be a change over at 10:00 PM. I stayed at the reception with him and the other police officer talking everything from politics to cost of living. I wish I could remember his name, I really enjoyed discussions with him.

At 10 PM indeed came a woman whom it seemed had been told about me and was pro ZANU (PF). After the others had gone he quickly gave me a menacing look and checked her register and asked me why I was still outside when I was supposed to be in the cells? I tried to tell him that I have been told to stay there and this is why I was not behind the bars. She quickly called other officers to reinforce as if I intended to escape. I was ordered to remove my shoes and belongings and off I was never a free man again. In this cell which was built to accommodate 2 people there were already 7 people excluding me. For about an hour I kept quiet listening to criminal gangs talking about how they survive and why they have been arrested, they even played judge and prosecutor in there. One man who looked very much experienced at ease with his surroundings, looked at me and smiled and asked whether I was not Pfebve the politician. I agreed and asked him as to how he knew my name. Bang came the revelation that he is a fanatic supporter of the MDC and a *robber*. Surely I got more that what I had bargained for. Here I was behind bars fighting fir robbers to be free, surely that didn't make sense to me. Everybody was keen to know my charge and when I told them that I was being charged with attempted murder they all sympathized with me. They all offered to protect me and later all those who were being put in the same cell were being searched. They told me that CIO were capable of sending one of their own to infiltrate and kill me in the cell, so they offered to protect me. 7 more people were brought in a cell which can barely fit 3 people, in total now we were 16. I was humbled by the respect I got in the cells and the extent of MDC support base, the entire night I was addressing a rally behind bars, and it was brilliant.

The following day, I was taken in a Defender truck with Inspector Dowa holding paperwork which was to be the sworn statement. There were only 3 of us the driver and Dowa himself. The truck was stopped at Corner House, Samora Machel Avenue where the office of attorney general is situated. Dowa jostled through people walking on pavements going to work and entered the entrance. I looked outside and discovered that on the Daily News main headlines read, "Pfebve arrested again". Curious to see what the papers were saying I asked the driver if I could check the newspapers, to my surprise he agreed. People in the newspaper queue recognized me and could not believe their luck, I managed to answer a few questions meanwhile a crowd had formed around me. I went back to the defender with the newspaper and started reading and the police officer whom I discovered had no clue about my case asked to know what crime I had committed. When I told him the whole story he got shocked and all he could do was to laugh, I began to observe a pattern that junior officers didn't like ZANU (PF) at all as they were suffering with economic meltdown but the high ranks still had food on the table. When Dowa came back his face had changed, asked the driver to drive back to Harare Central, glanced at my Daily news paper and never said a word. Back at the station I was left in the car alone for about 30 minutes and Dowa later came back alone and took over the driving seat. He drove me towards Eastlea a different direction to the court. When I challenged him he told me that he wanted to collect some papers but later on I got shocked when he parked the car by my door step and warned me to stay away from politics. He dropped me and drove off.

Meanwhile unknown to me at the Rotten Row court MDC supporters were running battles with police demonstrating against my arrest. The lawyers were also waiting in court and so were MDC senior executives. After being dropped I telephoned them to say that I was now a free man. It was hard to believe but it turned out that the attorney general Mr Yunus Patel refused to press charges because lack of evidence.

The whole episode lasted 48 hours and I was free again. I then went on to survive numerous assignation attempts. I have never taken leave of my fight for justice and until my people are free I will continue to put a spirited fight.

5 ARTICLES OF DEFIANCE

Ditch Mugabe at 82

As we prepare for the post Mugabe era, few of us are aware that Mugabe is not the only problem, but ZANU (PF) is. Mugabe is now 82, if he is not senile by the end of the next 12 months then he will be dead by then. While some prepare for his demise, few of us do realise that the current political and economic trauma will continue at least for some time, regardless of whoever will take over. Are we saying then that Zimbabwe will never be the same again, certainly yes, either for the better or for the worse.

There are all humane indications that Mugabe will not live to see the next election assuming it will be held in 2008 as proclaimed by law, and even if he does he will be another Kamuzu Banda, a human cabbage in a dock. At least the election will pass as a no event to him dead or alive. If ZANU (PF) wins which it is likely to through rigging, a new leader will be unlikely to remove the POSA, AIPPA and other oppressive draconian laws amended to keep ZANU (PF) in power. Where does it leave us all Zimbabweans? While we put more energy on Mugabe to go, let us not glorify ZANU (PF), because if Mugabe goes today, we will find ourselves with no visible enemy although in reality more hellish than before. The international community will embrace the new leader and mend targeted fences at the expense of freedom, peace and democracy. While this sounds absurd, there is nothing to stop the West, which since the end of the Cold War has transformed its imperialist ideology into humanitarian and liberal democratic discourse. The World is of the view that, Zimbabwe without Mugabe will be a better and rose one, easier said than done considering that in a classical flawed international intervention, the fall of Siad Barre in Somalia in 1991, which was to usher an ever lasting peace did instead degenerate into anarchy and statelessness. The international community committed themselves to undertake a peace process, the UN included, which went terribly wrong; they left a fragile peace process at the hands of War Lords. 15 years down the line, Somalia does not have a central government, banks, civil servants or parliament. This lesson teaches us that external assistance cannot be relied upon at the expense of homogeneously grown political dispensation and conflict resolution. Zimbabwe must start thinking ahead of Mugabe era and put in place a mechanism of the healing process, conflict resolution and post conflict reconstruction because Zimbabwe is at war with self. Thus in practice more than in theory Zimbabwe resembles any country at War in need of serious post-war reconstruction.

A mushroom of political parties is not the answer for conflict resolution on Zimbabwe but coalition of these parties is, remember, "united we stand and divided we fall" as the old revolutionary slogan of war goes. The onus is on the opposition parties to come together and deeply bisect this animal called ZANU (PF) and analyse what makes it win with or without supporters. As I see it, this requires an Independent Think Tank that becomes a fully fledged library where politicians can tape for an unbiased political wisdom. As things stand now, Mugabe has rigged elections before some of us were even born and no matter whether you put in a Rocket Scientist as Mugabe's opponent, the elections will be rigged. Part of the reason has been widely publicized by NGOs but they are as clueless to the remedy as we politicians, otherwise we could have claimed victory long back.

In trying to analyse the scientific political impedance to the Zimbabwean's self conflict transformation and resolution, I have come up with the following Models specific to Opposition parties and ZANU (PF.

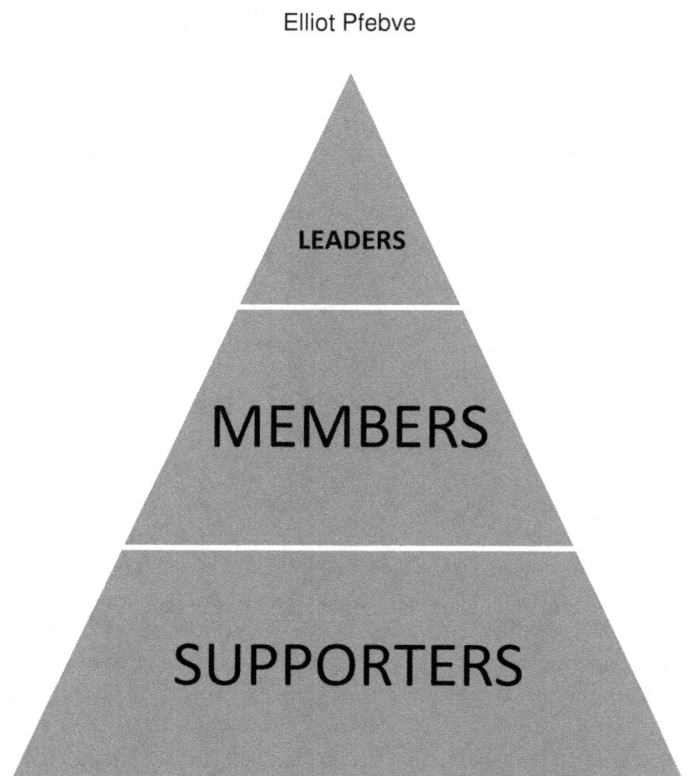

The Opposition political system Model A

The political parties are characterised by a wide support base followed by membership and finally a tip of leadership. A small leadership layer because of funding problems. The mistake that opposition has been making all along is to assume that supporters will automatically vote for them, as such they have wasted so much resource making rallies with its membership by so doing preaching to the converted. Remember supporters are not bound to vote for you and in American politics they call this constituency of people a swing vote. They will vote for any last minute campaigner who is convincing to them. Fortunately or unfortunately, ZANU (PF) has been clever on this layer, unable to convince them any further they use direct violence to swing the vote and it works. Meanwhile the opposition is counting numbers coming to their meetings, of course your members will come but not the supporters because after all they are only sympathisers of the cause and not the owners of it.

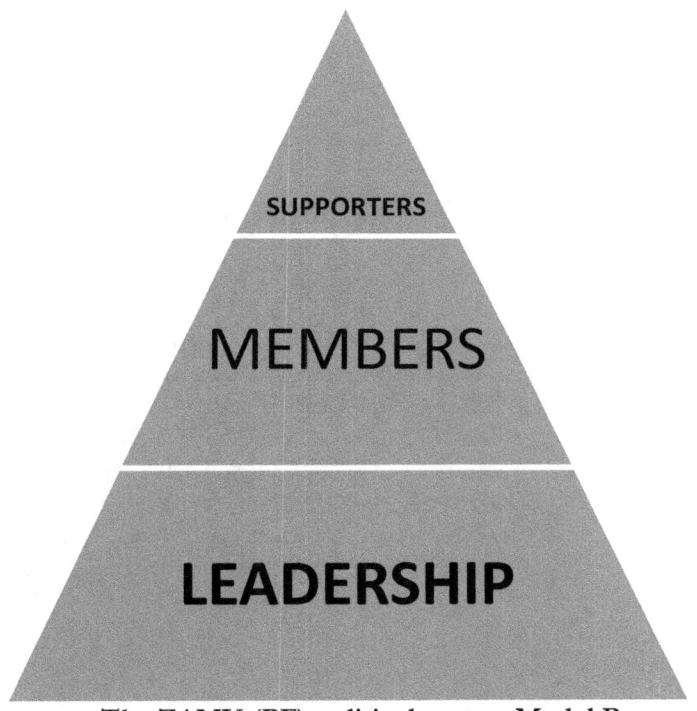

The ZANU (PF) political system Model B.

In theory ZANU (PF) has no supporters left but the leadership has remained intact through patronage. In Zimbabwe ZANU (PF) is the only party with a structure true to its constitutional meaning, Cell, Ward, District, Province, Central Committee and Politburo. Even though the structure might be left with no membership, the leadership is still there hence a bloated leadership at the bottom of the EP model B. The other reason is that it has a tendency of looting from state coffers to fund its wave of violence and payouts to its membership. ZANU has significantly lost its membership base to the opposition and almost the entire support base. ZANU is aware of this and knows the solution, bit opposition supporters towards election and you will have a swing vote by ginya.

Politicians must start being consumers of information rather than gatherers of information otherwise we will continue to be losers at every national election. ZANU (PF) is not sophisticated but effectively utilised a vast database of voters at their disposal. We must stop wasting resources on members and aim for the swing vote, the support base.

The Battle of the two Elliot's that never was!

The death of Elliot Manyika brings mixed feelings in the political landscape of Zimbabwe. Elliot Manyika, MP Bindura, Political Commissar (ZANU (PF)) killed by road accidents followed the death of Border Gezi, MP Bindura, Political Commissar (ZANU (PF)) by road accident ironically on the same Masvingo Road is no coincidence at all. What is by coincidence is that I am the ONLY person who contested against both evil men who died trying to revive an evil political party, ZANU (PF), led by an evil president Robert Mugabe. Is this the end of ZANU (PF)? Is there more infighting internally than what meets the eye? Has God finally answered our prayers? Who is going to be the next ZANU (PF) Political Commissar?

Killings and murders are not new in ZANU (PF), a party founded on revolutionary struggle concepts but failed to embrace change (after independence) in a fast changing global political sphere. Today we can safely conclude that ZANU (PF) the monster, is on a monstrous non recovery to doom, as it enters a new phase in a "struggle within struggles" If you live with evil you should be prepared to die by evil, while Elliot Manyika was playing both Satan and god's role, he failed to understand that above all there is GOD. He died doing the job he liked most murdering people and God saw it fit to reclaim His glory be recalling him to answer for his misdeeds. Imagine what would have become of Zimbabwe if Elliot Manyika successfully rejuvenated ZANU (PF) after the December Bindura Congress? Zimbabweans have suffered enough at the hands of ZANU (PF), unfortunately Robert Mugabe, the despot continues to live even beyond human expectation, and at 84 he seems to defy death. No doubt our prayers will continue to be answered.

I am the only person who had the privilege of contesting against these brutal citizens of Zimbabwe, Border Gezi and Elliot Manyika. Both men condemned me to death for mere exercising my democratic right to a better Zimbabwe, which was all I was committed to. And I still believe that, the same dream is closer now than when both men were still alive. This is a rare occasion where human beings can be more useful dead than alive. Border Gezi was the architecture of the Youth Militia and the setting up of torture camps, Elliot Mnyika exported them to other provinces where people were tortured, killed and women raped. Today those tactics remain the pillar of ZANU (PF)'s orgy of violence and campaign strategy. Some of you will remember the cold blooded murder of my brother Matthew at the hands of both Border Gezi and Elliot Manyika, the murder of Trymore Midzi, one of the campaign managers by Elliot Manyika. Between them Mashonaland Central saw the highest number of unexplained disappearances, murders and maiming of innocent civilians, I speak on behalf of an entire province traumatised. In July 2001 Elliot Manyika, personally plotted to assassinate me and Tsvangirai at Chiveso village in Bindura during the By-election. The military style ambush was meant to exert maximum casualty to MDC leadership since Manyika new that almost the top leadership of MDC was in the convoy. Had Manyika succeeded, he could have successfully disseminated MDC and we could be talking about different party at the moment. Many people were injured, although no confirmed death on the spot, many died from their injuries in hospital as a result of that incident.

I have included here a few citations from previous articles to show how Manyika played both the judge and the murderer;

"Trymore Midzi, an MDC youth leader in Bindura, about 60km (38

*miles) north of the capital, Harare, died after being beaten and slashed
through the head with a machete. Elliot Pfebve, the MDC spokesman,
said Mr Midzi's assailants were 20 supporters of the ruling ZANU-PF.
Mr Pfebve said the victim was taken to hospital after the assault on
Friday, then transferred to Harare and given 70 stitches to the head, before
dying there on Monday"* (The Independent December 27, 2001)

*"... the remains of Moffat Soka Chiwaura, an MDC supporter
abducted in Bindura in December, were found in January. (ZHR NGO
Forum February 2002)*
*"Elliot Manyika, an old-guard former diplomat, is contesting the seat for
ZANU-PF against the opposition's Elliot Pfebve, a young computer
engineer, in what is dubbed "The Battle of the Elliots".
Mr Manyika's supporters were out in force last weekend when they
ambushed Mr Tsvangirai as he travelled in a 15-car cavalcade to a rally
on the outskirts of Bindura.
Though Mr Tsvangirai emerged unhurt, five of his supporters were injured
and 10 vehicles were damaged, including one reduced to ashes after
ZANU-PF supporters set it ablaze"* (Telegraph July 29, 2001)

*"ZANU (PF) youths operating from seven bases in the Bindura constituency
are allegedly raping young girls and women, while assaulting suspected
supporters of the MDC as the campaign for the parliamentary by-election hots
up. ZANU (PF)'s Elliot Manyika is pitted against MDC's Elliot Pfebve.
The seat fell vacant following the death of Border Gezi in a car accident in
April. The by-election is set for 28 and 29 July"* Zimnews July 10, 2001

While my response to the death of Elliot Manyika (the other
Elliot) might dismay others who were benefiting from his brutality
and hold to power, let me remind them that Zimbabweans in
particular will not mourn a brutal leader who has been the
composer and singer of our deep rooted poverty. Comrade
Manyika, you failed to respect human life, when you were still alive,
you tried to kill me, you murdered my brother and now you are
dead, it's a price worth paying is it not it?

After all it was the battle of the two Elliot that never was!

A "leaked" letter from Mugabe

Dear Comrades in arms

Greetings from me here in New York at the United Nations Assembly, I can't believe that I am in the USA after all the battering they have been emphatically peddling around the World about me. Most of you will remember that they even have openly advocated for a regime change like what they did to Sadam Hussein in Iraq. Had it not been that they went for Sadam Hussein first and got their fingers burnt there, you and I probably could be history, and God is great you know! What they thought could be a day's war and they are still there now 6 years after they declared a victory, anyway back to business.

I have been invited by the CNN, I have no idea what they are going to ask me about but I have been told by our dear friend Comrade Chimurenga that the lady interviewing me is tough, I think her name is Amanpour or is it my aging memory, if so God forbid. I know they will talk about regime change disguised as GNU not working, their cousins whom we chased from farms causing, I admit here serious food shortages but who cares, they might even ask when I will retire, as if we have ever asked the Americans similar questions. Next time any American leader comes to Zimbabwe we must give him/her to Ruben Barwe and grill him/her of regime change, I think its fair comrades.

Here is how I intend to tackle the likely questions;

Government of National Unity (GNU):

As you aware this is a big issue, I have to be very careful on what I will say but with all the degrees in violence at my disposal, if she becomes noisy, I will unleash violence to her, I have the support of the Black February Movement. Some of you will remember comrade Chimurenga, whom we have always relied upon for Western Support.

I will tell the blood Americans that, it is none of their business, we have 14 nations behind us, I mean the SADC comrades. I will tell them that they should be lucky that we even invited their puppet MDC to plunder the riches of Zimbabwe. I will categorically deny that there are any outstanding issues in the implementation of the GPA or is it GNU. What else do they need, MDC's Biti is in control of Finance, if they are sincere then let the USA print money and send it to Harare after all we have a new reserve bank governor Johannes Tomana and a new attorney general Gideon Gono as they demanded, what else they want us to do. We even have an MDC prime minister, Morgan Tsvangirai yet they still complain. You all know that I was a Prime Minister before and Cannan Banana was my President but I didn't complain. If mai Mujuru have further information to add as acting president, I am more than happy to receive.

Land redistribution:

This will be an easy topic for me, because as you are aware this was the basis of our armed struggle. I have said it over and over again to them and they don't understand these Anglo-Saxons. I will remind them of the Lancaster House conference agreement, of course I will not mention that the money that we were given initially we plundered it on luxury for the chiefs, and after all it was payback for what we fought for. I will not backtrack on that, after all we have used this drum card successfully ever since and we got even some of the Europeans on our side like Hugo Chevaz, a powerful advocate of socialism.

I am going to tell them that we did not displace the farm labourers because they were blood illegal immigrants, we could not deport them like what they do because we don't have money so we asked them to leave peacefully or otherwise violently. If they want details of the operation I will refer them to Cde Chinos, can you confirm whether Chinos has now received a new mobile phone? As for the white farmers, I will remind them that we simply grabbed our stolen land. I know they will talk of title deeds, and I will simply pretend I didn't hear it and go ballistic on the need to exercise our sovereignty, because any link to them having supported MDC will justify an international criminal court proceeding which will be the worst thing for us all. The thrust should be on number 10 backtracking on its agreement as signed in 1979 at Lancaster house conference period.

I will deny that there was ever a food shortage in Zimbabwe and will never, ever, ever be. I will say those who are reported starving are as a result of sanctions which affected the weather pattern in Zimbabwe especially to the newly settled black farmers. The British I will allege have been sighted spraying the Zimbabwean airspace to ensure that no rain falls on newly settled farmers and I want the UN to issue a stern warning to the bloody British, especially to Tony Blair and Gordon Brown. I have already spoken to my comrades in arms, Ahmadinejad of Iran, Hugo Chevaz of Venezuela and Muhamar Al Ghadafi of Libya, and we are in agreement on that.

Economy:

They are likely to ask about the collapse of the Zimbabwean economy and the exodus of brain drain to the West. I will refuse that any Zimbabweans left with numbers except those that left due to the standard practice of immigration globally. After all Americans and British are all over the World including in Zimbabwe. I will also tell them that those who left for so called greener pastures are coming back home in droves after the credit crunch in the USA and UK, because we are fortunate we simply don't have a credit crunch in Zimbabwe. We have land, land is the economy and the economy is land, *handizvo here maComrades?* I will deny that the unemployment rate is over 80% although frankly speaking it might be in 3 figures, who goes to work in Zimbabwe except politicians? I will tell them to remove sanctions and people will get jobs, plenty jobs. We have our friends from the East, who are ready to invest in Zimbabwe as soon as sanctions are removed.

Why are they not removing travel sanctions, how do we do business without travelling, its ridiculous comrades. I am going to go nuts over this issue; I will not leave here without the sanctions having been removed. I am sure you all miss the comfort of western shopping.

Elections:

They are ill likely to ask me about rigging elections, who doesn't rig elections? I will remind them of GW Bush their outgoing president, he stole over 400,000 votes in Florida, more than twice the number of votes that I stole from Tsvangirai in March 2008. USA then can't preach democracy to us, I will tell them to go to hell! I will tell them elections don't always go to plan, sometimes ballot boxes disappear, sometimes election officials stammer in announcing results, resulting in unnecessary delays in releasing results, that is the reality, it has nothing to do with vaMugabe. After all they are countries that are friendly to the USA which don't run elections, look at Libya, every European country like them but they don't run elections. There is even Uganda to add to the list, so *urikutaura chiiko iwe?*

If there is any member of the Politburo who wants to contribute please pass your comments to the VP.

Cheers
President Gushungo

Zimbabwe social split at knife edge, an advice to GNU:

Zimbabwe social split at knife edge

Zimbabwe is deeply divided, we might not want to say it but it is a reality that those who left Zimbabwe more than 5 years ago will never be the same again and those who left represent a new face of Zimbabwe, a complete shift paradigm of Zimbabwean values due to the state sponsored mayhem. Strictly speaking there exists a two tier Zimbabwean society at odds with itself. Those who remain in Zimbabwe perceive those in the Western World as having a lavish lifestyle reminiscent of the Hollywood movies while those in Zimbabwe would take every opportunity if available to escape to the West. What then is the true picture?

In Zimbabwe, we lost another new generation to poverty and aids. According to the UN, there is over 1, 5 million orphans in Zimbabwe, an indeed worrying scenario. The collapse of the once prosperous nation meant that all these failed or is failing to access education. The GNU must move quickly to rescue these orphans before it becomes a ripple effect of the poverty cycle. There is no doubt that those who remained endured torrid hard times and most continue up to this day as the unemployment rate is still the highest in the World, over 90%. Many Zimbabweans have been pushed to limit in most cases experimenting with sins of the day to survive while politicians belly ballooned with corruption. No doubt this brings another social problem, crime! If you talk of 90% unemployment, you are talking about 90% with no formal economic means to survive; surely you can't blame the nation put to ransom by a blood filth junta.

If the truth is to be told the politicians had put the whole generation of skilled and talented Zimbabweans to waste. While a strong 500,000 plus graduate experts left Zimbabwe in the so called greener pastures for the past 10 years, many suffer from external inflicted deskilling, I mean they have not been near to their world of expertise ever since and only scratching a bare minimum survival to show it. Don't get me wrong some Zimbabweans run economies of scale in the so called powerful nations like US, Canada, UK, Germany, France, Russia, South Africa, Australia and New Zealand. Those professionals running these economies put together would make any European country envy with jealous, because when such expertise is fused no nation would come near to Zimbabwe. The only problem is that we Zimbabweans are so busy uplifting wrong nations, sometimes rogue once to notice our combined expertise of scale. But hang on who said we should be blamed, is it not only fair that when our politicians persecute experts and vilify academic institutions that it becomes a catalyst for self economic harm? , absolutely. The collapse of rule of law is a heaven for the lawlessness and social misfits and ironically ZANU (PF) for the past decade has been the bleeding ground for such calamity at a time when nations consolidate their economic gains with social security to their citizens.

There is no doubt that any government that comes into power today or tomorrow will have to ignore this problem at its own peril. What needs to be done by the GNU is to approach donor agencies to fund the return and subsequent setting up of companies that will benefit the general economy of Zimbabwe. Schemes could be explored where any company intending to invest in Zimbabwe can benefit from a tax incentive if it comes in with an investment partner who is an expert from the Diaspora (Zimbabwean). Giving food aid as what is happening now is only a short term solution but Zimbabweans must find a lasting solution while the food is still in the tummy.

As we prepare to heal the nation with words let us heal them first with deeds, then we can be sure that the words are not left to individual interpretation as sovereignty has always been in Zimbabwean context. No one person is more Zimbabwean than your fellow next door and it is only right that we look into the mirror before we can pass judgment to those we feel offended by their looks, who knows you might even discover that after all you do not have that face.

Zimbabweans in the Diaspora can shape the future of Zimbabwe.

Congratulations to the MDC for putting such a spectacular fight to the end, we wish the Prime Minster, his deputy and the cabinet every success. We hope the MDC government will live to its promise, people first, MDC is a people driven party. Let's utilise every expertise that we have to deliver the change that the people of Zimbabwe badly need. This is only the beginning, until we are in full government control, there must be no laxity.

The past 10 years saw millions of Zimbabweans migrating to other countries. The reasons were as varied as their destinations. South Africa is home to the highest number of Zimbabweans estimated to be more than 3.5 million; other regional countries had their share of this humanitarian catastrophe. Naturally English speaking countries like UK, USA, Canada, Australia and New Zealand where the highest foreign destinations outside Africa. The Diaspora has been a vanguard of the struggle for MDC and remains a key player both economically and politically, at least until now.

Under the new laws that forbid external funding for political parties strategically enacted to disposes MDC of its goodwill external sympathisers, the Zimbabweans in the Diaspora became the source of funding for many MDC activities. Diaspora all over the world has been vigorously putting the Zimbabwean struggle on the International agenda. We talk of the high flier case in USA courts which for the first time gave a vivid account of what the ZANU (PF) thugs where doing to opposition, to which Elliot Pfebve and Adela Chiminya spear headed, in response to the murder of Chiminya, Pfebve and others, we talk of Vigil outside the Zimbabwean embassy for the past 6 years, the list is endless. While we celebrate the GNU, we need to give every drop of blood for the lifeline of this new government to succeed, what comes to my mind is whether this government will take advantage of the Diaspora political and expertise talent? ZANU (PF) in 1980 recalled its Diaspora support base, some got cabinet posts, and some got posted in the embassy home countries that they were based already.

My advice, to the MDC new government is that diplomatic and consular services be restructured and strengthened in countries and regions where there is a large concentration of Zimbabweans in exile with the aim to encourage their participation in the national economy beyond just sending money. This has to be done in a sustained manner, government down approach policy formulation and not as a haphazard approach or an election gimmick. The Diaspora, has been sending money in the region of millions US dollars per month, surely the government can bring about policies that give incentives to Zimbabweans who intend to invest back home. We don't need any expatriates, Zimbabweans drive many economies world over and with the right incentives they will prefer to work in their country of birth.

Together we can build Zimbabwe that is tolerant and a mirror of emerging democracies. We can still reclaim our African jewel status in our lifetime.

Mugabe tops chart as the 8th richest person in Africa

Africa is home to million poverty stricken families yet it's not short of billionaires who exploit them. This rich list disturbing as it may, provokes debate as how a president of a poor country can end up being on the rich list without any investment portfolio?

That Robert Mugabe the President of Zimbabwe is US $3 Billion mega rich in a country which entirely depend on food aid baffles everybody. The next question is where are these billions and where did they come from. We can understand Strive Masiwa being a billionaire because he is an entrepreneur per excellent but what of Robert Mugabe, president of a self inflicted poverty stricken country?

Zimbabwe was at a blink of collapse before the Government of National Unity (GNU) in late 2008, cholera outbreak claimed thousands, hospitals grounded to halt, and water supply dwindled, electricity supply erratic and essential services collapsed, all because of a shortage of funding, while politicians stash money in offshore banks, Read on... (This list was correct as by the end of 2008)

1. Teodoro Obiang Nguema Mbasogo (est $65 Billion)
President of Equatorial Guinea since 1979
Born: 5 June 1942

2. Muammar al-Gaddafi ($56 Billion)
Leader and Guide of the Revolution
The Libyan Leader

3. Dr. Mike Adenuga ($27 Billion)
Dr. Mike Adenuga
Chairman of Globacom, a Telecommunications company
http://www.gloworld.com/

4. Onsi Sawiris ($20 Billion)
Onsi Sawiris, Egyptian Businessman who heads Orascom
a Telecommunications company
www.orascom.com

5. Mohammed Al Amoudi ($ 9 Billion)
Mohammed Al Amoudi
Ethiopian Business man
Oil, Gas, Mining, Hotels, Agriculture and hospitals

6. Aliko Dangote ($ 4 Billion)
Aliko Dangote
Nigerian Businessman
Dankotes businesses include food processing, cement manufacturing and freight
http://www.dangote-group.com/

7. Strive Masiyiwa ($ 3.5 Billion)
Strive Masiyiwa (aka "Bill Gates of Africa") is a Zimbabwean businessman

and cellphone pioneer, founding Econet Wireless.
econetwireless.com

8. Robert Mugabe ($ 3 Billion)
Robert Mugabe
President of Zimbabwe

9. Mohamed Fayed ($ 3 Billion)
Mohammed Fayed
Eqyptian Businessman
His Business interests include Harrods department store in London
and Fulham, an English
Premiership football club

10. Ibru Family ($ 2.5 Billion)
Hotels and Banking in Africa
Nigerian Businesses

11. Femi Otedola ($ 2 Billion)
Nigerian Businessman
Business interests include Zenon Oil and other Oil Products

12. Yoweri Museveni ($ 1.7 Billion)
President of Uganda

13. Olusegun Obasanjo ($ 1.3 Billion)
Olusegun Obasanjo
Former President of Nigeria

14. Anis Haggar ($ 1.3 Billion)
Sudanese industrialist
haggar-hf.com

15. Mo Ibrahim ($ 1.2 Billion)

16. Arap Moi ($ 1.2 Billion)
Daniel Toroitich Arap Moi

Former President of Kenya 1978 - 2002

17. Musa Danjuma (est $ 1.2 Billion)
Musa Danjuma
A Nigerian Businessman
Business Interests include real estate and shipping

18. Patrice Motsepe (est $ 1.2 Billion)
South African entrepreneur
has interests in gold, ferrous metals, base metals, and platinum.
www.arm.co.za

19. Madhvani Family (est $ 800 Million)
Roni Madvani
A Ugandan Business man
Business interests include Uganda Tourism Board and Hotels

20. Cyril Ramaphosa (est $ 600 Million)
Cyril Ramaphosa
South African business man and politician
Business interests include Shaduka Holdings, Bidvest Group, MTN
Group and SASRIA Limited

Forward Statement

Dear all

AS we prepare to celebrate the 10th anniversary of MDC's
formation, challenges and threats still exist, I urge you all to come
together this Saturday as a big family with one goal to unite and
refocus your energy on putting the party first.

I would like to take this opportunity to wish you all happy and
successful MDC anniversary celebrations, here in the UK on the
5th September in Milton Keynes. The party has come a long way,

along the way many have perished some maimed for life. The culmination of the GNU gives hope to an otherwise crippled country. We should continue to support our leadership through this difficult journey before the perceived next democratic elections after the new constitution.

Politics is not for selfish people, it is for those willing to forgive so that they can give, to meet the cause with endurance, tacit and loyalty to the founding principles of MDC. To those who cherish accountability to those whom they are suppose to serve. Above all it tests our resolve to unite in a common cause. We must be mindful of the fact that there are some who jump the boat to rock it and some who jump into it to save it but when all is said and done those with the party at heart must not stumble. As we unite against a common enemy we must remain resolute and vigilant that what we have collectively built, no man should put asunder.

MDC Ndizvo!!
Guqula Izenzo!!

She delivered change to us all then she died; Susan Tsvangirai.

The death of Mrs Susan Tsvangirai remains a shock to every peace loving Zimbabwean, not only because she was a visible fighter for peace and justice but that through her civic work, she touched many souls and minds. She was a pillar of hope and that for the first time Zimbabweans saw a figure head in the making that symbolised in every respect, the mother of a nation. She lived a simple life in a country torn strife with corrupt materialistic ergo. She was another Sally or should we say mother Teresa.

I am humbled to have met her personally, having met her at her house on numerous occasions as was all MDC officials. She was both welcoming and a rock to the party founded on none violence principles, not withstanding to her husband the Prime Minster Morgan Tsvangirai. I remember receiving her call on the day Border Gezi died in a car crash warning me to take extra care on the road. It came as a shock to me that she could take the pains to call me and warn me of possible danger; I felt her warmth and powerful guiding me through and through, it was touching.

I wish I could have done the same but I was not given the chance, she is dead. The accident that killed Mrs Tsvangirai and injured the Prime Minster, coming barely three weeks after he assumed the post of Prime Minster has already started raising eyebrows in both the media and within the Zimbabwean population. This fury and suspicion are justified in a country long bent on eliminating political opponents in bizarre incidents of a similar nature. While I am not suggesting a foul play, neither will I dismiss it.

No doubt that this incident shook an already shaky transitional government which Zimbabweans badly need. There have been never been a time when Zimbabweans placed so much hope for a new beginning and indeed a few weeks of the new MDC government had proved that indeed positive change is possible after all.

Nobody will deny that the accident will impact negatively on the GNU momentum, as deadlines will be missed as the nation mourns the fallen heroine of Susan Tsvangirai. Our greatest hope is that the Prime Minster will swiftly recover to continue where Mrs Tsvangirai left albeit a surmountable task.

The ZANU (PF) must move swiftly to lay bare all evidence to exonerate themselves from the incident, as I see it, fingers pointing at the hand of Mugabe government or is it pockets of resistance will not simply disappear. Investigations must prove beyond doubt that this was just a tragic accident otherwise the implication of the transitional government and subsequent recovery of Zimbabwe will be severely jeopardised. Nobody should go to sleep thinking that tomorrow it will simply disappear from people's minds because it simply won't.

To the mother of the nation, Mrs Susan Tsvangirai, R.I.P. and to the Prime Minster I wish you a fast recovery. To the Tsvangirai family I offer my deep sincere condolence.

So the Dogs are out again 29 March.

The election fever again! One might be forgiven to think that the mood of the electorate in Zimbabwe as we gear ourselves for the 29th March election has never happened before; it has at least during the June 2000 general elections and the subsequent presidential election of 2002. If this is correct then what has changed that makes it different this time for ZANU (PF) not to rig the upcoming elections? Who is likely to be the messiah Tsvangirai or Makoni? Are we heading for another disappointing long weekend? What if Mugabe rigs the election and be stores himself life president?

With all political signs compelling, we Zimbabweans must be prepared to brace for the worst disappointing weekend ever! The biggest question is whether we can be worse off than we are at the moment? An inflation rate of over 150,000%, 85% unemployment rate, life expectancy of just 34 years and an octogenarian president who plans to leave office at the age of 90 or is it 100 years. Surely if God does really exist this is the time that his testimony must be seen in the light of delivering salvation to the people of Zimbabwe long forgotten by everybody except nobody. The fact that we have been reduced to inhuman surrogates does not reflect what we are or who we are as an African nation, if it all we deserve better leadership now than we were a million years ago.

Mugabe has always made sure that those in charge of rigging him to power are well fed at least a few months before the election, is it not what is happening now? Ladies and gentlemen the dogs are out again! The service chiefs one by one will start giving allegiance to Mugabe's war credentials and even unashamedly declaring war if elections are won by any other than Mugabe, here is a few;

"Most of us in here are truly owners of the land. This is the sovereignty we should defend at all costs because for us to get at this point others had to lose their lives. At this point our gains should never be reversed," Chihuri said.

Harare - One of Zimbabwe's top defence forces chiefs says he will not salute former finance minister Simba Makoni or opposition leader Morgan Tsvangirai if either wins the March 29 presidential poll, it was reported Friday.

'I am giving you an order to vote for the President,' Zimondi told senior army officers at a ceremony in Harare on Thursday.

One needs to understand the structure of the army, CIO and the police. It is not the army chiefs or police chiefs expressing their opinion, no, they are expressing the whims of their master Robert Gabriel Mugabe. We all know that all top officers of each of the said units are appointed on partisan basis; you have to be ZANU (PF) both in blood and soul. Even in MDC we are making the same mistake, we have of late elected a former Senior Assistant Commissioner Chaora (shortly a number 3 man from Chihuri) to lead the party in the UK. He was the officer commanding the force that arrested and incarcerated me in Harare for giving Mugabe a finger. Surely it should be common sense that the man is still connected to his masters or is it his former masters after all he was appointed by Mugabe himself. How confidential is our records as a party now?

People must be made to know that in the event of Mugabe losing the elections; of course in a free and fair election he will lose, nothing will happen. Those are empty threats meant to divert us from the elections while Mugabe is busy rigging, no army can withstand the people's revolution whose time has come. As much as Mugabe went to war to fight injustice so can we! Zimbabweans out there, I urge you all to come out in your millions and vote for change, vote for an MDC government, lets save Zimbabwe. We can do it and the time is now!

Going back to Makoni, while many will not dispute that he stands out of the current ZANU (PF) crop of leadership, he cannot absolve himself from blame for as long as he claims to still belong to ZAN (PF). He is better off joining MDC where the grassroots are and I am sure MDC will put him to good use. It has never happened in Africa that you can win a presidential election as an independent worse still without grassroots support.

We know Mugabe is busy rigging, and he must be warned that we have the capacity to be free with or without him!

See you in Portugal, Bob

Zimbabweans from all over the World are urged to travel in mass to Portugal to demonstrate their displeasure at human rights violation by the despotic leader Robert Mugabe. His invitation to this important Summit is a slap in the face of peace-loving Zimbabweans who remain under the yoke of his brutal regime.

British Prime Minister Gordon Brown is boycotting the meeting in solidarity with the struggling people of Zimbabwe, well done Gordon! As for me, I am choosing the confrontational approach; if Mugabe goes to Lisbon then I am certainly going. I want him to address me before he lies to the World, I want him to look into my eye and tell me why he murdered my brother? I want him to tell me how many more years should the people of Zimbabwe suffer under his dictatorship?

Mugabe leaves behind a self-made trail of economic destruction and gross human rights violations. The life expectancy for a Zimbabwean has plummeted to 38 - except of course that of Mugabe who is now 84. Prisoners of conscience litter the filthy overcrowded jails, opposition and civic activists' limb with broken limbs from state sponsored brutality. Dripping with innocent blood, Mugabe wants to come to Portugal to preach good governance to the World, what a shame!

This trip is all about diverting the attention of the World from his brutal regime and its atrocities as we prepare towards a predetermined election next year. He is oiling his rigging mechanism in time for March or is it June elections.

Zimbabweans wherever you are, rise again to this occasion and show the World that although we might be down but we are not done. Remember it is only Zimbabweans who can liberate themselves.

Zimbabwe Victims of Violence Need Support ; Do you hear me bravo!!

The current crisis in Zimbabwe only works to demonstrate how much loyalty individuals have for their political parties. Everybody has a different opinion, but at the end of it all, we should all strive to harmoniously work together in a peace-building mission, stretch out olive branches, and be able to exercise reconciliation, in the interests of progressive development.

We should, therefore, challenge one another to chart a path of civility, reason, respect and consideration. That way, we can harvest more gains and develop our loving country.

The purpose of this communiqué is to amend torn relations, bridge animosity gaps, enhance the spirit of love and cooperation, while also promoting a way to allow a spirit of forgiveness among the victims and culprits of political violence.

If we allow the "eye-for-an-eye" concept to reign, we gear ourselves for an endless cycle of violence, which opens floodgates of poverty, destruction of infrastructure, loss of more precious lives, and hindrance to national development.

This is the opportune moment to bury our machetes, shake hands, and seriously realize that we are all Zimbabwean children. As such, we should strive to abstain from acts of savagery and barbarism, substituting those with reason, respect, love and understanding.

We need to rebuild our dear Zimbabwe for the purposes of progressive development and a better future not only for the current generation, but also for those to come.

GNU therefore comes at the ideal moment to help the victims of political violence, instil the elements of peace building amongst the parties involved, and promote a solid sense of patriotism.

Without unnecessarily assuming finger-pointing or a witch-hunt drive, the rational starting point is simply to cure the injured, clothe the naked, feed the hungry, give shelter to the displaced and teach all, victims and culprits, to forgive and forget. That way we forge ahead in love, building a solid nation with better values for a legacy that we challenge ourselves to leave behind.

By supporting GNU, anyone will prove to the world that, regardless of personal interests, background, or political affiliation, a Zimbabwean still needs a normal, stable, secure, pain-free and peaceful life. That kind of help be it in cash, in kind or otherwise, makes a difference to a distraught and anxious soul. That assistance alone restores hope!

Together, we can make a difference. Let us re-build our dear Zimbabwe

Zimbabwe a country at a crossroads

Let me first reflect on "talks about talks", whether it was good idea for MDC to participate? The major discussion point here is whether the agreement was in good faith and if so who is to blame? Many commentators blame the MDC for what they call a catalogue of blunders during the negotiations giving rise to the current impasse in the final agreement.

There is no doubt that any political standoff will end with negotiations, and possibly a peaceful transition or violent transition. If we all share this school of thought, then MDC must be applauded to engage head on with ZANU (PF) for the talks. A point of contention is whether we were powerful enough to drive our demands home and whether we came out winners or losers. Each part in a negotiation will bring to the table their positions with it compromises and counter compromises. Departing from the norm, I personally believe that the MDC could have done a better job. This is shared by many in the leadership of the MDC. The decision to sign the 15/09 agreement amid fanfare in front of the camera before the specific allocation of ministries was ill advised. We had no reason to trust ZANU (PF), an evil party led by a despotic leader of all times. If at all, it was more than being generous for MDC to share power with ZANU (PF) which has been the sole authors of national demise.

Which ministries should go to whom?

The fact that 2 months down the line we are still boggled with ministry allocations is baffling. ZANU (PF) has ruled this country for 29 years without sharing power with any political party, why now? ZANU (PF) is aware that they have no clue to turn around the fortune of Zimbabwe; in fact they have destroyed anything that was left of once a jewel of Africa. Their intention remains to safeguard their interests, negotiate for their immunity through managing the process, start using their stashed cash again and sharpen their violence machinery in time for the next elections. Contrary to what ZANU (PF) wants people to believe, the disagreement is not on the Ministry of Home Affairs, no! It's on the entire 31 ministries. ZANU (PF) wants finance so as to do what? , With what? We all know that they have no clue about running an economy; they want Foreign Affairs, so they can fly at will to expensive shopping trips, and they want all security ministries so that they can still hold Zimbabweans at ransom, a rule by military fear. They want agriculture, what a shame, is this not the fear of the unknown. If ZANU (PF) is genuine, it should get in the government as a junior partner because that's what they are as reflected by the March elections and worse still they are the minority in parliament. While I have respect to our neighbours in the SADC region, their decision for MDC to share the ministry of Home Affairs is a wrong precedent for fragile African democracies. If they can give us only one example where such an arrangement exists, I will be shocked. In fact how do you start talking about sharing a ministry with a party which is not negotiating in good faith, by the way Chinamasa admitted that he doctored the agreement, albeit in error, easier said than done? Any ministry which ZANU (PF) has failed to run must go to MDC without exception. If ZANU (PF) is not willing to concede power, and then just like what they have always been doing, let them govern. The MDC's time will come.

Amendment No. 19:

There are those who feel that article 19, must not even be talked about before the burning issue of ministries is addressed. The amendment does not address the allocation of ministries but address the constitutionality of the post of Prime Minister and his 2 deputies together with an intend to form a transitional government.

The current position of the MDC is that it will support the bill in parliament but stay put on demands for the equitable allocation of ministries before joining the government. On a personal note I have a problem with that, given the slippery nature of ZANU (PF). Would it not be appropriate to demand the ministries first and the amendment later, what will happen when Tsvangirai is sworn in as Prime Minister but fail to get ministries to supervise? It must also be noted that while many have found reason to criticize the MDC's position, you need to be in the leadership right under Mugabe's nose to appreciate what the current leadership is doing. As a leader

I believe you don't need to know it all, but to be surrounded by the right advisers, remember Barrack Obama

.

The Way forward:

We have reached a turning point, an apex of self destruction. The outbreak of cholera, in a country with no functioning health service is a monumental failure of the ZANU (PF) government. This is the moment that Mugabe should think of resigning and if not then we Zimbabweans must lead the way mobilizing for his imminent removal. In a country where fresh water rarely runs even in the capital Harare and yet the government still clings to power is sincerely madness. Here is a chance for Zimbabweans of all party affiliations or none partisan to come up with strategies to sink this boat carrying a toxic cargo.

The fact that Mugabe extended Gideon Gono's term for a further 5 years for his blatant incompetence is a sign that Mugabe is not even imagining himself sharing power with anybody. Botswana must be applauded for leading the way in isolating Mugabe. As David Moore once lamented, "the only problem that we have is that none of the SADC regional leaders openly support Morgan Tsvangirai except Botswana". We should move quickly diplomatically to make sense into our neighbours.

I would like to leave a challenge to you all. What do you think of a government in exile in the SADC region? Is a military solution a reality in Zimbabwe? Can ZANU (PF) be trusted to share the ministry of Home Affairs with Chihuri as head?

By the way the only good news is the death of Elliot Manyika, remember "the battle of the 2 Elliots in Bindura" what a brutal man he was!

Mugabe lost the state house keys

Never have a head of state been politically marooned like what Bob is at the moment. The drastic metamorphosis from a freedom fighter to a despot is equally shocking. Zimbabwe has not and will never run short of credible leaders. There are too numerous statesmen to mention.

Political commentators and political scientists will agree with me that there is nothing new of Mugabe's past that can make him see social sense where there is no political self centring. That being that paints a gloomy picture for Zimbabweans; we believe in earnest that what civic pressure groups had failed inflation would succeed, *'acharohwa nezveusiku gore rino'.*

I am not predicting that Mugabe will rule till Jesus comes but wait a minute, how old is Mugabe for argument's sake? Most of us would prefer waiting for his natural death which if I am right was 48 years ago, considering that the life expectance for Zimbabweans is 35 years. Albeit Mugabe seem to defy every scientific norm. What makes him we without our concern? What makes him breathe without oxygen? What makes him win without votes? What makes him young without youth? What makes him Zimbabwean without being one? May be he has lost the keys to the state house? *'Kunyika kwedu hatingadaro'*

In a book "Confronting authority" written by Derrick Bell, a black American who took 1 year unpaid leave to confront the US authority on behalf of the disadvantaged black woman, at Harvard Law School, noted," even those who are considering confrontation as an alternative to passive acceptance, there are no ten easy steps to adopting a more aggressive stance to the indignities suffered by individuals or groups you wish to defend" This shows why Zimbabwe is now 40 years backwards although we have more political parties and civic pressure groups than in any peaceful country living although still devoid of any political effect. There is simply no easy step to confronting and defying authority. Furthermore Mugabe belongs to a class of his own, a complex mixture of naivety and political mongering, devoid of reason and humanity.

The dilemma that we Zimbabweans face is that African states continue to have solidarity with the head of states rather than the people of individual countries, further more governments in Africa do not necessarily include the electorate but the elected or self imposed. Opposition though progressive have found themselves incapacitated by a windfall of repressive legislations hurriedly passed to ensure a crackdown on all progressive forces. The war on terror has subsequently added a blow to opposition worldwide, as rogue governments can crackdown on the opposition in the name of the war on terror privy of the Western World.

Zimbabwe will be free and is going to be free, Mugabe or no Mugabe. We should actively debate on Zimbabwe after Mugabe because that is the reality now than ever. Mugabe will not be president come 2008 elections, mark my words. As much as we have wanted to see him go forcefully at least I am one of them for a specific reason which even Mugabe knows better, I feel the inflation has a more ferocious fire power than all wishful thinking put together now than anticipated, *'dzawira mutsvanda kaidzi mhanduwe'*. Each time I look at Zimbabwe's economy and political mayhem, the more I personally take the entire ZANU(PF) leadership to blame, how on earth somebody elected by the people forsake the same electorate and instead look after the interest of a ghost like Mugabe or Mkabe forgive me for the lack of knowledge as to where he comes from? As far as I am concerned, only Simba Makoni has voiced his concern about the state of Zimbabwe, the rest let's send them to hell together with Mugabe.

I still believe strongly that the opposition in Zimbabwe needs to unite for the good of the nation. All opposition leaders in Zimbabwe must understand that they owe what they are to the people of Zimbabwe and not to themselves, at least no one is more intelligent than the Zimbabwean electorate, if you think so then don't seek our votes, come on guys, this is our country and not your country. We owe it to the generation to come and not to our selfish political gains. Mugabe is an example of a political venture which went wrong, we don't need another example, be warned!

African Union where U?

When will Africa become truly African?
Addis Ababa, Zimbabwe is burning, where is Africa? Where is the spirit of Emperor Halie Selassie, Ndugu Mwalimu Nyerere, Kwame Nkrumah, Mzee Jomo Kenyata, Seku Toure and Gamel Abdel Nasser? Zimbabweans must know the cloud that does not bear water, Zimbabwe is burning. What happened to the charter of freedom, equality, justice and peace? Who signed the charter for Zimbabwe? Africa will never be Africa without Zimbabwe, the Tea Pot that all Africans drink from, Zimbabwe, Zimba remangwe.

Olusegun Obasanjo where are you, Abdoulaye Wade, do you hear me? South Africa is to Thabo Mbeki, Malawi is to Bingu Wamudarika, Zambia is to Levy Mwanawasa, Mozambique is to Armando Guebuza, Tanzani is to Banjamin Mkapa, Kenya is to Mwai Kibaki and Mugabe is to Mugabe. Africa where are you. People crying, people dying, people shot, people hungry, people running, Africa where are you? Let the spirit of fallen heroes guide us through this 29 March 2008 joint parliamentary & presidential elections as we unshackle the chains of bondage from a self proclaimed "Black Hitler", Robert Mugabe. Zimbabwe must be free, I want to be free to be free!

The fall of a gallant fighter Getrude Mthombeni
Her smiles still vivid in my thoughts and she used to call me Border, jokingly of course, as a pseudo name derived from the brutal ZANU(PF) madzibaba whom I contested with in June 2000 parliamentary election. Getrude was the finest woman politician I have ever met, mixing jokes and political stature. What then went wrong sister? I learnt with regret that she passed away on Saturday 19 January 2008 after a short illness.

We were the same age group yet she was privileged to have made a leadership impact earlier than me. I looked to her as my mentor, speaking to her one would hardly notice her feminine side, she was frank to the point that sometimes you would wish you would apply the brakes on her behalf, yes that was her inner being that mattered. She was a tough woman and when I heard that she was contesting to be a Vice President of MDC, I was sure that it was going to be a tough contest. I had had the privilege of working with both women, Thoko and Getrude, I would be lying to say any one of them was taller in thought than the other, wonder why the delegates had a tough choice.

She was a simple woman who always preferred a bald head with a natural Ndebele traditional beauty. I have such poor Ndebele language vocabulary and she was more than willing to teach me the basics, which I am, grateful for. As I was a National member, I had to travel throughout Zimbabwe and this was to prove very helpful. Soon I was to find myself working for the party in Matebeleland and the people I met more often were Getrude Mthombeni and Steve Mudenda of Bulawayo and Matebeleland North respectively. I worked extensively with these politicians such that we had personal numbers of each other. It was not surprising to receive a call in the middle of the night from Getrude or Steve. They all sympathised with my situation in Bindura which was the HQ of the militia and a haven of brutality.

To those who have known Getrude we have been robbed of the true cadre of the struggle in MDC. Her departure will be felt and the replacement difficult to find. I say to Getrude R.I.P. We salute you; we envy your political pathway.

Your death is not in vain we will continue the struggle where you left until victory. Such a loss tends to strengthen us knowing it very well that victory is on our side.

My strength within me is enshrined in my political philosophy school of thought outlined below;

"Politicians risk being irrelevant for advocating strategies out of their political capacity. This is not a game of loosely knitted words, it is about action and indeed shouldering surmountable risks. Politics is not a business; it is about building a viable national pride against all odds, bulldozing the obstacles along the way no matter what it takes"

Pfebve family abducted 13 May 2008- Media Alert!

ZANU (PF) thugs descended on the Nyakatondo village in MT Darwin on Tuesday evening and rounded the entire village. The area is a strong support base to MDC and home to Pfebve family which has been influential in the opposition politics ever since MDC formation. Information received by an eyewitness who managed to escape indicates that 2 people were murdered and scores of property were burnt to the ground as a government sponsored militia take retribution to new heights. At about 8 PM and abducted my parents, tied their hands with ropes and flog marched them to a torture camp at the Nyakatondo Primary School.

Fireson Pfebve (brother) who escaped to contact me on Wednesday managed to reach Harare talked of a desperate situation on the ground as scores of people were rounded up and beaten, the fate of those captured could not be ascertained at the time of writing this article. My parents an elderly couple in their late 70s are being accused by ZANU (PF) of having natured opposition members to government of Robert Mugabe in a country purportedly to be democratic. As I speak their fate is not known and so is the fate of other family members reported missing in action. My fear is the trauma that these law abiding elders of society is going through for having voted for a government of their choice. They have done nothing wrong, Mugabe set the election date, printed the ballot papers albeit with opposition leaders printed on them, Mugabe did employee the polling officers and did the counting. Why then should my parents and family members be punished? Communication in this area has been difficult as ZANU (PF) has cut off all forms of communication. Road blocks have been set up to prevent opposition members or aid workers reaching them. Livestock belonging to opposition members have been confiscated and are being slaughtered to provide food for

Mugabe militia. Many more people said to have been injured and there are reports of targeted rape against members of the opposition.

Less than 90 days to a forced run-off, this incident is not new, official figure put the dead to 38 since 2 May but this number is a grossly underestimate as many remain un accounted for. In rural remote, where communication is poor, this will take time to be known. There are reports of ZAN (PF) burying the murdered in shallow graves to cover up their heinous crimes. The wave of violence has spread to all 8 provinces and this proves that the government is fully behind the logistics of it, no one criminal gang can replicate its self covering such a wide area operating with impunity without government support and logistics. Many people in Zimbabwe rural today have fled their properties and are living in the mountains in a country not at war other than at war with its own government. Politicians talk of a run-off, we must be joking really!

Surely this is not consistent with a government willing to accept defeat in the event that MDC wins the run-off. I think as a nation we have to accept that no matter how we vote Mugabe has no intention to concede defeat. What then is left for us young generation if an 84 year old decides to drive us into extinction by a calculated genocide? I hate war but how do we deny it when Mugabe has already declared war on his own people? For how long are we going to remain victims of our own government, the very one which is supposed to protect us

Show me your back Bob

Looking at the political impasse in Zimbabwean election; it is important to revisit the preceding event before the 29 March election. How did we end up with such a retrogressive law, that a winning presidential candidate has to garner more than 50% of the total votes which has proved to be a thorn in the flesh? What happened next or what is not to happen next because doing nothing in politics is indeed doing something?

The dialogue brokered by Thabo Mbeki under the SADCC initiative started in March 2007. All major Zimbabwean political stakeholders were to be consulted in the process, preceding the harmonized presidential and parliamentary elections. Thabo Mbeki facilitation team of Minister Sydney Mufamadi, the Director General Rev Frank Chikane and the Presidential Legal Adviser Advocate Mojanku Gumbi indeed managed to bring to negotiation table the two MDC factions and ZANU (PF). On June 18 2007, both parties agreed on amendments to electoral laws, security laws, media laws and a draft constitution which was to form the basis of public consultations before the elections.

The facilitation team tried hard to bring the principal negotiators together namely, Robert Mugabe, Arthur Mutambara and Morgan Tsvangirai. Both Tsvangirai and Mutambara agreed to the proposal but Mugabe being stubborn as he is, refused to personally participate in a face to face dialogue with other principal stakeholders. While the negotiating teams had agreed on other burning issues to be included in the draft constitution, such as the establishment of an independent electoral commission, ZANU (PF) was buying time on ttimetablentation time table and the logistical framework. While both parties were waiting for ZANU (PF) to honour their part in the negotiations, Mugabe proclaimed 29 March 2008 as the date of harmonized election plunging the country in a constitutional crisis. Mugabe went further as to draft amendment number 18 to captivate half backed electoral reforms to hoodwink the SADCC and the facilitation team. Mugabe knew that given a political level ground he would lose dismally yet this is what the SADCC and the opposition were asking him to do, to part with his traditional murderous tactics. MDC had suggested a postponement of the election to about June 2008 to allow meaningful electoral reforms to take place. The date of the election was actually part of the negotiation and for Mugabe to jump the gun and announce the date of an election, before the agreement was reached is detrimental to staging a coup, one political commentator was quoted;

SADLY and regrettably, the dialogue between the MDC and ZANU (PF) /the government of Zimbabwe which President Mbeki was mandated to facilitate by the SADCC Heads of State and Government on 29 March 200) ended in failure when ZANU (PF)/government of Zimbabwe repudiated the principles and the spirit of the dialogue by unilaterally proclaiming 29 March 2008 as the date of the election, when that very issue was a subject of deadlock at the talks.

ZANU (PF) went on public describing the negotiations as being a success and asked the opposition to support the amendment number 18 which among the changes was the creation of the Zimbabwe Election Commission (ZEC), which today over a month after the 29 March election has failed to announce the crucial presidential election.

Analysing the above it is clear that what we now face is Mugabe the old man in limbo. He rushed to announce the election date so as not to allow opposition parties the slightest chance to win. The MDC opposition was actually mooting a boycott of the election on that basis. Doesn't it sound sordid that the man who rushed us into an election that we were ill prepared should today cry foul when he is beaten? What Mugabe must understand is that MDC need not have campaigned for them to win because everything that could have gone wrong in a classical misrule have gone wrong under his rule Zimbabwe. Look at the economy, the infrastructure, social services and hyperinflation; surely assuming you're still sane, do you think given the option people would choose misery over the hope of a meaningful change?

Before I pen off; I have just a few words for the former president Robert Mugabe. There is no point for you to use violence anymore; the people of Zimbabwe have made their decision to see your back. You should be grateful for the people of Zimbabwe who are the most peaceful, more docile and intelligent people in the World; they chose a pen instead of a gun. There is no need for a run-off or off-run after 28 years of iron rule, it's not rocket science Bob and we are fed up with you! What if you steal the election in a run-off, what do you what to achieve at 84 years which you failed at 56 years plus 28 years in power.

Any delay in handing over power to the people of Zimbabwe must be seen in the light of treason and gross violation of the constitution of Zimbabwe. In essence the law must take its course.

Zimbabwe: My prayer

I ASK for your divine intervention in Zimbabwe.

I have come to understand that we Zimbabweans lack the righteous capacity to unshackle the chains of bondage we now find ourselves in. Thousands of quasi organizations have mushroomed over the years to come with a unifying position against the regime but all what these organizations have achieved, has been to enrich the founding members at the expense of the struggling masses. The opposition parties have come and gone. Those still championing the cause remained toothless and clueless against a highly sophisticated regime.

Oh! Lord in case you forget, the basic commodities remain elusive in Zimbabwe. No-one seems determined for a cause as we do to the endless queues. In case our prayers have not reached you my Lord, we remain banned to discuss matters pertinent to development and governance. China remains our friendliest nation donating numerous electronic gadgets to monitor our movements and loyalty to a regime long bent on sadistic rule and acrimony. The only new development worth noting is the purchase of 2 MA60 passenger aircrafts through a 'buy two get one free' deal, although my Lord, I understand that the free one failed to complete a 400 km return trip from Bulawayo. We remain forced to look east even though the sun no longer shines on Zimbabwe. My Lord when the regime committed itself to looking East, progressive forces celebrated thinking that we were going to emulate Mozambique our Eastern neighbour, knowing pretty well that Mozambique remains the envy of the region. Of late they have one of the best human rights record, they commit themselves to free and fair elections and have been actively promoting sound agrarian policies.

Zimbabwe remain divided deliberately or otherwise. Most churches in Zimbabwe are now being run by ZANU (PF). I am surprised that, Almighty, you could have allowed that to happen...to have your Holly House used to further repressive regimes. The only man of the cloth worth mentioning in Zimbabwe is Pius Ncube who remains focused. I pray that you give us more Pius Ncubes and arm them with your hand of supremacy to deliver THY KINGDOM. In case you have forgotten us, more than a quarter of us Zimbabweans live in the Diaspora where we suffer trauma due to lack of identity and decadence of social fabric.

Zimbabweans remain among the most educated on the land, most courageous, most resourceful, most skilful yet most oppressed. My Lord when all is said and done, there is no reason why MDC can run out of ideas or ZANU (PF) can run out of ideas. Our problem, my Lord, remains shameful, that those who first cross the line of power immediately close the doors behind them. In unwittingly closing the doors, they close the doors to the voice of reason.

Finally, my Lord, I beg you to use your powers to descend on Zimbabwe and curse the tyranny. Zimbabwe remains our only Promised Land generation after generation, unfortunately Mugabe sees himself as all generations wrapped into one. How on earth can this be allowed. I offer myself, body and soul, to be used by the Holy Spirit to deliver salvation to the people of Zimbabwe, through you my Lord can this be done.

Through this palm I shall change my destiny

The prophets of doom must be reminded that MDC is here to stay, prosper and rule Zimbabwe come what may as the Birmingham meeting had shown. Sometimes you need serious problems like the ones befalling MDC to select the seeds from the chuff if a struggle is to succeed. When the MDC was formed it had its humble beginnings embedded in mass boycott and civic activism. The past 6 years had seen the true colours of Zimbabwean politics that it is dirty and enduring. Like "struggle within struggle" (in ZANU) by Masipula Sithole, MDC is no exception. We all learn from mistakes and through crisis management, nations prosper.

The Birmingham MDC meeting of 8 January 2006 drew participants from all over the UK. For the first time I have never seen so many women at a District Level both in the UK and Zimbabwe. Many of those who were present are well known activists who have been dormant for a long time and finally had vowed that the 2006 is the year and the year is 2006, for change and no less. I have to admit that in this meeting there were more heads than there were bodies, believe me you. It reminded me of the early 2000 when the MDC was still in its infancy with virgin energy to overthrow the regime. We danced, ululated and cried for our mother land even though the exchange rate was $1 to 44. We gave our best, risking all for the country and the party. Today the exchange rate is $1 to 1000 yet we are no longer crying, what a shame. There we were in the middle of UK toyi toying, crying for our mother land. We were closer to each other than a baby is to a mother. Suddenly MDC was re-born thousands of kilometres away from Zimbabwe, MDC UK, well done.

We call upon Zimbabweans all over the World to unite and rally behind MDC to reclaim what is rightfully our struggle. To those with wounds and scars come open and guide us through for you have convincing tales to share with us. We are no longer guided by democracy where there is none but by fury and love of one's country. Together we have seen it go, together let us see it come.

We came, we danced and we spoke, and then let us commit ourselves. Let us give our leaders awakenings call that MDC ndeyeropa, least they forget. Those who aspire to be leaders of today and tomorrow must be reminded that it is not by personal wisdom that they succeed but by the blessings of true MDC members. If what I saw in Birmingham is repeated in Zimbabwe, then Mugabe must be warned that, MDC here we come! We have only our bare hands to fight with but no amount of firepower will save him and his corrupt government. We have started the first step, like a baby we will not crawl back, until we reach our destination, old age.

Chinja Maitiro, maitiro chinja. Gucula Izenzo, Izenzo Gucula.

The argon of sharing a birthday with a dictator

Ever thought of sharing a birthday cake with a dictator? Certainly unthinkable if you are a Zimbabwean in limbo. But believe me you I share the same month with the dictator Robert Mugabe. While I wish myself many more years, I will be wishing him the same.

Mugabe will be 82 years on the 21st February 2006 and I will be xx. My friends and wife have always laughed at me for the obvious reason. I used to have many friends and relatives joining me in the celebration, today no one wants to celebrate with me anymore. I have not managed to find new friends but more than half of my old friends are dead at the age of 35, they were lucky to reach the Zimbabwean life expectancy. I am like a benchmark for a new era, a sad thing indeed. I am not going into detail about what you Zimbabweans should expect this year, because none indeed.

I have been doing a research in a dictatorship. I am not going to dwell on Mugabe because, doing so would give him unnecessary

publicity. In 82 we should not waste our time in discussing about
when he will leave the office. Mugabe is a liability in Zimbabwe we
all know that.

As a political researcher, I was interested on how rather than
why? Most dictators throughout the World have one thing in
common, they are all human beings but born between 20th and
30th of the month. Some of you might think otherwise but here
are the results;

Dictator	Date of Birth
Robert Gabriel Mugabe	21-02-1924
Benito Mussolini	29-07-1883
Saddam Hussein	28-04-1937
Idi Amin	17-05-1928
Adolf Hitler	20-041889
Augusto Pinochet	25-11-1915

Mugabe rest in peace no one needs you anymore.

Tribute to Makuwaza and Efurida Pfebve

EFURIDA Pfebve, sister, fighter for justice, former chairperson of
MDC Mt. Darwin North is no more.

She passed away on September 24, after being taken ill a day
before she met her death. She became another victim of a failed
health system in Zimbabwe among others.

This comes less than four weeks after Remus Makuwaza, a long
time friend, MDC director of elections died without realising his
dream of a free Zimbabwe. Losing freedom is one thing, losing
fighters of that freedom makes the whole struggle a surmountable
task.

Such has become a common scenario in Zimbabwe today; one
after the other, Zimbabweans has succumbed to a crumbling health
system. Losing two comrades in arms in less than four weeks have
left me devastated and grief stricken.

Against all these odds, ladies and gentlemen, comrades and friends the struggle must continue unabated. With the conviction and guidance of the Almighty, victory is certain.

I worked with Makuwaza from the formation of the MDC, in structure building and mobilisation. We were all members of the National Executive, we shared common problems in the 2000 Parliamentary Elections. Makuwaza was contesting against Moven Mahachi in Makoni West and I was against Border Gezi in Bindura. These men were regarded as the most dangerous in ZANU (PF) hence we had a common difficult task. Remus and I were soon nicknamed Mahachi and Gezi respectively. We both escaped numerous attempts on our lives. By coincidence, yet not of our own making, both men died in car accidents after rigging the elections. They were victims of the struggle within struggles in ZANU (PF). Makuwaza my friend rest in peace.

Condolences for Efurida continue to pour in from three continents, from those whose work she touched to those who knew her well both in a personal capacity.

I remember receiving a phone call three days after the Presidential elections in March 2002 notifying me about 11 members of the MDC who were arrested and in detention at Mukumbura Police Station in MT. Darwin. Knowing the area to be politically volatile, I took with me some youths and travelled to Mukumbura Police Station passing through a barrage of ambushes along the way from ZANU (PF) militia. I was shocked to see Efurida being the only woman in custody among the 11 MDC supporters. They were being held for an alleged attack on a war veteran. Although the other 10 supporters were not admitting taking part in the said crime, Efuida remained adamant that she acted in self defence against ZANU (PF) supporters who waylaid her and others for being MDC supporters.

For the first time I saw her courage and determination flowing through her veins refusing to compromise her liberty and prepared to go to jail for what she thought was her right of political association. Those who know MT Darwin area will agree with me that very few people had taken an open stance against ZANU (PF) there, yet there she was a symbol of a new Zimbabwe among jackals of ZANU (PF) patronage. Even after the murder of my brother Mathew, Efurida refused to move away from the area preferring instead to lead the women's wing from the grassroots against all odds. Efurida was present when my brother was murdered yet escaped only to meet her death last week.

She was determined to carve the future for all Zimbabweans even if it meant sacrificing her own life. She died a miserable woman knowing that the struggle she so committed herself to, has now moved from a political to a constitutional crisis with Robert Mugabe getting a firm hand of every system living and gone.

Efurida, sister and politician rest in peace.

Today, 5 years ago Mugabe killed my brother

TODAY the 30th of April in 2000, my brother retired Inspector Mathew Pfebve was murdered by Robert Mugabe in cold blood.

Mathew a family man and a symbol of the Pfebve family were murdered by ZANU (PF) in cold blood. His crime, being a brother to Elliot Pfebve, the MDC political National Executive member and MP candidate for Bindura.

He was murdered 2 months after having retired from the ZRP after having served the same government that killed him for 21 years. Today Mathew could have been 50, energetic and contributing to the development of his country.

His Death Certificate number 672017 registered at MT Darwin District Office confirmed the cause of his death as, "Massive brain injury from trauma, assault and laceration of right lung" and this was signed by Dr. Kabanda and countersigned by the informant

Officer- In- Charge Mkumbura Police, Inspector Daniel Dennis Makaure.

Five years after he was murdered, nobody has been brought to book for the murder despite the fact that the people who murdered him are well known and moving freely doing their normal business, scaring and probably murdering more people in Zimbabwe.

"I salute all those who have been murdered in cold blood in pursuit of a true democratic Zimbabwe. I salute those who voted in the past election against the Lord of Darkness"

Robert Mugabe and his ZANU (PF) government did not issue any statement to condemn those who murdered my brother other than unilaterally declaring an amnesty to all those who could have been involved in political crimes and murders. Five years down the line more and more people continue to die, are maimed, raped and displaced from a country of their birth.

The massive exodus of Zimbabweans fleeing the country means that Zimbabwe will never be the same again. The impact this has on social and economic factors is beyond human imagination yet today the international community has watched from the terrace while Zimbabweans continue to live under the yoke of the tyrant and systematic persecution. Zimbabwe today has even been rewarded by being elected to the UN Human Rights Commission in New York on the 27 April 2005. What this means is Mugabe for the next three years will advise the UN on Human Rights issues in the region and beyond, what a shame!

I dream of a Zimbabwe where the young get charged and the old get change. I believe in a country where the President is from the people and by the people. I believe in a new Zimbabwe where the people of Zimbabwe are free to be free. I believe in a world of peace, liberty and stability. I don't believe in politics of patronage, I believe in a natural selection of leadership which is democratically changeable. At 81, we Zimbabweans are fighting with our ancestors. I salute all those who have been murdered in cold blood in pursuit of a true democratic Zimbabwe. I salute those who languish in filthy jails serving for politically motivated crimes they did not commit. I salute those who voted in the past election against the Lord of Darkness.

Long live Zimbabwe! Long live the struggle for peace and justice! Long live civil disobedience against tyranny! Long live the march to victory!! Aluta continua!!

Why the Zimbabwe 'stay away' failed

In a country where over 70% are jobless, it is unthinkable to expect the few still privileged to have a job to risk losing further. Last week's efforts by the Broad Alliance to mobilise people for a job boycott however, must be applauded, although against a background of ill fated strategies and underestimated consequences.

After over 22,000 people were detained for defending their property amid no resistance from the impoverished populace, politicians should have devised a better strategy of harnessing people's anger there-and-then rather than wait and even when the enemy of a stay away.

In the Western World this could have had a profound impact but don't forget this is Zimbabwe. Our greatest weakness as a people is that, we are more spiritual than religious, hence lacking holy confrontational capacity of other nations.

Mugabe would not give a toss if the economy was brought to its knees because the economy is already on its stomach anywhere. One would be forgiven to think that for a leader with more degrees than his fingers, he should know better that governance and economic development are mutually exclusive.

What are the lessons learned and where can we go from here?

The civic groups missed a golden chance by not harnessing people's anger at the massive demolition sites by the government. We seem to be good at being reactive rather than being proactive. A statement by the Broader Alliance that people should simply stay indoors to avoid being pounced by police was irresponsible and insensitive to the thousands of people toiling in detentions for having stood up solo against the wanton destructions of their properties by Mugabe.

People should simply stand up and fight back, POSA or no POSA. How do we respect the same laws that we are condemned as being barbaric and oppressive? What we have succeeded in doing is to legitimise the POSA and the fraudulent Mugabe regime. What is needed is spontaneous confrontations with Mugabe were ever we are, and by whatever means.

Politicians risk irrelevance for advocating strategies out of their political capacity. This is not a game of loosely knitted words, it is about action and indeed shouldering surmountable risks. Politics is not a business; it is about building a viable national pride against all odds, bulldozing the obstacles along the way no matter what it takes.

Mugabe is making a mockery of the African Union and the UN. When every leader is committed to eradicate poverty, Mugabe is committing himself to state-sponsored poverty. Where is Mugabe getting the fuel to move such an army to destroy people's homes and livelihood in a country with no fuel?

I cannot believe that all people in ZANU (PF) are so solid stupid as not to see beyond Mugabe. How can these people continue to support such unpopular actions against the very electorate they intend to vote them back into power in the next election?

Only Zimbabweans remain capable of rescuing the country from this morass.

LET'S TALK ABOUT TALKS

What is this mumbo jumbo of talks about talks? Is there any need for talks in Zimbabwe and if so who should talk and to whom and about what?

There is no doubt that any stand-off in politics will always assume two dimensions, one of the use of force, which I shall call the Bush theorem and dialogue or simply the Annan theorem. But before parties can talk, there must be a reason to talk and not only that but that demands are clearly outlined for the negotiating team. The logic of negotiation dictates that the person with more fire power gets the lion's share because he/she is negotiating from a point of advantage. The weaker party will settle for the political leftovers, caught between demise and duress. Is it possible to enter a political settlement where both parties are at a win-win situation? That being rare in fully fledged democratic societies, makes it even a sad reading for a politically fragile country like Zimbabwe. For the success of the talks about talks, one party must be prepared to surrender its identity and go through a political metamorphosis for the sack of national survival. Will this be ZANU (PF) or MDC?

Although coming to a negotiating table is a sign of political maturity and relevance, neither MDC nor ZANU (PF)**Error! Bookmark not defined.** have any reason to negotiate. ZANU (PF) claims to have won more than 2/3 majority in the March 2005 parliamentary elections, and they are right because we have accepted it both in theory and in practice, stolen or not stolen it's time to shut-up. MDC claims the elections were rigged of course they were and will always be for as long as ZANU (PF) is in power. Are we negotiating for a rerun of the elections if so then we risk being in the political oblivion for being not squaring up for the political grade. Are we suggesting that we get a quarter system of the cabinet posts if so why? Under whose presidency? We are negotiating at the time we have fewer parliamentary seats than the first aborted talks, at a time that Mugabe can change the constitution using his 2/3 majority in parliament and worse still against a successful operation murambatsvina to which no body raised a finger.

The only reason why ZANU (PF) will want to negotiate is not much for the power which they have but for the economic reason. Mugabe intends to use MDC to prop up a bartered image internationally. Get the IMF and World Bank to resume its financial rescue packages. Oh! By the way, Grace also misses shopping in London, New York and Paris, this can only come about if MDC baptise the marooned ZANU (PF) into a born again child. I do not think ZANU (PF) needs any rescue financial package when they are busy destroying the production line turning the country into a nation of food aid recipients.

The demands for negotiations should be narrowed to 3 specifics, that Mugabe must go, that a new constitution must be enacted and pass through a referendum, and finally there must be the restoration of the rule of law. There will be a transitional process to which all stakeholders must be involved, the NCA, the Churches, Civic organizations and political parties. Unfortunately the process will have a ZANU (PF) moderate as the head of state if ever there are any moderates in ZANU (PF). Of course ZANU (PF) would not want to be seen to have lost everything in the process. Whether it is acceptable to have a ZANU (PF) head under a close scrutiny by a transition committee bound by a new constitutional framework is debatable.

We must also learn from the previous talks, the Lancaster Conference of 1979, the ZAPU-ZANU talks of the 1988. What if Mugabe decides to merge with MDC? Although of political mirage, it will work out in favour of the MDC. Those on the table must ensure that the new party be called MDC. The party symbol must change from a clenched fist into an open palm. The Headquarters of the new party must be moved to Mbare to give it a face lift that it needs most. The retiring age for the president must be 65 years. Party president must not exceed two terms whether for party or national position. Let us make sure that it's Mugabe who demands talks not MDC.

I SMELL A SURPRISE VICTORY IN THE AIR?

What then are the chances for a win for MDC?

There is no doubt that MDC's spirit is high and the support base gearing for a victory, but I have seen that before. MDC rallies continue to manifest its popularity but I have seen that before. Morgan Tsvangirai**Error! Bookmark not defined.** is as charismatic as ever but I have seen that before. T-shirts are everywhere but I have seen
that before. To my fellow citizens, MDC members and the handpicked observers, the elections have been rigged, are being rigged and will be rigged.

The 3,5 million people scattered all over the world are opposition
supporters and have been denied their birthright to vote, that is already the biggest rigging exercise since the concept of one man one vote was adopted by progressive forces world over. What if the 3 million people horrendously exiled by Mugabe are allowed to vote? What if the people decide to reclaim their power by massive civil disobedience? If we analyse the Zimbabwe political past and present, these elections are more just what if than being a new turning point for a new Zimbabwe.

Let's listen to Pius Ncube but let us not overburden his courage. All Zimbabweans world over must unite, irrespective of party lines and demand that meaningful change be delivered to the bleeding country. Let's all Zimbabweans safeguard their vote! We have been docile to the point of being stupid, I see no choice between death and starvation.

Is ZANU (PF) sincere about preaching a peaceful campaign leading to March election?

Is the violence statistics lower than the previous 4 years?

Zimbabwe what went wrong?

1. They will never be a prospect of a free and fair election in Zimbabwe on the 31 March 2005. The reasons are clear, the political landscape is tilted in favour of ZANU (PF), and they hold the state machinery which they have been used to murder, maim and rob its own citizens for the past 5 years. Even if they might appear to be less violent election than the previous one, the fear embedded into people's minds is real and is harvest time for ZANU (PF). They are still harvesting from the proceeds of a brutal and violent tenure. SADC election guidelines lack the balance and checks of an enforceable regional legislation. They only guide the willing and watch the unwilling. Mugabe is seeking a fortune turn around by becoming the first leader to adopt the SADC guidelines albeit cosmetically and lip service at most.

The massive exodus of eligible voters to the tune of around 3 million, 95% of which if accorded the chance to vote would vote for the opposition, they cannot vote for a party that had, against their will sent them into exile. This is more than half the legible voters in this coming election.

The deployment of the feared army to monitor and supervise elections all of which adds to the fear already in many rural people cannot be over emphasised. These factors and much more will not make   this   election   free   and fair.

2. ZANU (PF) is not sincere in preaching about a peaceful election. If we revisit all past elections, 1995 against ZUM, 2000 against MDC and 2002 against MDC, you will find a pattern of systematic persecution of perceived opponents of ZANU (PF). Mugabe has never participated peacefully in an election he is convinced he will lose without using violence. He has always used violence where it suited him most. How does he know whether he will lose or win an election? Remember Mugabe is the only President   in   Africa with a first world class security service in a third world country. The CIO is the only organization whose operation is windfall

funded by the state. It has been used to sustain the regime since 1980. They have structures with a high alert warning system to warn Mugabe of a pending victory or loss. If there is any achievement that we Zimbabweans have done is to prove beyond doubt that Mugabe has been the architecture, director and coordinator of violence. There is no way he could have stopped the violence if he was not the leader of its origin. In short we have a historic landmark here where history must judge him harshly for causing impeccable suffering of his people. When your liberator turned oppressor your will have very little chance of survival.

3. What triggered the violence in the 2000 election? A combination of fear of defeat and a bankruptcy of a political solution to the woes of the country by the present regime. There is no doubt that Mugabe used to be a hero of my peace loving Zimbabweans in the early years of his rule, yet we all know that everybody has his hay days, by 1998 Mugabe has reached a sell by date of his usefulness to the people of Zimbabwe. His defeat in the referendum, the upcoming of an alternative viable opposition party, MDC and the final straw of showing support of white farmers to the MDC was a blow to Mugabe.

The battle ground was drawn and the hiring of the mad professor, Jonathan Moyo to prop up his lost popularity coupled with the use of the war veterans marked the beginning of a dark history in Zimbabwe. Mugabe new he will lose the election this is why he postponed the 2000 elections twice before settling for June 2000 date. Mugabe did not have any solution to the crumbling economy, high inflation rate and massive unemployment rate of more than 70% other than to use violence. More than 200 people were recorded murdered between 2000 and 2002. All bye- elections turned into battlegrounds.

4. Zimbabwe what went wrong? Everything had gone wrong in Zimbabwe. While one man has held 12 million people at ransom,

you and I cannot escape the blame for not standing up for a cause early enough and effective enough. 2002 was the year, presidential election was the event and Mugabe could have found very little breathing space to continue against people's wishes. This was the only election Mugabe was not sure whether he would survive. Even after the results, business remained closed, some for 2 days, police were even nowhere to be seen on the streets, there was confusion. We needed only 1000 people in Harare to march to the State House. We had no plan B. ZANU (PF) will go, it might not be this coming election but the conviction of a pending defeat is imminent. Victory is in the air; the journey might be long but let us begin.

Mugabe begs to join the West!

The news that the IMF has postponed its decision to expel Zimbabwe from the International Monetary Fund should have come as a relief to Robert Mugabe but certainly not to the multitudes of poverty stricken Zimbabweans. That Mugabe can afford to raise US120 million over night to pay back IMF under the current economic meltdown comes as a shock to us all. The burning question is where did the money come from and how much is still left in this mysterious green bank source? Why is Mugabe more concerned about pacifying IMF more than his own people? Who owns IMF?

Mugabe blames USA and Britain for sabotaging Zimbabwe's economy that is rubbish! Mugabe should know it better that the IMF is USA and Britain among other economic giants like Japan, France and Germany. USA is the only country with veto power over IMF due to its 17.08% shareholding capacity of the IMF. Why should then Mugabe be much concerned with paying the same countries such huge sums of money? Is it not only logical that if you borrow any amount of capital then you should be prepared to pay back? It does not require a rocket scientist to understand that borrowers cannot be the lenders. Mugabe has been the sole leader since Independence from Britain in 1980; he cannot therefore blame anybody for his both political and economic failure.

Why did Mugabe pay the US 120 million in the first place at a time the country is financially bankruptcy? Mugabe is known for playing political double standards blaming everything to the West. Zimbabwe joined the IMF on its free will just like the 184 member states who are shareholders in it. Mugabe knows very well the benefits of being an IMF member and this is why he had gone out of his way to borrow money to meet the IMF balance of payments. Established December 1945, its primary purpose was to avoid an economic meltdown that leads to the Great Depression of the 1930s. The core business for IMF thus is to promote international monetary cooperation, exchange stability, orderly exchange arrangements, foster economic growth and high levels of employment, provide temporary financial assistance to countries to easy balance of payment adjustments. It is affiliated to the United Nations and its top ownership is USA, Japan, Germany, France and UK. South Africa is the biggest IMF shareholder in Africa with 0.85%. Ironically Mugabe wants to borrow from South Africa, the biggest African shareholder of the IMF so as to pay IMF. It will not be surprising that the money South Africa intends to lend to Zimbabwe is directly coming from IMF attached with specific home grown demands. Whatever is the case, South Africa must continue to demand stringent political reforms as a precondition to releasing the money. By extending a financial credit to Zimbabwe, South Africa is increasing its credit rating from the IMF to which it is part. Zimbabwe's voting rights was suspended from IMF on June 6 2003 joining Liberia which was suspended March 5 the same year. Zimbabwe remains the only country in Southern Africa with no voting rights capacity in the IMF.

What we have is Mugabe is trying to borrow from Peter to pay Paul. The government is just buying time from a looming economic meltdown with a political disastrous consequence; it is a beggar- thy-neighbour-to-feed-thy-neighbour affair.

Mugabe's fear is that Zimbabwe will be internationally alienated, which literally already it is. He must know better that Zimbabwe was one of the most promising economies in the World when he took over power from Britain in 1980, yet he rocked it down to bottom low single handed. He must stop blaming IMF and the West, and fully accept the blame and gracefully resign, that he is resigning within the next 2 ½ years is not news at all. Mugabe at 81 will naturally cease to function mentally any time from now but he is determined to go on until the end of his disputed term in 2008. Looking at him during a recent TV interview, he looked terribly socially exhausted not withstanding furrows of political erosion reminiscent of a dictator on the trail. He even had gusts to reiterate that after retiring, he will continue to be behind the scenes in ZANU (PF), what a shame. In saying that Mugabe is even refusing to let ZANU (PF) go, he regards it as his personal asset. What Zimbabweans should note is that there will be no hope of a better Zimbabwe within ZANU (PF). What is needed is a complete change of government, only then can we start talking about a turnaround in the fortunes of Zimbabwe. No matter how much you hate the West, you will still go back on your knees begging. Mugabe must be warned that you cannot fool everybody all the time without playing fool yourself.

Zimbabwe who will fire the first shot?

This week has been of particular frustration to all Zimbabweans where ever they are and whatever they are doing. Too many people, the images of the past week do not come as a surprise but the graphical illustration of the mayhem is astonishing. Seeing is believing! While the World is agape that civilised people in this 21st century can stoop so low as to be subdued by one man, Robert Gabriel Catholic Mugabe, few does understand the scale of Zimbabwean problem. If the World new, they would not have placed Iraq ahead of Zimbabwe because during Sadam Hussein, at least food and sanity was available to the Iraqis. Mugabe is a moving grave surrounded by blood thirst vipers fed on blood and corrupt money. In case you forget, China, Russia and Iran remain his closest allies. In the absence of Africa backing, where would one seek pad for a democratic regime change. By forsaking Zimbabweans, Africa is colluding with Mugabe in the hope that if they become dictators in the making African brotherhood will prevail.

I have written many articles on the Zimbabwe crisis, all hardcore militant as to motivate people to take a collective and perpetual civil defiance even if it means an armed struggle. Only writing is not enough but I put my head on the block contesting with Border Gezi the architecture of Green Bombers, Elliot Manyika the brutal Mugabe intelligence. Many Zimbabweans today do not know that the Green Bomber were initially setup specifically for me. By the way I have a constituency to represent, I have a grave right at my door step having lost my brother, a father with a permanent injury due to a murderous ZANU(PF) and a business empire ransacked to feed Green Bombers under Mugabe's instruction. God answered our prayers and Border Gezi did not live to enjoy the fruits of his brutality albeit Mugabe did.

In October 2000, Adela Chiminya and I sued Robert Mugabe on gross violations of human rights, albeit even the USA presidency (George Bush) did not support us, actually the state department appealed on behalf of Mugabe, whatever the reason, I don't what to know, but USA employs double standards and I am very much convinced that the USA is behind the collusion with Mugabe. Mugabe would not have survived even for a year if he has fallen out with USA and Europe; I stand to be corrected here.

So 2008 we are going for dual Presidential and parliamentary elections? DID I get it correct that the opposition agreed with ZANU (PF) to?

Increase the parliamentary seats from 120 to 210
Accessible advertisement for all parties
The president will now be able to appoint a successor
Bla-a-a-a-ar

If this is true, then MDC has lost sanity. Even before commenting on the above, let me hasten to say as a postgraduate of Civil Conflict Resolution, I was appalled by the speed at which we opposition agreed to everything ZANU (PF). Zimbabwe has one of the most educated people in Africa, and a mere consultation would have put the struggle on the track. This is utter rubbish! Who does not know that the over 4 million people who left Zimbabwe were from urban areas and who are opposition supporters. The delimitation commission by Tobaiwa Mudede will simply put the majority of the 90 seats in rural areas, everybody knows that. By agreeing to Mugabe forfeiting the 30 seats he appoints and give him leeway to appoint further 90 indirectly is lunatic to say the least. We have always protested that the civil servant is bloated and needs trimming, we can't even find money to pay the current 120 MPs adequately, where are we going to get the money to pay late alone 210, this is rubbish! I remain defiant that Robert Mugabe must go and MDC has no business to nurse him in his transition to hell, "ngatisaputsa chirongo tasvika veduwe" In 2002 we were allowed to advertise but mind you the decision for the content still remained with Mugabe and he never publish anything because he did not agree with it, what makes us think that this will be different this time. The agreement is silent on POSA, AIPPA, Green Bombers and the Political Funding ACT. These sections mean more to the current fear than meets the eye. If you remove them then you have democracy in Zimbabwe.

Zimbabweans all over the World are fighting this struggle, I hope the opposition realise this. This is not a lone struggle and consultation is important. We must fight Mugabe on sea, on air, on land and cyberspace; remember he will be turning 84, where on earth, for God's sake an 84 year old has ruled a country with sanity. Mugabe needs to be confronted with all fire power the World can produce. The opposition by agreeing to constitutional changes no. 18, risk perpetuating a Mugabe dynasty. What will stop Mugabe from passing power to Grace Mugabe (the brutal wife) or to his 10 year old son in the name of the constitution? You don't need a degree to understand that!

I am in favour of not only removing Mugabe but the uprooting of everything ZANU (PF) "ndipo panonyaya ipapo". Change is in the air but it can only come from Zimbabweans and not Thambo Mbeki. I am proud to be a Zimbabwean and I will die for that cause.

Robert, your honeymoon is over

The daggers have been drawn between the World's most powerful man and the World's most despotic leader albeit they are all Africans. Robert Mugabe visas Koffi Annan, Anna Tibaijuku is the referee. Whether it was by coincidence that UN envoy Anna Tibaijuku from Tanzania (an African) or by design and intend was given the job of investigating the Operation Murambatsvina, it indeed signal a new era in African politics. She will go down in History as the bullet that killed the giant monster to save millions of fellow Africans from mayhem.

The report was exhaustive, frank and unbiased, reporting it as it is. Her choice of words was more than the bullet could have achieved, ricocheting right into the Mugabe regime's twisted minds. Words like, "disastrous venture, brutal and horrific", are the strongest words coming from the UN since Mugabe went berserk. The fact that Mugabe has always hid behind a race card in his barbaric disastrous ventures makes it an interesting scenario now that it is the powerful sons and daughters of Africa telling him to shut up or else. May be Mugabe will label Anna Tibaijuku as a white woman in a black jacket. What will he say about Koffi Annan? Who have described the report as being, "profoundly distressing ...Indiscriminate actions carried out with disquieting indifference to human suffering" Koffi Annan want the International Community to intervene in Zimbabwe, too good to be true for all Zimbabweans out there. He wants the Operation Murambatsvina to stop and those who master minded the operation to be brought to book. Being a Zimbabwean and political analyst, I know pretty well that there was nowhere any Minster could have ordered such an ambitious wanton destruction of property without being ordered to do so by the Executive President. Remember Mugabe is not only a President but is an Executive President whose actions by virtue of his title are exonerated by the law. He personally spoke of his support of the operations only as a formality.

Not surprising that the government reacted with utter shock of the report because they have become paranoid of reasoning. Simbarashe Mumbengegwi describe the report as an inbuilt bias against the government and operation and he even unashamedly described it as , "upholding a pro –opposition tone" Mr. Minster, if you think you are the Jonathan Moyo in the making, you are only displaying your utter stupidity against logic. You allowed Anna Tibaijuku to see for herself want your government had done to its people. She was only compiling facts as she saw them on the ground. You did not provide alternative accommodation did you? Did you clean your messy after destroying the houses? Tell us where you housed them after you destroyed their habitat? You and Robert still sleep in the state funded mansions, what a shame. You expected a report sympathetic to your barbaric government, you must be joking. I have profound outrage of your shallow mind next time just shut up!

What if it was Thabo Mbeki empowered to investigate the operation? He certainly would have submitted a blank report to the UN. I mean how do you expect him to have managed to get the answers that Tibaijuku got if he believes in quiet diplomacy? I say to Thabo Mbeki, you are becoming a liability to Pan-Africanism. Unashamedly, Mbeki speaks of not allowing Zimbabwe to collapse because that would mean South Africa inherits the consequences. I thought you have always been aware of this Mr President and why has it taken Tibaijuku to knock sense into you. South Africa owes the region all the wisdom it inherited from its colonial master as is Nigeria to West Africa. Let's start thinking of an African Think Tank Committee (ATTC), to which sons and daughters of Africa like Anna Tibaijuku patriotic to their motherland will champion the cause for conflict resolution and post conflict rehabilitation. The AU has dismally failed Zimbabweans and hence an Independent ATTC watch- dog.

A month ago I wrote a prayer about Zimbabwe, calling for a divine intervention, at least my prayers has been answered! Well done Ms Tibaijuku.

Elliot Pfebve

Zimbabwe: the stolen Christmas

I looked at the sun, it was about 11am on Christmas Day. I was getting late, for this was a day of showing off. I have to rush to the Shopping Centre where people of all ages were celebrating the traditional Christmas.

I needed to show off my new clothes to the rest of the village. Everybody was happy, I mean happy! There were no politics in the air. As far as I was concerned I was my own liberator, MP, Minister and Prime Minister rolled into one. This was the first Christmas after attaining Independence, a test of African rule in Rhodesia indeed. I was 9.

I was tall and slender, my friends used to mock me saying I was tall seated than standing. I had no bad feelings. I wished there was a big looking glass to cover my whole body but that was a luxury not to be seen in a village.

I was wearing a new pair of black Tenderfoot from BATA, a Paramount English khaki suit from ENBE, Moffat Street. It was slightly oversize but stone robust and thick. I looked like an 1890 Brakwasha without a cap, it was brilliant!

My father, a carpenter by the way gave me some spending money, Z$1.00. I was the luckiest child because not many families would raise Z$1.00 in rural areas, let alone giving it to a 9-year-old. I was dressed to kill, and I felt lucky. The whole Christmas wear costed $5.00, very expensive indeed considering the value of the Zimbabwean dollar then.

As was the tradition, I passed through relatives' houses showing off my new clothes and feasting. Almost all families would afford meat and bread on Christmas. Not only bread but this was the only time that families bought dozens and dozens of bread and tins of Sun Jam.

Munongotumira vana kuhondo/kuhondo iwe/kuhondo iwe/aha wedza muchadura/kuhodo iwe/kuhondo iwe hwedza muchadura (Shona Lilics), I suddenly find myself dancing to the tune.

I had no idea who sang the song but all the same it gave me that conviction of a forgotten struggle. Suddenly I felt courage flowing through me, I wished the war would start again so that I could be in the thick of it all brandishing an AK47 and a Bazooka, breaking the enemy lines. How I wished I was old enough to have gone to war. I had the greatest respect for the Comrades, "vana mukoma". With my $1.00, I was able to buy a box of Lebena biscuits, a bottle of Coco-Cola, tinned beef and still remained with 70 cents. We danced to a host of musicians, Ngwaru Mapundu, Thomas Mapfumo, Marshal Munhumumwe, Oliver Mutukudzi and the Ngwenya Brothers, it was brilliant! I watched people dancing, bare footed, people crying for more. There was that human bond of a nation in the making. Zimbabwe or Rhodesia, as was still the confusion, was my home not that I owed it a favour but that it owed me a favour for bringing me to life.

Back home, my mother was waiting for me patiently. I had dust all over me and my Khaki suit was wet with Sweat in the searing heat as I was dancing. I sat down and settled for the Mazowe Orange drink, sweet and full of flavour. There was plenty of food everywhere, everybody was happy. What I didn't know was whether the happiness was brought by Mugabe or Ian Smith. I did not like politics by then, I was too young to understand it.

By the way, I understand Paramount Garments have since closed down and so has the Coca-Cola Company. The cheapest pair of shoes cost not less than Z$1, 000,000.00. Bread is now $32,000.00. A shirt costs more than a pair of trousers at over $1,200,000.00. Rent for a decent house now costs not less than $6,000,000.00. I understand that calculators no longer work in Zimbabwe because there are just too many digits more than 8 digits it was designed for.

In 1999, 80% of the population were literate. Today that figure is down to 50%. The rest can hardly count their earnings, it's just too many zeros. I understand that there are no more pick pocketers in Zimbabwe because anything in a purse won't buy even a sweet, you need a carrier bag full of money to buy a pint of beer.

Zimbabwe is a country where everybody is a millionaire. We must be the richest nation in the World!

As I remember that Christmas Day when I was 9, my eyes swell up with tears for a lost nation. Where we should have consolidated, we brought destruction. I keep wondering when it will, if ever it does, return to the good old days.

I voted MDC because I have AIDS

One of the many victims of southern Africa's no 1 killer, AIDS.

HARARE - More than three years have passed since the last Presidential election. No hope has come to me except the loss of my husband in 2004 and the recent loss of my only daughter Medusa. They all died of AIDS, they say. Although I am not a doctor, this might be true because as I speak now, I am just a heap of bones waiting to rot. All I can remember is that I voted for MDC in 2002 and 2005.

In the queue there I was, coughing and spitting blood, determined to cast my vote. I could hear people saying that your vote is your secret - for me it was your vote is your cure. I didn't vote for Tsvangirai or MDC but I was voting for antiviral drugs or just medicines to ease my pain. I knew my only hope was a change of government because how on earth could the west give medicines to Mugabe? If there was any hope it was going to come through Tsvangirai.

I talked to my MP who assured me that an MDC government would make health for all a reality. I understand in the western world an AIDS patient can live a normal life if he/she lives positively with it. I was determined to vote for my life. I have not seen my MP since I voted for him, not that I expect the medicine from him - just a last goodbye for I will not last to vote for him again. I can feel my lungs collapsing and I just bedridden.

I don't know whether the politicians know that we are an important constituency. If my facts are right, a quarter of us Zimbabweans are infected with AIDS. In a population of 12 million, this gives us 3 million people living with AIDS. If we look at the total votes for presidential election, 1, 6 million voted for ZANU (PF) and 1,2 million for MDC. The total number of people who voted was 2, 8 million. It is likely that all those who voted are living with AIDS for there are 3 million people living with AIDS more than the number of people who voted. I have no doubt that going by the statistics, one of the presidential candidates might be living with AIDS, and I don't know who that candidate is but how much I wish that could be Robert Mugabe. Not because I hate him but because he would give our health a priority over land redistribution and Operation Murambatsvina.

I understand that Mugabe, as an Executive President, can easily flood this country with medicines overnight and stop the brain drain of doctors to neighbouring countries. I am only 25 years, I don't deserve to die, I have been clinging to dear life for long, my hands are now tired I might give up any time now. I understand that life expectancy is now 32 - only five years ago we used to say life begins at 40.

I hear this nonsense about talks against talks. Mugabe once again is globe-trotting - what happened to the targeted sanctions? I understand that Mugabe was promised Chinese medicine but failed to understand the Chinese language and ended up refusing out of ignorance.

I am staring at the wall of my house, which I am told the sheriff came today to attach because of unpaid mortgage. I had two structures at the back of my house for rent which was able to pay my mortgage and at least one meal a day but the government has demolished everything and the lodgers have deserted me. I am not working, relatives and friends have deserted me, and how much I wish my husband was still alive. I did not choose to be a victim of AIDS. I graduated at the University of Zimbabwe with BSc (Hons) in Engineering, my picture still hangs on the wall, in a gown smiling and innocent, receiving my degree.

Zimbabwe never gave me a chance. The economy collapsed under my feet. I needed to survive, the system let me down and my only survival was to get married. Like everybody else in Zimbabwe, I had to choose a husband with 3 C's (Car, Care & Cash). Back then, he was healthier than a doctor.

I think it's time to leave my will before I die. I have no child and no husband left. My only will is for you all Zimbabweans. Vote for a presidential candidate who will openly admit to having AIDS, that way you are assured that 3 million people on the verge of extinction will survive.

6 THE BAD AND THE GOOD

ZIMBABWE HEROES AND VILLAINS

11 August, every year is the time we reflect our revolutionary beliefs for which our forebears fought for and pay allegiance to the fallen heroes of all times. Every nation draws its pride and strength from its historical past of vanguard sons and daughters whose contribution to economic, social and political cohesion merits thus. Zimbabwe although in limbo is no exception. We have our heroes and villains. While we owe the reversal of imperialism to our heroes, political independence remains elusive as villains continue to clog the wheels of fortunes with disastrous political quagmire.

Today, 25 years have passed, we remain 1 step forward and 10 steps backwards.

Who is then a hero and who is a villain? We salute the sons and daughters whose bodies lay scattered worldwide in pursuit of freedom in Zimbabwe. The beacon of our grief and pride is the tomb of the Unknown Soldier. Unknown, because we remain ignorant of their resting places and anguish they went through as they met their gruesome death. Josiah Magamba Tongogara, Ziyapapa Moyo, Chief Rekai Tangwena, George Silundika, Leopold Takawira, Herbet Chitepo, Joshua Nkomo, Ndabaningi Sithole, Jairos Jiri and Sally Mugabe just to mention a few. Zimbabwe is littered with heroes too many to mention whose heroism has been erased because of the politics of patronage. Who should declare one a hero or a villain has always been a cause for concern given the irony that villains have given themselves power of attorney over the issue, neither you nor me will ever be heroes no matter what impact we will bring to Zimbabwe. The only person living who is assured of a place at National Hero's Acre is Robert Mugabe, who has already booked a grave in his solemn name. How does Mugabe know that he will die a hero? Where do we draw a line between a true hero and one fallen from grace? Let's look at the definition of a hero, the Collins English dictionary defines a hero as a man (sic) distinguished by exceptional courage, nobility and fortitude. By all purposes it includes consistent high morals coupled with a positive contribution to national building and values, surely the same cannot be said of my grandfather Robert Mugabe.

Every Zimbabwean will find it difficult to deny that Mugabe is a liberator cum dictator. Liberator because he is and dictator because will continue to be. Mugabe used to be my political icon, actually if there is a person who gave me a positive influence into joining the turbulent world of politics then its Mugabe himself. I wanted to understand him and I have to admit he has been too elusive for my academic taste. We Zimbabwean missed a golden chance in 1980, we should have rehabilitated Mugabe and a transition from bush to office must not have been left to the grace of God alone. Mugabe knows what is right for Zimbabweans and so is ZANU (PF) but the problem that we have is that they seem to have found a new school of politics, arrogance and brutal, despotic and myopic. Otherwise there is no justifiable reason why the butterfly Mugabe of 1980 should be the poisonous larvae of today. As far as I am concerned, there are no heroes left in the ZANU (PF) of today. Mugabe's combative threats of what he called hypocrisy within his party criticising the operation clean up, highlights a new understanding of what is going on in the closed doors of ZANU (PF). Mugabe behaves like a School Headmaster who bullies his pupils wily nil. He accepts no advice and takes no nonsense from his cabinet or perceived advisers. He is in full control of his demise.

As we mourn our heroes let us worn our tormentors that we fully take them responsible for our anguish knowing very well that history is on our side.

List of ZANU (PF) names targeted for sanctions by EU.

(Acts adopted under Title V of the Treaty on European Union)
COUNCIL DECISION 2005/592/CFSP
of 29 July 2005:

**Implementing   Common   Position   2004/161/CFSP
renewing restrictive measures against Zimbabwe
List of persons referred to in Articles 4 and 5 of Common
Position 2004/161/CFSP**

1. Mugabe, Robert Gabriel President, born 21.2.1924
2. Bonyongwe, Happyton Director-General Central Intelligence Organisation, born 6.11.1960
3. Buka (a.k.a. Bhuka), Flora Minister for Special Affairs responsible for Land and Resettlement
Programmes (Former Minister of State in the Vice-President's Office
and former Minister of State for the Land Reform Programme in the
President's Office), born 25.2.1968
4. Bvudzijena, Wayne Assistant Police Commissioner, Police Spokesman
5. Chapfika, David Deputy Minister of Finance (former Deputy Minister of Finance and
Economic Development), born 7.4.1957
6. Charamba, George Permanent Secretary Department for Information and Publicity, born
4.4.1963
7. Charumbira, Fortune Zefanaya Former Deputy Minister for Local Government, Public Works and
National Housing, born 10.6.1962
8. Chigudu, Tinaye Provincial Governor: Manicaland
9. Chigwedere, Aeneas Soko Minister of Education, Sports and Culture, born 25.11.1939

10. Chihota, Phineas Deputy Minister for Industry and International Trade
11. Chihuri, Augustine Police Commissioner, born 10.3.1953
12. Chimbudzi, Alice ZANU (PF) Politburo Committee Member
13. Chimutengwende, Chen Minister of State for Public and Interactive Affairs (former Minister of
Post and Telecommunications), born 28.8.1943
14. Chinamasa, Patrick Anthony Minister of Justice, Legal and Parliamentary Affairs, born 25.1.1947
15. Chindori-Chininga, Edward Takaruza Former Minister of Mines and Mining Development, born 14.3.1955
16. Chipanga, Tongesai Shadreck Former Deputy Minister of Home Affairs, born 10.10.1946
17. Chitepo, Victoria ZANU (PF) Politburo Committee Member, born 27.3.1928
18. Chiwenga, Constantine Commander Zimbabwe Defence Forces, General (former Army
Commander, Lieutenant General), born 25.8.1956
19. Chiweshe, George Chairman, ZEC (Supreme Court Judge and Chairman of the controversial
delimitation committee), born 4.6.1953
20. Chiwewe, Willard Provincial Governor: Masvingo (former Senior Secretary responsible for
Special Affairs in the President's Office), born 19.3.1949
21. Chombo, Ignatius Morgan Chininya Minister of Local Government, Public Works and National Housing,
born 1.8.1952
30.7.2005 EN Official Journal of the European Union L 200/99
22. Dabengwa, Dumiso ZANU (PF) Politburo Senior Committee Member, born 1939
23. Damasane, Abigail Deputy Minister for Women's Affairs, Gender and Community Development
24. Goche, Nicholas Tasunungurwa Minister of Public Service, Labour and Social Welfare (former Minister
of State for National Security in the President's Office), born 1.8.1946

173

25. Gombe, G Chairman, Electoral Supervisory Commission

26. Gula-Ndebele, Sobuza Former Chairman of Electoral Supervisory Commission

27. Gumbo, Rugare Eleck Ngidi Minister of Economic Development (former Minister of State for State Enterprises and Parastatals in the President's Office), born 8.3.1940

28. Hove, Richard ZANU (PF) Politburo Secretary for Economic Affairs, born 1935

29. Hungwe, Josaya (a.k.a. Josiah) Dunira Former Provincial Governor: Masvingo, born 7.11.1935

30. Jokonya, Tichaona Minister of Information and Publicity, born 27.12.1938

31. Kangai, Kumbirai ZANU (PF) Politburo Committee Member, born 17.2.1938

32. Karimanzira, David Ishemunyoro Godi Provincial Governor: Harare and ZANU (PF) Politburo Secretary for Finance, born 25.5.1947

33. Kasukuwere, Saviour Deputy Minister for Youth Development & Employment Creation and ZANU (PF) Politburo Deputy-Secretary for Youth Affairs, born 23.10.1970

34. Kaukonde, Ray Provincial Governor: Mashonaland East, born 4.3.1963

35. Kuruneri, Christopher Tichaona Former Minister of Finance and Economic Development, born 4.4.1949. NB currently in remand

36. Langa, Andrew Deputy Minister of Environment and Tourism and former Deputy Minister of Transport and Communications

37. Lesabe, Thenjiwe V. ZANU (PF) Politburo Secretary for Women's Affairs, born 1933

38. Machaya, Jason (a.k.a. Jaison) Max Kokerai Former Deputy Minister of Mines and Mining Development, born 13.6.1952

39. Made, Joseph Mtakwese Minister of Agriculture and Rural Development (former Minister of
Lands, Agricultural and Rural Resettlement), born 21.11.1954
40. Madzongwe, Edna (a.k.a. Edina) ZANU (PF) Politburo Deputy Secretary for Production and Labour, born
11.7.1943
41. Mahofa, Shuvai Ben Former Deputy Minister for Youth Development, Gender and
Employment Creation, born 4.4.1941
42. Mahoso, Tafataona Chair, Media Information Commission
L 200/100 EN Official Journal of the European Union 30.7.2005
43. Makoni, Simbarashe ZANU (PF) Politburo Deputy Secretary General for Economic Affairs
(former Minister of Finance), born 22.3.1950
44. Makwavarara, Sekesai Acting Mayor of Harare (ZANU-PF)
45. Malinga, Joshua ZANU (PF) Politburo Deputy Secretary for Disabled and Disadvantaged,
born 28.4.1944
46. Mangwana, Paul Munyaradzi Minister of State (former Minister of Public Service, Labour and Social
Welfare), born 10.8.1961
47. Manyika, Elliot Tapfumanei Minister without Portfolio (former Minister of Youth Development,
Gender and Employment Creation), born 30.7.1955
48. Manyonda, Kenneth Vhundukai Former Deputy Minister of Industry and International Trade, born
10.8.1934
49. Marumahoko, Rueben Deputy Minister for Home Affairs (former Deputy Minister of Energy
and Power Development), born 4.4.1948
50. Masawi, Eprahim Sango Provincial Governor: Mashonaland Central
51. Masuku, Angeline Provincial Governor: Matabeleland South (ZANU (PF) Politburo
Secretary for Disabled and Disadvantaged), born 14.10.1936
52. Mathema, Cain Provincial Governor: Bulawayo

53. Mathuthu, Thokozile Provincial Governor: Matabeleland North and ZANU (PF) Politburo
Deputy Secretary for Transport and Social Welfare
54. Matiza, Joel Biggie Deputy Minister for Rural Housing and Social Amenities, born
17.8.1960
55. Matonga, Brighton Deputy Minister for Information and Publicity, born 1969
56. Matshalaga, Obert Deputy Minister of Foreign Affairs
57. Matshiya, Melusi (Mike) Permanent Secretary, Ministry of Home Affairs
58. Mbiriri, Partson Permanent Secretary, Ministry of Local Government, Public Works and
Urban Development
59. Midzi, Amos Bernard (Mugenva) Minister of Mines and Mining Development (former Minister of Energy
and Power Development), born 4.7.1952
60. Mnangagwa, Emmerson Dambudzo Minister of Rural Housing and Social Amenities (former Speaker of
Parliament), born 15.9.1946
61. Mohadi, Kembo Campbell Dugishi Minister of Home Affairs (former Deputy Minister of Local
Government, Public Works and National Housing), born 15.11.1949
62. Moyo, Jonathan Former Minister of State for Information and Publicity in the President's
Office, born 12.1.1957
63. Moyo, July Gabarari Former Minister of Energy and Power Development (former Minister of
Public Service, Labour and Social Welfare), born 7.5.1950
30.7.2005 EN Official Journal of the European Union L 200/101
64. Moyo, Simon Khaya ZANU (PF) Politburo Deputy Secretary for Legal Affairs, born 1945. NB
Ambassador to South Africa
65. Mpofu, Obert Moses Minister for Industry and International Trade (former Provincial
Governor: Matabeleland North) (ZANU (PF) Politburo Deputy

Secretary for National Security), born 12.10.1951

66. Msika, Joseph W. Vice-President, born 6.12.1923

67. Msipa, Cephas George Provincial Governor: Midlands, born 7.7.1931

68. Muchena, Olivia Nyembesi
(a.k.a. Nyembezi)
Minister of State for Science and Technology in the President's Office
(former Minister of State in Vice-President Msika's Office), born
18.8.1946

69. Muchinguri, Oppah Chamu Zvipange Minister for Women's Affairs, Gender and Community Development
ZANU (PF) Politburo Secretary for Gender and Culture, born
14.12.1958

70. Mudede, Tobaiwa (Tonneth) Registrar General, born 22.12.1942

71. Mudenge, Isack Stanilaus Gorerazvo Minister of Higher Tertiary Education (former Minister of Foreign
Affairs), born 17.12.1941

72. Mugabe, Grace Spouse of Robert Gabriel Mugabe, born 23.7.1965

73. Mugabe, Sabina ZANU (PF) Politburo Senior Committee Member, born 14.10.1934

74. Muguti, Edwin Deputy Minister for Health and Child Welfare, born 1965

75. Mujuru, Joyce Teurai Ropa Vice-President (former Minister of Water Resources and Infrastructural
Development), born 15.4.1955

76. Mujuru, Solomon T.R. ZANU (PF) Politburo Senior Committee Member, born 1.5.1949

77. Mumbengegwi, Samuel Creighton Former Minister of Industry and International Trade, born 23.10.1942

78. Mumbengegwi, Simbarashe Minister of Foreign Affairs, born 20.7.1945

79. Murerwa, Herbert Muchemwa Minister of Finance (former Minister of Higher and Tertiary Education),
born 31.7.1941

80. Musariri, Munyaradzi Assistant Police Commissioner
81. Mushohwe, Christopher Chindoti Minister of Transport and Communications (former Deputy Minister of Transport and Communications), born 6.2.1954
82. Mutasa, Didymus Noel Edwin Minister for National Security (former Minister of Special Affairs in the President's Office in charge of the Anti-Corruption and Anti-Monopolies Programme and former ZANU (PF) Politburo Secretary for External Relations), born 27.7.1935
83. Mutezo, Munacho Minister for Water Resources and Infrastructural Development
84. Mutinhiri, Ambros (a.k.a. Ambrose) Minister of Youth Development, Gender and Employment Creation, Retired Brigadier L 200/102 EN Official Journal of the European Union 30.7.2005
85. Mutiwekuziva, Kenneth Kaparadza Deputy Minister of Small and Medium Enterprises Development and Employment Creation, (former Deputy Minister of Small and Medium Enterprises Development, born 27.5.1948
86. Muzenda, Tsitsi V. ZANU (PF) Politburo Senior Committee Member, born 28.10.1922
87. Muzonzini, Elisha Brigadier (former Director-General Central Intelligence Organisation), born 24.6.1957
88. Ncube, Abedinico Deputy Minister of Public Service, Labour and Social Welfare (former Deputy Minister of Foreign Affairs), born 13.10.1954
89. Ndlovu, Naison K. ZANU (PF) Politburo Secretary for Production and Labour, born 22.10.1930
90. Ndlovu, Richard ZANU (PF) Politburo Deputy Commissariat, born 20.6.1942
91. Ndlovu, Sikhanyiso ZANU (PF) Politburo Deputy Secretary for Commissariat, born 20.9.1949

92. Nguni, Sylvester Deputy Minister for Agriculture, born 4.8.1955

93. Nhema, Francis Minister of Environment and Tourism, born 17.4.1959

94. Nkomo, John Landa Speaker of Parliament (former Minister of Special Affairs in the President's
Office), born 22.8.1934

95. Nyambuya, Michael Reuben Minister for Energy and Power Development (former Lieutenant
General, Provincial Governor: Manicaland), born 23.7.1955

96. Nyanhongo, Magadzire Hubert Deputy Minister of Transport and Communications

97. Nyathi, George ZANU (PF) Politburo Deputy Secretary of Science and Technology

98. Nyoni, Sithembiso Gile Glad Minister of Small and Medium Enterprises Development and
Employment Creation (former Minister of Small and Medium Enterprises
Development), born 20.9.1949

99. Parirenyatwa, David Pagwese Minister of Health and Child Welfare (former Deputy Minister), born
2.8.1950

100. Patel, Khantibhal ZANU (PF) Politburo Deputy Secretary for Finance, born 28.10.1928

101. Pote, Selina M. ZANU (PF) Politburo Deputy Secretary for Gender and Culture

102. Rusere, Tino Deputy Minister for Mines and Mining Development (former Deputy
Minister for Water Resources and Infrastructural Development), born
10.5.1945

103. Sakabuya, Morris Deputy Minister for Local Government, Public Works and Urban Development

104. Sakupwanya, Stanley ZANU (PF) Politburo Deputy Secretary for Health and Child Welfare

105. Samkange, Nelson Tapera Crispen Provincial Governor: Mashonaland West

30.7.2005 EN Official Journal of the European Union L 200/103

106. Sandi ou Sachi, E. (?) ZANU (PF) Politburo Deputy Secretary for Women's Affairs

107. Savanhu, Tendai ZANU (PF) Deputy Secretary for Transport and Social Welfare, born 21.3.1968

108. Sekeramayi, Sydney (a.k.a. Sidney) Tigere Minister of Defence, born 30.3.1944

109. Sekeremayi, Lovemore Chief Elections Officer

110. Shamu, Webster Minister of State for Policy Implementation (former Minister of State for Policy Implementation in the President's Office), born 6.6.1945

111. Shamuyarira, Nathan Marwirakuwa ZANU (PF) Politburo Secretary for Information and Publicity, born 29.9.1928

112. Shiri, Perence Air Marshal (Air Force), born 1.11.1955

113. Shumba, Isaiah Masvayamwando Deputy Minister of Education, Sports and Culture, born 3.1.1949

114. Sibanda, Jabulani Former Chair, National War Veterans Association, born 31.12.1970

115. Sibanda, Misheck Julius Mpande Cabinet Secretary (successor to No.122 Charles Utete), born 3.5.1949

116. Sibanda, Phillip Valerio (a.k.a. Valentine) Commander Zimbabwe National Army, Lieutenant General, born 25.8.1956

117. Sikosana, Absolom ZANU (PF) Politburo Secretary for Youth Affairs

118. Stamps, Timothy Health Advisor in the Office of the President, born 15.10.1936

119. Tawengwa, Solomon Chirume ZANU (PF) Politburo Deputy Secretary for Finance, born 15.6.1940

120. Tungamirai, Josiah T. Minister of State for Indigenisation and Empowerment, Retired Air Marshall (former ZANU (PF) Politburo Secretary for Empowerment and Indigenisation), born 8.10.1948

121. Udenge, Samuel Deputy Minister of Economic Development

122. Utete, Charles Chairman of the Presidential Land Review Committee (former Cabinet

Secretary), born 30.10.1938

123. Veterai, Edmore Senior Assistant Police Commissioner, Officer Commanding Harare

124. Zimonte, Paradzai Prisons Director, born 4.3.1947

125. Zhuwao, Patrick Deputy Minister for Science and Technology (NB Mugabe's nephew)

126. Zvinavashe, Vitalis Retired General (former Chief of Defence Staff), born 27.9.1943

L 200/104 EN Official Journal of the European Union 30.7.2005

7 PICTURES OF DEFIANCE

Pictures of defiance

With former US Presidential Candidate and Human Rights
leader, The Right Rev. Jesse Jackson, October 2010

Addressing an MDC gathering in Bedford, UK

With Morgan Tsvangirai, MDC President at a function in London.

In memory of my murdered brother Mathew Pfebve and those fallen during a heroes commemoration in August 2009

All is red, the MDC show force of solidarity

The late Brutal Governor Border Gezi with his PA, Mrs Jones.

First MDC Star Rally in Bindura 2000 general elections, part of a 40,000 strong crowd000 the show ground at show ground, ZANU (PF) disputed the figure and pegged it at 25,000, and then I got 11,500 votes!

Deep in the rural of Musana, rural part of Bindura
Constituency 2000.

Supporters enjoy the MDC dance after the rally in Bindura.

Rural campaigns in Mashonaland Central province 2000

Working as a campaign team, Loice Mabande looking into the camera and Tapera Macheka wearing an MDC T-Shirt keep a watchful eye in the volatile Mashonaland Central province, home to Border Gezi the brute.

Listening to the grass roots and support base was one of the reasons MDC took ZANU (PF) by surprise.

As ZANU (PF) militia disrupts the meeting supporters scramble in all directions, but for the faithful music plays on.

The by-election heats up as I address a crowd, my Mazda truck behind with visible damages from ambushes and attempted assassinations, 2001.

Happy to be free at last after being arrested, detained and released on 30 July 2001 Bye-election

My parents, Sinoia and Serina a few days after their release, who were abducted 14 May 2008 by Mugabe militia, a repeat of 29 May 2000 attack that left my brother Matthew dead and my father with serious injuries

The team that took Mugabe to court in USA, New York Federal Court, back row; Elliot Pfebve and the US Attorney, Front row; Adela Chiminya and Maria Stevens .

The photographs above show the charred remains of farm workers' homes on Muniya Farm. Muniya Panganai, a war veteran who seized the farm in 2006 from the former white owner, began evictions on April 15, 2008 as "punishment" because the area had voted overwhelmingly for MDC.

Farm workers made destitute after Mugabe's farm invasions and eviction making up the bulk of Internally Displaced Persons (IDPs). Elderly, women and children with no shelter is a common place in Zimbabwe.

Looking after the orphans and displaced children were left to the NGOs and Mugabe's government was no way to be seen.

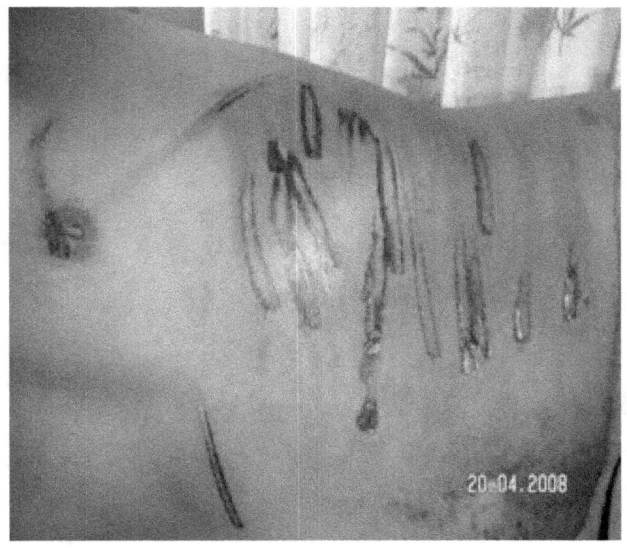

This young man was beaten by militia in military camouflage in broad daylight for supporting the opposition party MDC.

Penhalonga, Mutare MDC supporters were equally beaten and their properties destroyed.

The carnage has been everywhere as Mugabe announced that he had degrees in violence! People were desperate to leave their homelands from one part of the country to another adding to IDPs.

Hopeless and dejected, the signs of a dictator taking toll on his own people are everywhere. These people were punished for voting for the "wrong party."

Some people were not lucky, as this man lay murdered for supporting the MDC party.

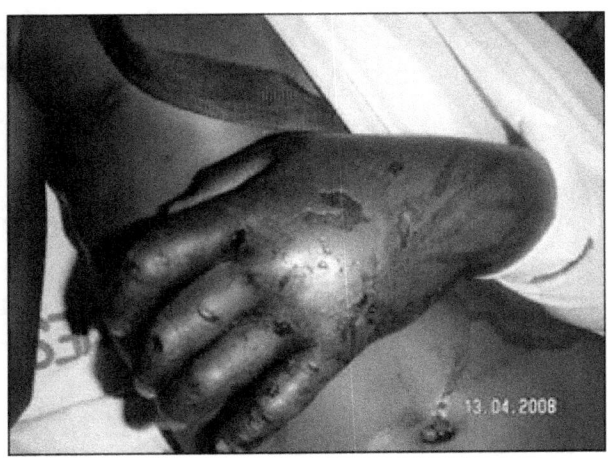

A businessman from Mudzi, Mutoko in agony after ZANU (PF) thugs looted his shop, burnt his hands and smashed his hands to make sure he will not vote again.

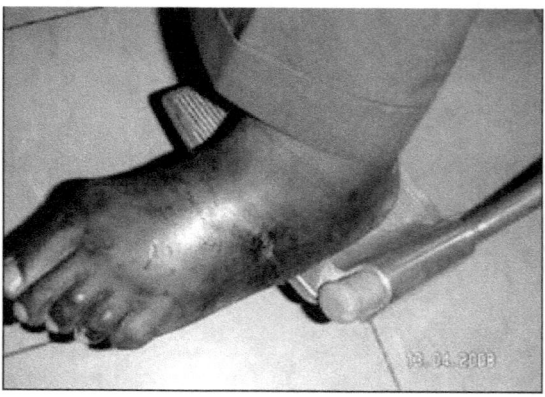

The leg broken for supporting and voting MDC, this old man has 2 teeth knocked off and lips split by Mugabe's thugs.

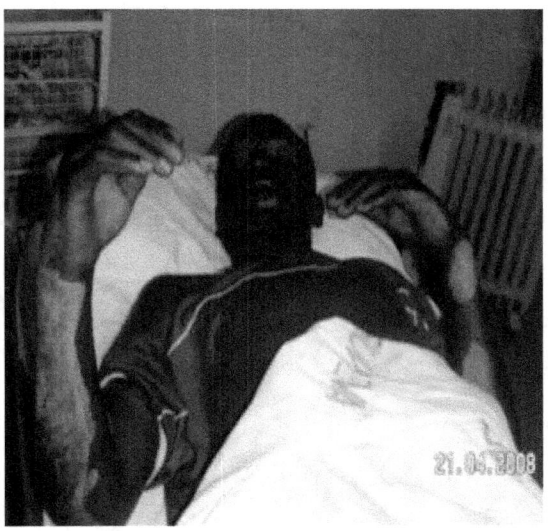

A man from UMP (Uzumba Maramba Pfungwe) area was tied to his hut door by militia and then set alight.

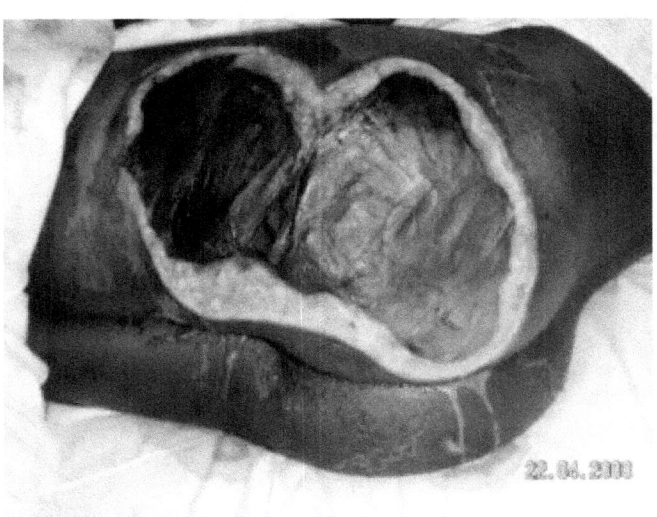

This man from the Mudzi area, Mashonaland East was brutally beaten on the buttocks by ZANU PF militia for being an MDC supporter.

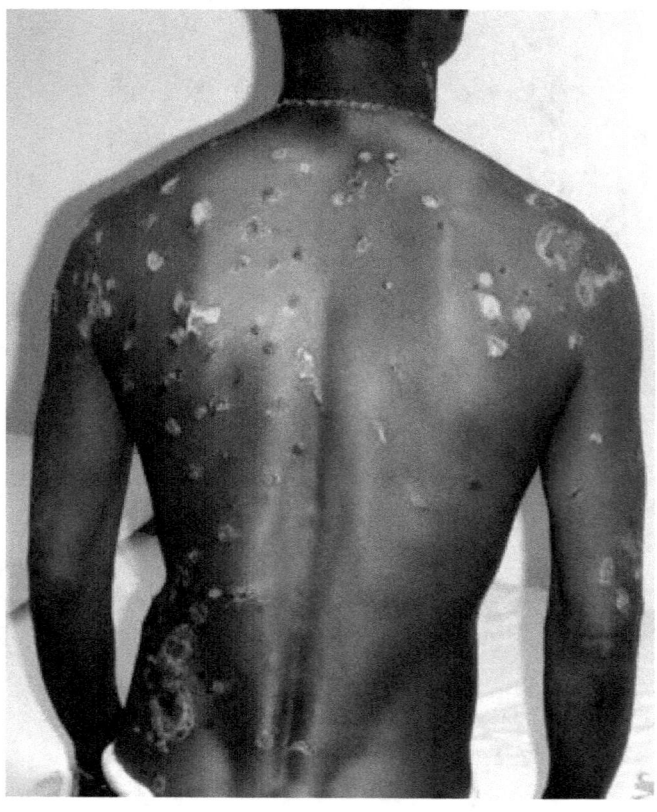

This man had burning plastic put on his back and arms. His home was burned and his animals were doused in diesel and burned alive.

With Zimbabweans, Mr Mutasa (Branch Chairman) and
Zimbabwean campaigners in Bristol, UK after a Zimbabwean
Community Forum.

Outside Zimbabwe, MDC activities have been visible, the aim,
a Zimbabwe free of violence and dictatorship.

Taking a scenic view in Geneva, Switzerland after addressing the office of UNHCR on current issues in Zimbabwe, 2000.

Solidarity with deputy minister of Foreign Affairs of Malawi in 1999, David Katsonga.

"Mugabe" gets dirty a role play in Portugal

Elliot Pfebve

Visual campaign against Mugabe's torture in Zimbabwe,
Portugal December 2007

A global campaign to stop torture in Portugal during the
EU/AU summit 2007.

ZANU (PF) die hard hold a Mugabe banner in Portugal in
December 2007

Dr Makumbe "joins ZANU (PF)" in Portugal.

With fellow campaigners, Sanderson Makombe and others in Portugal.

Save the children had a powerful message to the leaders of
EU/AU summit

Mugabe hired whites to show the world that he is not racist

With Bridgett, an MP in Swedish government, demanding fair elections in Zimbabwe, was putting up a global fight.

In Portugal with Makuvise and Dr. Makumbe (UZ Lecturer)

8 THE US COURT CASE

The Mugabe US court case
USA Court Serialisation

Well come back since my last article, I have been inundated by calls from all over the world wanting to know more about the political situation in Zimbabwe to the USA court against Mugabe. While this proves a wider readership for this newspaper, it is also a wakeup call for Mugabe that all is not lost for Zimbabweans to fight for peace and justice. One day even Mugabe will be free!

In further articles I shall dwell on both political and Human Rights issues for the future Independent Zimbabwe. For today I will take you over to the Court Case. Let me hasten to say contrary to many people that Zimbabweans seem to have slumped into submission against Robert Mugabe's continual denial of fundamental human rights, this is totally untrue. Believe me you, thousands of people day in day out are giving up their lives to give a voice for the voiceless and justice for the oppressed in Zimbabwe. The fantastic work being done by the Zimbabwe Human Rights Forum NGO, the vanguard Independent Newspapers, the work of the Opposition Parties, Civic Societies, Churches, International Organizations and the languishing in jail of Zimbabweans for standing up on their rights is a testimony of an era about to happen. The court case against Mugabe and ZANU (PF) was another milestone by Zimbabweans to Internationalise the Human Rights abuse in Zimbabwe after a denial of recourse by the same regime. For your own information even though Mugabe wants to be seen outwardly as Rambo bravado, inwardly he is a Mickey Mouse when it comes to Big Brother Watching him. No sane leader can lock horns forever with the international community against international will. To many Zimbabweans it is like a mouse confronted by a cat trying to argue its right to life, liberty and happiness.

The USA court case against Mugabe was based on an Alien Tort Claims Act which is over 400 years old. It was a class action against Mugabe and ZANU (PF) for crimes against humanity. They were five plaintiffs in the court case myself, Adella, Maria, Efuridah and Everlyn. Of the five only Adela and I made it to the USA court for cross-examinations. The court case remains up to now the biggest legal circuit in the World drawing over 18 senior lawyers worldwide and submissions of tones and tones of evidence to prove the case against the defendant (Mugabe). Every corner of Zimbabwe had a legal sample of evidence to prove a systematic persecution of Zimbabweans by their government which constitutionally has the duty to protect them.

Mugabe had the summons served on him at 09:15 (New York Time) on 07/09/2000 at the Harlem church where he was guest speaker at a ZANU (PF) fund raising party by an NGO known as the December Movement, some of you might remember that the organizer, Cde Chimurenga (an American) was eventually rewarded with a farm during the farm invention. Mugabe accepted the summons. Stan Mudenge was served at 13:45 (New York Time) on 08/09/2000 and declined to accept the papers but were placed in front of his feet. By US law placing the papers in front of the defendant's feet constitutes a legal serving. Despite the serving of the papers and subsequent legal proceedings that followed, Jonathan Moyo the then Minister of Information emphatically issued a denial of ever such an incident having happened although Jonathan Moyo was with the delegation in the USA at the time of the summons. Many of you will not be surprised by the spin doctor's denial as he had become the professor of prophets of doom. Reporters who reported the cover story were arrested and detained for "irresponsible journalism."

ZANU (PF), Mandenge and Mugabe were issued with a summons to answer charges for violations of human rights on the 24th October 2000 at Manhattan District Federal court before Judge Victor Marrero. Mugabe did not oppose the case nor did he send any representative. With Mugabe's arrogance, none of us were surprised. Adela and I took turns to give evidence. Many people up to now do not understand how this court case changed the lives of millions of Zimbabweans who by now could have been murdered unknown by the Human Rights watch dogs. In the court was even a map of Africa and that of Zimbabwe bloated to assist the jury as to familiarise with where Zimbabwe was and Bindura which was under immense scrutiny, a little known issue by then. A default judgement was issued by Judge Victor Marrero after the clerk of court Mr. James Parkinson issued a certificate confirming proof of service having been filed on 13 September 2000. This case, took me to UNHCR in Geneva in October 2000 to convince the UN to take a combative stand against Human Rights abuses in Zimbabwe. It took me to the Amnesty International Secretariat HQ to highlight the need for a Zimbabwe Human Rights strategy, US Senate, Washington on Africa (a coalition of Churches for Africa), International Human Rights Lawyers Group among many more. There were not many of these organizations then knowledgeable of the Zimbabwe situation. In a way this was the beginning of a new chapter in a painful struggle for a peaceful and just Zimbabwe. Meanwhile I leave you to flip through the pages of misery.

ADELLA CHIMINYA TACHIONA, on her own behalf on behalf of her late husband TAPFUMA CHIMINYA TACHIONA, and on behalf of all others similarly situated,
EFRIDAH PFEBVE, on her own behalf and on behalf of her late brother METTHEW PFEBVE,

ELLIOT PFEBVE, on his own behalf and on behalf of his brother METTHEW PFEBVE,

EVELYN MASAITI, on her own behalf, and

MARIA DEL CARMEN STEVENS, on her own behalf, on behalf of her late husband DAVID YENDALL STEVENS, and on behalf of all others similarly situated,

SOUTHERN DISTRICT OF NEW YORK

Civil Action No.

COMPLAINT

CLASS ACTION

JURY TRIAL DEMANDED

UNDER SEAL UNTIL SERVICE ON DEFENDANTS COMPLETED

Plaintiffs, by their undersigned counsel for their Class Action Complaint in this action, aver, by direct knowledge as to themselves and on information and belief as to all others, as follows:

PRELIMINARY STATEMENT

This is an action for compensatory and punitive damages for personal injuries and destruction of property inflicted in direct violation of a United States statute and in violation of international law. The injuries suffered by plaintiffs and other unnamed members of the class are due to extrajudicial killing, torture, terrorism, politically motivated violence, racially motivated violence, and other gross violations of the fundamental norms of international human rights law and of specific United States statutory law.

Plaintiffs bring this action against defendant Robert Mugabe in his individual capacity and as First Secretary and President of the Zimbabwe African National Union Patriotic Front ("ZANU-PF"), the political party that currently controls the Zimbabwean Government. In his private capacity and in his capacity as First Secretary of ZANU-PF, defendant Mugabe has orchestrated and directed a widespread campaign of violence and terror against the people of his own country based purely on their peaceful expression of political opposition to ZANU-PF.

Defendant Mugabe has directed officials within the ZANU-PF party to organize targeted violence against political opponents and their families and supporters, assassinations and assassination attempts, kidnappings, tortures, rapes, beatings, mass destruction of property, and mob riots in a consistent and focused campaign of terror designed to crush political opposition to ZANU-PF.

Defendant Mugabe has also authorized criminal acts and gross violations of international human rights law by the Zimbabwe War Veterans' Association ("ZWVA") and its president, Dr. Chenjerayi Hunzvi, who operates under his own adopted middle name of "Hitler." Led by Hitler, the ZWVA had illegally occupied over 1,600 farms by end-June 2000 and has assisted ZANU-PF members and supporters in the campaign to terrorize, assault, and in some cases to extrajudicially murder farmers, farm workers, and any others suspected of supporting the Movement for Democratic Change ("the MDC"), the emerging opposition political party to ZANU-PF.

Defendant Mugabe has also improperly and without legal authority directed the Zimbabwean military, the Zimbabwean Central Intelligence Organization ("CIO"), and the Zimbabwean Republic Police to assist ZANU-PF and the ZWVA in their illegal campaign to terrorize political opponents of ZANU-PF and to murder, torture, rape, brutalize, and destroy the property of farmers, farm workers, and other supporters of the MDC.

The actions directed by defendant Mugabe, and implemented by defendant ZANU-PF and other, unknown, named individual defendant-officers of ZANU-PF, to be identified and served following initial discovery, constituted conduct that is actionable in a civil case in a United States District Court under the clear provisions and precedents of 28 U.S.C. section 1350.

Elliot Pfebve

JURISDICTION AND VENUE

This Court has jurisdiction under 28 U.S.C. Sections 1331 and 1350, and under principles of supplemental jurisdiction, 28 U.S.C. section 1367.

Specifically, the Torture Victim Protection Act ("TVPA"), Pub. L. No. 102-256, 106 Stat. 78 (1992), found at 28 U.S.C. section 1350 (Note), provides that an individual shall be liable in a civil action in federal court for acts of torture and extrajudicial killing committed under color of foreign state authority, without regard to where those actions occurred or whether the victims were U.S. citizens or aliens.

In addition, the Alien Tort Claims Act ("ATCA"), 28 U.S.C. section 1350, provides federal jurisdiction for "any civil action by an alien for a tort only, committed in violation of the law of nations."

Plaintiffs' causes of action arise under the TVPA and the ATCA as well as fundamental and non-derogable norms of international law as stated in, among others, the 1949 Geneva Conventions, Convention Against Torture and Other Cruel, Inhuman, or Degrading Treatment or Punishment, United Nations Charter, Universal Declaration of Human Rights, and the International Covenant on Civil and Political Rights.

Defendant Mugabe and defendant ZANU-PF, as represented by defendant Mugabe who is the First Secretary and President of ZANU-PF, are currently physically present in the United States, availing themselves and their property of the security and sanctuary of the United States and the state of New York, engaging in press and other activities.

Defendant Mugabe and is liable in this civil case for conduct taken by him, in his private capacity and in his capacity as First Secretary of ZANU-PF, that was specifically designed to perpetuate his personal position of power and the position of power held by ZANU-PF in Zimbabwe. Likewise, defendants Moyo and Mudenge are liable in this civil case for conduct taken by them, in their private capacity and in their capacities as Senior Officials in ZANU-PF, that was specifically designed to perpetuate their positions of power and the position of power held by ZANU-PF in Zimbabwe. This case is not an action against the Government of Zimbabwe, nor against any of its officers in their official capacity so as to merit either sovereign immunity or head of state immunity as a defense to this Court's jurisdiction over this action.

Defendant ZANU-PF is liable for orchestrating a campaign of violence and terror, and for gross violations of fundamental norms of the international law of human rights, actionable in this Court under the ATCA.

The United States District Court for the Southern District of New York is the proper venue of this action pursuant to 28 U.S.C. Section 1391(b)(3).

PARTIES

Defendant Robert Mugabe is the First Secretary and President of ZANU-PF, a political party in Zimbabwe. As leader of ZANU-PF, he has, and at all times relevant to this Complaint had, command authority over all ZANU-PF officials, members, and supporters. Acting under his command and control, these ZANU-PF officials, members, and supporters have inflicted a brutal campaign of murder, torture, terrorism, rape, beatings, and destruction of property against Zimbabwean citizens and residents suspected of supporting the opposition political party, MDC. Through his leadership of ZANU-PF, which for all practical purposes has been the only political party in Zimbabwe for two decades, defendant Mugabe has also directed and commanded the leadership and members of the ZWVA to occupy and appropriate privately-owned farmlands in violation of Zimbabwean law and international law, and to murder, terrorize, brutalize, rape and inflict physical violence on farmers, farm workers, and any suspected supporters of the MDC.

Defendant Robert Mugabe is also President of the Republic of Zimbabwe. Over the course of the past several years, but in particular during the months since February, 2000, defendant Mugabe has illegally and improperly acted outside of his constitutional authority under the Zimbabwean constitution, and has relied upon his position of unrivalled power as leader of ZANU-PF in illegally directing the military and police to assist in the unlawful activities of ZANU-PF and ZWVA.

Defendant ZANU-PF is the political party that has controlled the executive and legislative branches of the Zimbabwean Government since 1980. It operates under the control of its First Secretary, defendant Mugabe, and through its other officers and members. Under the leadership of defendant Mugabe, ZANU-PF has relied on its position as the unrivalled and dominant force in the Government to illegally direct and force the military and police to assist in the unlawful activities of ZANU-PF and ZWVA.

Defendant Isack Mudenge is a senior ZANU-PF official and the Minister for Foreign Affairs for Zimbabwe. On information and belief, he has been complicit in and supportive of the campaign of terror and violence orchestrated by defendant Mugabe and defendant ZANU-PF, and has assisted in attempting to conceal the true extent and nature of the crimes and violations of international law committed under the auspices of ZANU-PF.

Defendant Jonathan Moyo is a senior ZANU-PF official and the Minister for Information and Publicity in Zimbabwe. On information and belief, he has been complicit in and supportive of the campaign of terror and violence orchestrated by defendant Mugabe and defendant ZANU-PF, and has assisted in attempting to conceal the true extent and nature of the crimes and violations of international law committed under the auspices of ZANU-PF.

Unknown Named Senior Officers In ZANU-PF are such Senior Officers as are engaged with defendant Mugabe and defendant ZANU-PF in perpetrating the systematic acts of violence, intimidation, and other gross violations of fundamental international human rights that ZANU-PF has orchestrated over the past eight months in order to suppress all political opposition to ZANU-PF.

Plaintiff Adella Chiminya Tachiona (nee Mutero), is a citizen of Zimbabwe. She is the 34-year-old widow of the late Tapfuma Chiminya Tachiona. She sues on her behalf and on behalf of her late husband's estate for the extrajudicial killing of Tapfuma Chiminya Tachiona, who was killed April 15, 2000, while campaigning for MDC leader Morgan Tsvangirai, by ZANU-PF members and supporters acting under color of state authority and under the direction of defendant Mugabe.

Plaintiff Efridah Pfebve is a 28-year-old resident of Nyakatondo Village in Mount Darwin North in Zimbabwe. She sues on behalf of herself and on behalf of the estate of her murdered brother, Matthew Pfebve, who was extrajudicially killed by ZANU-PF and ZWVA members and supporters acting under color of state authority and under the direction of defendant Mugabe on April 29, 2000.

Plaintiff Elliot Pfebve is a citizen of Zimbabwe and an executive member of the MDC. Mr. Pfebve stood as the MDC candidate in the Zimbabwe National Parliamentary Elections on the 24th and 25th of June 2000 in the Bindura Constituency for Mashonaland Central Province. He sues on behalf of himself for the repeated and targeted attacks made against him personally in an attempt to assassinate him and to intimidate him against standing for election, and on behalf of the estate of his murdered brother Metthew Pfebve.

Plaintiff Evelyn Masaiti is a 35-year-old citizen of Zimbabwe who resides in Mutare, Zimbabwe. Ms. Masaiti stood as an MDC candidate for Mutasa in the province of Manicaland during the June 24th and 25th Zimbabwe National Parliamentary Elections, and who as a result of those elections was elected to the post of Member of Parliament for Mutasa District. She sues on behalf of herself for the repeated acts of violence, attempted assassination, and terrorism to which she was subjected during the period of time leading up to the June 2000 elections.

Plaintiff Maria Del Carmen Stevens is a commercial farmer residing in Zimbabwe. She sues on behalf of herself and her late husband, David Yendall Stevens, who was extrajudicially murdered by ZANU-PF members on April 15, 2000.

CLASS ALLEGATIONS

Plaintiffs bring this action on behalf of themselves and all others similarly situated, pursuant to Rules 23(a), 23(b)(1)(B), and 23(b)(3) of the Federal Rules of Civil Procedure.

The class consists of all men and women who suffered extrajudicial murder, torture, terrorism, rape, beatings, or other acts of politically or racially motivated violence or cruel, inhuman or degrading treatment inflicted by ZANU-PF members or supporters acting under the command, control, and direction of defendants.

The exact number of class members is not known, but it is estimated that the class includes several thousand families living and working on farms that were occupied and attacked under defendants' directions and who were subject to gross violations of international human rights. The class is so numerous that joinder of individual plaintiffs is impracticable.

The claims of the plaintiffs, the class representatives, are typical of the class. Plaintiffs are able to, and will, fairly and adequately protect the interests of the class.

There are common questions of law and fact in this action that relate to and affect each member of the class, namely:

whether defendants knew or should have known that ZANU-PF, ZWVA, military and police forces under their direct or indirect control and authority were murdering, torturing, raping, beating and terrorizing men and women who were farmers, worked on farms, or were suspected of supporting the MDC;

whether defendants' actions give rise to liability under the TVPA, the ATCA, and the applicable international law.

This action is properly maintained as a class action because (a) the prosecution of separate actions by individual members of the class would create a risk of adjudications which could as a practical matter be dispositive of the interests of the other members or would substantially impair or confuse their ability to protect their interests, and/or (b) questions of law and fact common to the members of the class predominate over questions affecting individual members and a class action is superior to other available methods for the fair and efficient adjudication of the controversy.

ALLEGATIONS COMMON TO ALL COUNTS OF THE COMPLAINT

Defendant Robert Mugabe co-founded the predecessor organization of ZANU-PF in 1963, and has been the leader of the party since that time. Since 1980, defendant Mugabe and ZANU-PF have controlled the Government of Zimbabwe.

The ZANU-PF regime in Zimbabwe is not a dictatorship and is not operating under martial law. Nevertheless, defendant ZANU-PF and defendant Mugabe have on numerous occasions shown outright disregard and contempt for the Zimbabwean Constitution, the legal system of Zimbabwe, and the rulings of the Zimbabwe judiciary, including the Zimbabwe High Court.

In particular, defendants have historically demonstrated that they will violate the basic laws of their country as well as fundamental international human rights norms in order to punish and suppress peaceful expressions of political dissent or opposition. For example, in January of 1999, two journalists, Ray Choto and Mark Chavunduka, both of the privately owned Standard weekly newspaper, were unlawfully detained by the military solely for their publication of an article on January 10, 1999, that was critical of the ruling party. While in military detention, these two individuals were allegedly subjected to brutal torture and intimidation.

Because of their positions of unrivalled and dominant political power for the past two decades, the defendants' lawless actions to suppress political dissent and to crush and punish political opponents are committed under color of state authority.

In addition, defendant Mugabe has illegally abused his position of power within the government and within ZANU-PF in order to amass an unauthorized and illegal fortune. Specifically, defendant Mugabe is reported to now have a personal fortune estimated in hundreds of millions of pounds sterling. According to reports published in the Sunday Times of London on May 1, 2000, he owns a hotel in Switzerland, a holiday mansion near Cape Town, three palatial homes in Zimbabwe, two previously privately-owned farms, off-shore companies and numbered bank accounts. There is also a castle in Scotland reputed to have been paid for with a gold mining concession.

On information and belief, this fortune is comprised of assets stolen from the Zimbabwean people and from the legitimate functions and budgets of the Zimbabwean government. On information an belief, this fortune also is likely to comprise assets wrongfully and illegally taken from assistance and development funds provided by numerous foreign governments, including the United States.

In January 2000, reflecting the growing discontent among the people of Zimbabwe with the ZANU-PF regime, the MDC was formally launched as an opposition party that was increasingly perceived as a serious challenge to ZANU-PF's totalitarian dominance over the Government.

In an effort to further consolidate his power and to advance his political goals, in February 2000 defendant Mugabe, through his hand-picked legislature, offered a national referendum which would have extended defendant Mugabe's presidential term by up to an additional 12 years and would have provided defendant Mugabe with the constitutional authority to seize white-owned farms without compensation. On February 13, 2000, the Zimbabwean electorate soundly rejected that referendum. The illegal invasion of white-owned farms by ZANU-PF loyalists began the next week.

Due to the threats of forced and illegal expropriation of farmland consistently made by ZANU-PF and defendant Mugabe over the past year, many farmers and farm workers have become strong supporters of the MDC.

In response to the threat posed by the MDC in the national parliamentary elections scheduled for June 2000, defendant Mugabe and defendant ZANU-PF initiated and orchestrated a campaign of deliberate and systematic violence and terror that accompanied the farm occupations, and that consisted of the physical intimidation and murders of members, sympathizers, and supporters of the democratic opposition, as well as of farmers and farm workers.

The violence was mainly directed at MDC supporters and at farmers, but other opposition parties were also targeted. There were 18,000 incidents of violence during the campaign, which have been recorded by the Amani Trust, a Non-Governmental Organization ("NGO") set up to help victims of political violence.

The land occupations have been taken in direct contravention to Zimbabwean law and to the rulings of the Zimbabwean High Court, and have been part of a coordinated plan and policy to attack farmers and farm workers for purely political reasons.

On information and belief, defendant ZANU-PF illegally engaged the ZWVA to spearhead the party's election campaign and the land occupations. Under defendant Mugabe's direction, defendant ZANU-PF paid or undertook to pay ZWVA $20 million for this purpose in direct contravention of Zimbabwean statute. In accordance with defendants' plans, the ZWVA members formed armed groups of militia including unemployed youths to occupy commercial farms, particularly those operated by MDC supporters, and set up militia bases where the youths were supplied by ZANU-PF with food, drink and money to enable them to corruptly influence persons on each farm and in the surrounding areas to give their vote to ZANU-PF and/or refrain from giving their vote to the MDC, all in direct contravention of Zimbabwean law and international law.

On information and belief, the land invaders were an organized force put together by the highest levels of ZANU-PF leadership, including defendants, and were comprised of roughly 1,500 war veteran members of ZWVA, 1,000 soldiers of the notorious 5th Brigade, 300 to 400 CIO operatives, certain members of the police force, and a group of about 7000 ZANU-PF members who volunteered and were paid a per diem directly for their services in implementing the unlawful land occupations and the campaign of violence and terror against farmers and the political opposition.

On information and belief, the notorious 5th Brigade was responsible under defendant Mugabe's direction, and under the immediate command of Mr. Perence Shiri, for tens of thousands of extrajudicial murders in

Matabeleland during the 1980s as part of a systematic effort to suppress political opposition.

On information and belief, the invasions were fully supported by government transport. Moreover, local CIO officers have provided communications and coordination facilities. Mr. Perence Shiri, Head of the Air Force and commander of the 5th Brigade, which carried out the killings in Matabeleland in 1983-84, is allegedly exercising command at the behest of defendant Mugabe.

Various concrete examples of defendants' involvement in orchestrating this strategy of violence during the pre-polling period are available as a matter of public record.

On Sunday, February 27, 2000, at a ZANU-PF campaign meeting in Rusape, Zimbabwe, Didymus Noel Edwin Mutasa, the ZANU-PF National Secretary for Administration, publicly outlined a strategy of violence to be adopted by his party against those seen to support the MDC. On information and belief, Mr. Mutasa is said to have stated the following: that his party had changed its slogan from that which said, Down with those who do not understand. Instead, Mr. Mutasa stated, the new slogan was that those who did not understand should be beaten to make them understand, that it was not too late to make them understand, and the only way to do this was to assault them. In addition, this ZANU-PF official stated that no one would protect the opponents from such assaults because ZANU-PF is the ruling party.

Another example is given by the statements made by Moven Mahachi, Minister of Defense, who on several occasions referred to the brutal murder of MDC campaign manager Chiminya, who had been extrajudicially murdered by ZANU-PF members (see below). On information and belief, these statements by Minister Mahachi included the following:

On May 31, 2000, at a ZANU-PF campaign rally of 400 persons in Mukamba, Mahachi singled out 3 MDC supporters and stated that if they "followed that road" (voting for MDC) they would die for nothing, that they were lucky to be alive and that Chiminya had been fooling them to follow MDC.

On June 2, 2000, at a rally in Chiundu, he referred again to the fate that would befall MDC supporters, stating that if MDC supporters did not surrender MDC T-shirts and cards, "we will move door to door killing like we did with Chiminya. Mind you, I am the Minister responsible for defense. Therefore I am capable of killing. When you go to vote there will be computers which will identify you and tell us which party you have voted for, so we will know if you have voted for MDC. We will then later take action against you."

On June 3, 2000, at a rally at Murowa Business Center, Mahachi stated the following: *"We killed Chiminya. What happened to us? Nothing. [..] We have our machines that will see where you voted. After the elections we will follow all MDC members and kill them. At every polling station we will have a person there who knows you."* In reference to MDC supporters, Mahachi stated that *"if you meet them, you have to kill them."*

On June 4, 2000, at a gathering at Shangwe Shopping Centre, Mahachi stated that *"MDC supporters must be reminded that I am the Minister responsible for defense. We will not hesitate to kill those who detract ZANU-PF, especially people like Remus Makuwaza. A good example is what we did to Chiminya."*

On June 4, 2000 at a village meeting called by ZANU-PF, Mahachi stated that *"if you are going to vote for MDC we will see what you have voted for, because we will have machines in these polling stations. After the elections we will move around from door to door at every house beating you."* Threats against property were also issued against MDC supporters: *"For those who are in the resettlement area, because I was the minister responsible for resettlement at that time, we will have to take that land back, because it was not easy to get the land."*

On information and belief, the statements and actions of senior ZANU-PF officials such as Secretary Mutasa and Minister Mahachi, explicitly and overtly designed to physically threaten and terrorize political opponents of ZANU-PF, would not and could not have been taken and made without the clear, expressed direction of the long-established leader, First Secretary and President of ZANU-PF, defendant Mugabe.

In addition, Defendant Mugabe has himself on numerous occasions made openly public statements directly threatening physical violence to political opponents of the ZANU-PF regime:

On March 16, 2000, on occasion of the opening of the Pungwe-Mutare pipeline in Mutare, defendant Mugabe publicly made the following statement, in the Shona language so as to be understood by the broadest segment of the population: *"Those who try to cause disunity among our people must watch out because death will befall them."*

On April 7, 2000 defendant Mugabe publicly threatened voters that if they voted MDC "my ghost (chidhamo) will come after you."

On April 18, 2000 at the Independence Day Celebrations defendant Mugabe publicly stated that by allying themselves with the MDC, white farmers had made themselves "enemies of the State."

On information and belief, in addition to orchestrating the campaign of violence against the political opposition, defendant Mugabe has directed ZANU-PF and the ZWVA to occupy and effectively appropriate over 1,600 privately owned farms. These land occupations have been associated with deliberate targeting of white farmers who supported the MDC. On information and belief, there is evidence that the extrajudicial murders of 10 different white farmers were authorized by defendants. One of these killings involved the murder of a white farmer by an army officer in civilian clothes, with 100 thugs in attendance and the police standing by without intervening.

On information and belief, the ZANU-PF code name for the organized campaign of violence against farmers, farmworkers, and MDC supporters was "Operation Tsuro." Tsuro is a word from Zimbabwe's dominant tribal language of Shona meaning "hare" or "rabbit."

According to a special report described by the Sunday Times of London on May 21, 2000, defendant Mugabe had full knowledge of and encouraged the activities of the so-called "Operation Tsuro," which systematically set out to brutalize and kill MDC supporters. Henchmen of the ruling Zanu-PF party in the operation were promised payment on a sliding scale, from £379 ($570) for killing an opposition member to £117 ($175) for burning a house.

According to the Sunday Times, young party members were selected by their local branches and sent for seven days of training and indoctrination at the King George VI (KG6) army barracks in Harare. They were taught assassination skills and paramilitary maneuvers. They were shown how to stab someone in the chest and advised to throw their knife in a river or sewerage drain so that it could not be traced. The recruits were also given instructions on burning the homes of opponents. They were then sent out at night in small squads to kill members of the MDC or burn their houses.

According to the Sunday Times, the details of Operation Tsuro were disclosed by Bright Salani, a teacher in his forties who was recruited in his hometown of Checheche, near Zimbabwe's border with Mozambique.

Police in Checheche, working with ZANU-PF, arrested him hours before he was due to meet the journalist from the Sunday Times of London to discuss Operation Tsuro. Party members had searched his house, accusing him of being a traitor. Salani feared he would be held or killed, so left a written statement. He also told a friend about his experience.

It was known that the occupation of farms and the intimidation of MDC supporters had been ordered at a high level and implemented by the state security services after voters rejected Mugabe's proposed constitutional reform in February. But Salani's story shows it was directly orchestrated by the president. Defendant Mugabe himself was the speaker at their "graduation" ceremony at the Sheraton hotel in Harare. His words left them in no doubt as to their duty. According to Salani, the president made the following statement in Shona: "When we are speaking of the struggle, we are talking about killing people so the country can be free."

According to the Sunday Times, defendant Mugabe is also reported to have made the following statement during this speech: "Now we are at war again . . . If one of you is asked why you are killing, you say it is not us, it is the president. But behave like hares. The baboons have a big build, but the hares are more clever."

Defendant Mugabe has on several occasions publicly stated his knowledge of and support for the terrorizing and illegal actions being undertaken by the ZWVA:

On May 18, 2000 in Mauritius, defendant Mugabe expressed his support for the war veterans saying they had a just cause.

On May 29, 2000, Dr. Chenjerai "Hitler" Hunzvi stated that the war veterans would only leave the farms if defendant Mugabe asked them to do so.

On June 1, 2000 defendant Mugabe expressed his satisfaction with the invasions of farms by war veterans.

On June 8, 2000 defendant Mugabe stated at a public rally in Gutu that if farmers tried to resist war veterans taking their farms, they (the war veterans) would kill the farmers.

On June 11, 2000 defendant Mugabe expressed his gratitude to the war veterans and said they should not vacate farms and the police would not harass them.

On June 15, 2000, the Zimbabwe newspaper "The Herald" reported the following: "President Mugabe yesterday described as nonsense the High Court ruling that war veterans should leave the farms they are occupying and reiterated that he would never send the Police or the army to evict them."

The role of defendant Mugabe acting as leader of ZANU-PF in orchestrating the recent campaign of terror and violence against the people of Zimbabwe and the supporters of the MDC has been well documented by journalists and others who have investigated the situation in Zimbabwe.

The United States Senate passed a bill on June 23, 2000, S. 2677, entitled the Zimbabwe Democracy Act of 2000. In this bill, the following explicit findings, among others, are made:

Deliberate and systematic violence, intimidation, and killings have been orchestrated and supported by the Government of Zimbabwe and the ruling ZANU-PF party against members, sympathizers, and supporters of the democratic opposition; farmers; and employees. The violence has resulted in death, a breakdown in the rule of law, and further collapse of the Zimbabwean economy.

The lawlessness, harassment, violence, intimidation, and killings directed at the opposition and their supporters, farmers, and farm employees continues at President Mugabe's explicit and public urging despite two court rulings that the land occupations by the so-called war veterans are illegal and must be ended.

The breakdown of the rule of law has jeopardized Zimbabwe's future, including international support for programs that provide land ownership for the large number of poor and landless Zimbabweans, other donor programs, economic stability, and direct investment.

The orchestrated violence and intimidation directed at opposition supporters has created and fostered an environment that seriously compromises the possibility of free and fair elections.

As of the end of June, 2000, the total number of commercial farms that have been invaded and occupied exceeded 1,600. The Commercial Farmers Union has recorded close to 8,000 human rights violations directly associated with these occupations and with defendants' politically-motivated campaign of violence. Of these violations, 606 have been perpetrated directly against farmers, and the remaining 6,614 have been perpetrated against farm workers.

On information and belief, defendants Mudenge and Moyo have both assisted defendant Mugabe and defendant ZANU-PF in carrying out the gross violations of international law set forth in this Complaint, and are complicit in the tortious and criminal conduct alleged that is actionable under the ATCA and the TVPA.

In part, this complicity has taken the form of defending the actions of defendant ZANU-PF. For example, defendant Moyo is reported to have accused the MDC of having instigated the violence that all other accounts and reported investigations, including those underlying the findings of the U.S. Senate, have attributed directly to defendant ZANU-PF.

Similarly, according to the BBC World Service, defendant Mudenge on June 12, 2000, publicly accused the United States and Britain of being responsible for the destablization in Zimbabwe.

The actions described in S. 2677 that have been taken by ZANU-PF members, supporters, and sympathizers at defendant Mugabe's repeated and explicit public urging, are taken under color of state authority. While the acts are illegal under Zimbabwean law as well as under international law and United States law, they are taken at the direction of the First Secretary of ZANU-PF, defendant Mugabe, who is also the President of Zimbabwe, and under the auspices of ZANU-PF, the ruling party for two decades.

The actions taken by defendant Mugabe to initiate, direct, and urge the orchestrated campaign of violence against MDC supporters, farmers, and farm workers have been taken with the direct and specific goal of eliminating ZANU-PF's political opposition. These actions are not in furtherance of any policy of the Government of Zimbabwe, lawful or otherwise, and, moreover, are illegal and unauthorized under Zimbabwean law. Defendant Mugabe's actions that are the subject of this Complaint were therefore taken in his individual, personal capacity and in his capacity as First Secretary of ZANU-PF, and not in his official capacity as President of Zimbabwe.

ALLEGATIONS OF SPECIFIC PLAINTIFFS
ADELLA CHIMINYA TACHIONA

Ms. Chiminya is the 34-year-old widow of Tapfuma Chiminya Tachiona, who held the position of National Youth Organizer for the MDC.

Mr. Chiminya was a close companion of Morgan Tsvangirai, the President of the MDC and chief political rival to defendant Mugabe.

On April 15, 2000, Mr. Chiminya was campaigning for Mr. Tsvangirai at Murambinda Growth Point, in the Buhera District of

Zimbabwe, with two other individuals, Ms. Talent Mabika and Mr. Sanderson Makombe, as well as other MDC supporters.

Mr. Chiminya and his companions were traveling on their way home in a Mazda pick-up truck.

On information and belief, while stopped at a gasoline station, they were approached by members of the ZANU-PF party, driving a white Nissan double cab, vehicle registration number 755-878F, upon which was emblazoned the emblem and name "ZANU-PF" on the front driver and passenger doors.

On information and belief, these ZANU-PF members/supporters attacked Mr. Chiminya and his colleagues. A member of the Central Intelligence Organization named "Mwale" led the ZANU-PF members.

On information and belief, Mr. Chiminya was wearing an MDC T-shirt, which Mwale tore off, stating, "Who do you think you are? Today it is over!" The ZANU-PF members then assaulted both Mr. Chiminya and the other MDC supporters.

Mr. Chiminya managed to escape and to take one of the injured MDC supporters, who was seriously injured, to the hospital.

After leaving the hospital, Mr. Chiminya and his colleagues went to the police station to report the incident, and duly filled out a report of what happened. A number of police then followed Mr. Chiminya and his friends in a separate vehicle.

While traveling back to their homes, Mr. Chiminya and his friends were stopped on the road by Mwale and the ZANU-PF members operating with him. While many of the MDC supporters immediately fled, Mr. Chiminya, Ms. Mabika, and Mr. Makombe were not able to escape.

Mr. Chiminya, Ms. Mabika, and Mr. Makombe were all then severely beaten with metal bars, stones, clenched fists, and booted feet.

Mr. Chiminya was beaten unconscious. While he was lying on the ground, members of the ZANU-PF party, who had perpetrated the assault, doused him with gasoline. At the same time, they doused Ms. Mabika.

Both Mr. Chiminya and Ms. Mabika were then set on fire. Mr. Makombe was able to break free and escape into the surrounding bush.

Mr. Chiminya died on the road where he had been beaten and was set on fire. Ms. Mabika managed to run a few meters down the road before she collapsed.

Throughout the entire assault, the Zimbabwe Republic Police vehicle that had followed Mr. Chiminya remained parked in the vicinity, observing the incident. These police officers did absolutely nothing to intervene, but instead waited until the ZANU-PF members departed before they sought to assist any of the victims.

After the ZANU-PF members had departed, the police officers approached the place where Ms. Mabika had collapsed, but were too late to render assistance. She had died from the burns suffered.

A report was made to the Zimbabwe Republic Police and various witnesses came forward identifying the perpetrators of these brutal beatings and politically motivated murders. In addition, a number of police officers also witnessed the murders. Nevertheless, none of the accused have been apprehended or charged with any crime in relation to this incident.

Ms. Chiminya has been told that there are individuals who have given the police the exact identification of the specific individuals who poured gasoline onto Mr. Chiminya and Ms. Mabika and set them both on fire.

Despite this information, the police have done nothing further to attempt to apprehend the killers of Mr. Chiminya and Ms. Mabika.

On information and belief, this specific act of violence, like many others committed in Zimbabwe over the course of the past several months, was carried out on the instruction of senior members of the ZANU-PF party, including defendant Mugabe.

By acting as members and supporters of ZANU-PF and for purposes clearly articulated as ZANU-PF's political purpose of intimidating and putting a stop to the MDC's political challenge, the perpetrators of the assault against Mr. Chiminya and his companions were clearly acting under color of state authority. Their actions represented the orchestrated action of the ruling party as directly guided and directed by the President of the country and First Secretary of the ZANU-PF party. The inaction of the police likewise confirms that these actions, while patently unlawful and beyond the legal authority of any official to authorize, were taken under color of actual state power.

Mr. Chiminya was a close friend and political supporter of Morgan Tsvangirai, president of the MDC, and traditionally accompanied him whenever they traveled. On information and belief, the attack on Mr. Chiminya was either a direct assassination attempt on Mr. Tsvangirai or an effort to intimidate him through the assassination of one of his close supporters and companions.

THE PFEBVE PLAINTIFFS

Ms. Efridah Pfebve is the 28-year-old younger sister of the late Mr. Metthew[1] Pfebve. She resides in a family village in Nyakatondo Village, Mount Darwin North.

Mr. Elliot Pfebve is the brother of Ms. Efridah Pfebve and the late Mr. Metthew Pfebve. He is an executive member of the MDC, and he stood as an MDC candidate in the Zimbabwe National Parliamentary Elections on the 24th and 25th of June, 2000, in the Bindura Constituency for Mashonaland Central Province.

Mr. Elliot Pfebve's opponent in the election was Mr. Border Gezi, the candidate for ZANU-PF. Mr. Gezi was prior to the election, and is now, the Member of Parliament for the Bindura Constiuency. He was also the Provincial Chairman of ZANU-PF during the election campaign.

During the run-up to the June 2000, elections, the Mashonaland Central Province witnessed an extremely high level of politically-motivated violence and death. On information and belief, Mr. Pfebve believes Mr. Gezi orchestrated this violence on the direct instructions of defendant Mugabe.

In February 2000, after the National Referendum (described above), defendant Mugabe appeared together with Mr. Gezi at a rally at Manhenga Business Center, in the Bindura Constuency. At this rally, defendant Mugabe categorically stated that the MDC was an enemy of his government and his party, and that ZANU-PF would therefore deal with its supporters accordingly.

Prior to this February 2000 rally, the Bindura constituency had been remarkably free of violence. This rally was attended by a number of senior leaders of the ZANU-PF party for the region. After this rally, the incidence of violence in the Bindura Constituency increased remarkably.

On information and belief, this increase in violence was clearly the direct result of defendant Mugabe's statements and instructions. Defendant Mugabe is believed to have given specific instructions to conduct this campaign of violence and terror in an effort to intimidate voters into voting for ZANU-PF or into not voting at all.

---

[1] The spelling "Metthew" may not be correct, but is the spelling that appears on Mr. Pfebve's death certificate.

It was made very clear to Mr. Pfebve, in particular, by informants and other individuals, that he was a principal target of this violence. He was the candidate for Bindura, the regional capital and a traditional ZANU-PF stronghold.

(A) ZANU-PF ATTACKS AGAINST MR. E. PFEBVE

On February 20, 2000, Mr. Pfebve was scheduled to give a speech at a rally at Shutu Business Center, Chiweshe Communal Lands, Mazowe East. Prior to this rally, approximately 150 ZANU-PF youths wearing ZANU-PF T-shirts, chanting ZANU-PF slogans, and armed with spears, axes, sticks, and stones attacked the gathered MDC supporters.

Mr. Pfebve was advised, after the attack, that the principal reason for the attack had been to assassinate him. This was not accomplished only because Mr. Pfebve had a firearm that he was able to use to threaten the attackers and to hold them at bay.

Among the ringleaders of the ZANU-PF mob was Bernard Nyangoni Chimutengwende, who is the younger brother of Chen Chimutengwende, the Minister of Information and a senior leader of ZANU-PF.

The participants in the ZANU-PF mob that attacked this rally were all wearing T-shirts emblazoned with the ZANU-PF symbol and the face of Chen Chimutengwende.

Mr. Pfebve was attacked by another ZANU-PF group of about 90 similarly armed and clad supporters at another political rally at the Rukope Business Center in Bindura Constiuency. On information and belief, these attackers had been hired by Mr. Gezi to travel from Mashonaland East to disrupt the rally. Mr. Gezi is believed to have instructed Mr. Padi Zhanda, the Provincial Chairman of ZANU-PF, Mashonaland East, to gather this force and to transport them to the rally.

These ZANU-PF attackers seriously injured at least six MDC supporters gathered at the rally. Mr. Pfebve was attacked by these ZANU-PF assailants in his car, and managed to protect himself again by showing his firearm and threatening his assailants. The Zimbabwe Republic Police also appeared and assisted Mr. Pfebve, and on this occasion actually arrested some of the assailants.

However, all of the ZANU-PF assailants that were arrested were released without being charged with any offenses. This release is believed to have occurred at the specific direction of Mr. Gezi. Mr. Pfebve was advised by the officer-in-charge of Smava Station, where the arrested ZANU-PF assailants were taken, that he had been given specific instructions by the Bindura Police Station, his superiors within the Zimbabwe Republic Police force, to release all of these ZANU-PF attackers without charge. This is believed to have occurred as a direct result of interference by Mr. Gezi.

An additional incident of ZANU-PF violence against Mr. Pfebve occurred in April 2000 at Glendale Township in Mazowe East.

Mr. Pfebve was walking with two MDC supporters. The three were approached by a group of about 30 ZANU-PF members wearing ZANU-PF T-shirts. Mr. Pfebve and his companions were attacked by these youths, most of whom were armed with knives. One of Mr. Pfebve's companions suffered three serious stab wounds and was left unconscious by this ZANU-PF group.

This assault was reported to the police. Nevertheless, to date, no arrests have been made in connection with this incident.

Mr. Pfebve was once again attacked after addressing a rally at the Mount Darwin School. On this occasion, he was traveling from Rushinga Town with a number of supporters when approximately 700 ZANU-PF youths, ZWVA war veterans, and members of the Central Intelligence Organization attacked them. These attackers were armed with sticks, axes, spears, stones, and, in some instances, with firearms.

Mr. Pfebve was able to escape on this occasion because he was in a motor vehicle and was assisted by police. Nevertheless, others were injured, including his driver Nixon Makaure who was severely assaulted and lost his right eye.

Mr. Pfebve repeatedly received death threats from ZANU-PF throughout the run-up to the June 2000 election.

On April 29, 2000, while he was in Bindura campaigning, a group of approximately 300 ZANU-PF assailants attacked his home and family and murdered his brother, Metthew Pfebve.

(B) THE APRIL 29 ATTACK ON THE PFEBVE HOME

Ms. Efridah Pfebve was present at the family village on April 29, 2000, the day that her brother Metthew was murdered by ZANU-PF members.

At about 6:00 p.m. on the evening of April 29, 2000, while Ms. Pfebve's mother was preparing the family meal, the family heard the sound of a large group of people converging on their home.

This group of people consisted of approximately 300 ZANU-PF members and supporters, ZWVA members, and ZANU-PF youths or operatives. The group was armed with various weapons, including axes, spears, sticks, and stones, and were wearing ZANU-PF T-shirts and chanting ZANU-PF slogans.

Seeing that the group's intentions were violent, the Pfebve family attempted to flee. Ms. Pfebve's mother managed to hide in the outside toilet, which was then stoned by members of the group. Ms. Pfebve believes that they stopped stoning only because they believed her mother to have been killed.

The ZANU-PF group then attacked both Ms. Pfebve's father and brother Metthew Pfebve with sticks, stones and fists. They dragged them both away from the home, dropping Ms. Pfebve's father as he fell unconscious. They continued carrying Ms. Pfebve's brother, Metthew Pfebve.

Ms. Pfebve's father, who is 70 years of age, has suffered deep lacerations to his head and two broken fingers.

On the next day, Sunday April 30, 2000, Mr. Metthew Pfebve was found in the middle of the road between the Pfebve's village and the Kamutsenzere Primary School, approximately one and a half kilometers from the Pfebve home. Mr. Metthew Pfebve had been severely beaten and murdered, and was left lying naked in the middle of the road.

Mr. Elliot Pfebve has been told by informants that the purpose of this attack on his home was to kill him.

On information and belief, Mr. Elliot Pfebve asserts that his brother's extrajudicial murder was a direct result of a deliberate campaign of violence instituted by defendant Mugabe.

(C) THE KAMUTZENZERE PRIMARY SCHOOL

During the election period, the Kamutsenzere Primary School was set up as a torture camp.

The camp commander was John Karikoga, a ZWVA war veteran and ZANU-PF councilor in the region.

Mr. Pfebve knows of at least two individuals, Mr. Paul Chaziya and Mr. Revas Chimudze, who were held and tortured at this camp by ZANU-PF or ZWVA members, acting under the direction of senior

ZANU-PF officials, including the defendant, and therefore acting under color of state law and authority.

On information and belief, Mr. Metthew Pfebve was likely tortured at or near this camp prior to his murder by members of ZANU-PF, acting at the direction of or under the actual or constructive knowledge of defendant Mugabe, under color of state law and authority.

EVELYN MASAITI

Ms. Masaiti is a 35-year-old woman residing in Mutare, Zimbabwe.

Ms. Masaiti stood in the June 2000 elections against the ZANU-PF candidate, Mandy Chimene, a former member of the Central Intelligence Organization. Ms. Chimene is married to Shadreck Beta, the ZANU-PF Provincial Chairman.

Ms. Masaiti won her June 2000 election and therefore is a Member of Parliament for Mutasa District.

Prior to the election, Ms. Masaiti was subjected to a number of acts of violence perpetrated by members of ZANU-PF and ZWVA acting under color of state authority.

On April 23, 2000, at Gatsbi Business Center in the Honde Valley, Manicaland, Ms. Masaiti's motor vehicle was stoned by ZANU-PF supporters.

On April 24, 2000, Ms. Masaiti was traveling to the Zimbabwe Republic Ruda Police Station to make a report. Her car was stopped by approximately 25 ZANU-PF supporters, two of whom, one by the name of Tambudzai Chinyengwa and a war veteran by the name of Madzitire, physically assaulted her with clenched-fist punches to the face.

On this occasion, Ms. Masaiti's husband was also assaulted by two or three ZANU-PF members.

Ms. Masaiti reported the two individuals who assaulted her to the police. Notwithstanding this, the police have taken no action and no one has been arrested in connection with the assault on Ms. Masaiti and her husband.

During this pre-election period of several months, a number of ZWVA ex-combatants were camped at the Gatsbi Business Center. They made it clear that it was not possible to travel to this area for any and all MDC supporters or members, notwithstanding that it was a part of Ms. Masaiti's rural village.

On May 27, 2000, at around 9:00 p.m., Ms. Msaiti, her husband, and several other family members were standing on the patio of their home when they were warned that Tendai Samanga, a ZWVA ex-combatant and the local ZANU-PF councilor for Samanga A Ward in the Mutasa constituency, was walking around their home carrying a bottle which he was attempting to conceal.

Shortly after the warning, a bottle full of petrol was thrown directly at the group standing on the patio and exploded at their feet. Ms. Masaiti suffered lacerations on her left leg, but otherwise escaped serious injury only because the bomb did not explode to its full capacity.

Ms. Masaiti was able to identify the bomb-throwers, both Mr. Samanga and Dekaurendo (another war veteran) and Patrick Mandigara. While these three individuals have been reported to the police and while multiple written statements about the crime have been submitted by all of the witnesses, no arrests have been made.

A far more severe attack occurred on May 29, 2000. On this day, Ms. Masaiti was informed that ZANU-PF planned a serious attack on her home. As a result, she fled her home and spent the night in the bush.

That evening, both Ms. Masaiti's rural home and her communal home were in fact attacked and destroyed. The rural home, Gatsi Homestead, situated at Kwesha Kraal, together with her automobile, were set on fire by members of the ZANU-PF party, in the company of war veterans.

Three different structures on Ms. Masaiti's property were set on fire and destroyed. All of her possessions were destroyed, as was the granary that stored the family's maize crop for the entire season.

Two of Ms. Masaiti's supporters were severely assaulted by the ZANU-PF group, as were her in-laws. The homes of six additional MDC supporters were also set on fire and destroyed.

Ms. Masaiti has been advised by an informant that she was the planned target of the attack. She was also informed that Mandy Chimere, her ZANU-PF opponent in the election, had transported the war veterans into the area in her Landrover Discovery.

The existence of approximately 70 war veterans in the Mutasa Constituency is extremely unusual. This area is mainly communal land, with only 2 commercial farms in the whole district. Since the war veterans are directed to occupy commercial farms, it is highly unusual for them to be found in such a predominantly communal area.

On information and belief, Ms. Masaiti asserts that these 70 veterans were sent by ZANU-PF to this remote part of the country to carry out a campaign of intimidation and violence in an effort to intimidate the local voters against voting for the MDC.

The member-in-charge of Ruda Police Station is a ZANU-PF member and is believed to be an ex-combatant himself. On information and belief, Ms. Masaiti asserts that this fact is the reason that he has not followed through on his investigations relating to the various reports of violence, destruction of property and other crimes committed by ZANU-PF against MDC supporters.

Because of ZANU-PF's dominant position in the Government, because of defendant Mugabe's role as leader of the ZANU-PF party and as President of the Government, and because of the inaction of the police force in defending Ms. Masaiti or in apprehending her assailants, it is clear that the campaign of terror and violence against her was undertaken under color of state authority.

On information and belief, Ms. Masaiti asserts that the ZANU-PF and war veteran groups that attacked her and that destroyed her homes and the property of other MDC supporters were acting on direct instructions from senior members of ZANU-PF and in particular from defendant Mugabe.

PLAINTIFF MARIA DEL CARMEN STEVENS

Maria Del Carmen Stevens is the 39-year old widow of the late David Yendall Stevens, a private commercial farmer who was tortured and murdered by ZANU-PF and ZWVA members on April 15, 2000.

David Stevens was actively involved in the Macheke area MDC.

Maria Stevens and her late husband were farmers in the Macheke area of Zimbabwe. Their farm was invaded by the ZWVA and by ZANU-PF on or about February 12, 2000.

After the February 12, 2000, invasion of the Stevens' farm, there have been a number of incidents of violence involving approximately 26 different invaders. On at least two occasions, young teenage girls working or living on the farm were assaulted, and in at least one case one of these girls was raped, by the invaders.

Reports of these incidents have been filed with the police, but to date no arrests have been made.

On Saturday, April 15, 2000, ZANU-PF and ZWVA members entered the homestead area of the farm, shot one of the dogs on the homestead, and kidnapped Mr. Stevens.

A number of the Stevens' neighbors saw Mr. Stevens being driven from his farm to Murehwa. He was being driven in a convoy of three vehicles filled with ZANU-PF and ZWVA members.

Mr. Stevens was taken to the Murehwa Police Station. From there he was abducted again by ZANU-PF and ZWVA members, along with five other individuals. This abduction was observed by the Zimbabwe Republic Police who made no effort to stop it.

All six of these individuals were severely beaten and tortured. As part of this torture, Mr. Stevens was forced to drink diesel oil.

On information and belief, sometime late in the day on April 15, 2000, Mr. Stevens was summarily executed. The shots were heard by one of the other individuals who had been kidnapped and had been abandoned by the side of the road.

Despite an extensive report of this incident being given to the Zimbabwe Republic Police, including numerous eyewitness accounts, no one has been arrested for this horrific atrocity and extrajudicial murder.

When interviewed by the Zimbabwean press about David Stevens' murder, defendant Mugabe stated that Mr. Stevens was armed and started the "war," and implied that Mr. Stevens got what he deserved and that white farmers should not try to resist attacks.

Mrs. Stevens attests to the fact that her husband was not in fact armed, that the only weapon on their farm was an old shotgun used for vermin-control held in the possession of the individual responsible for such duties, and that Mr. Stevens abhorred violence and in no way precipitated the violence that befell him.

On information and belief, defendants directly orchestrated the attack and occupation of the Stevens' farm and authorized the use of violence and the extrajudicial murder of the occupants of that farm.

INADEQUACY AND UNAVAILABILITY OF LOCAL REMEDIES

Defendant Mugabe has on at least two occasions shown a total and complete disregard for the clear rulings of the Zimbabwean High Court regarding the illegality of the occupations of farms by ZWVA and ZANU-PF supporters.

In or about February, 2000, the High Court ruled that the farm occupations were illegal. Defendant Mugabe's response was to publicly encourage farm occupations and related violence throughout the ensuing six to eight months.

Similarly, on March 17, 2000, the High Court affirmatively ordered the Zimbabwean Government to take affirmative action to remove the ZANU-PF and ZWVA squatters from the commercial farms they were occupying. That order has been ignored despite the Southern African Development Community Lawyers Association also urging the Zimbabwe Government to take action.

In addition to the Zimbabwe Government's complete disregard for High Court rulings, local police stations of the Zimbabwe Republic Police have been ineffectual in combating, if not complicit in committing, the crimes authorized and perpetrated by defendants and their agents.

On August 15, 2000, lawyers from the Law Society of Zimbabwe attempted to present to defendant Mugabe a petition of complaints, but were told by the police at defendant's office that no such petition could be accepted, nor would any of the lawyers be allowed in the building.

Based on the forgoing facts, it is patently clear that there are no adequate remedies available to plaintiffs to redress the wrongs suffered at the hands of defendant.

FIRST CLAIM FOR RELIEF

(Extrajudicial Killing In Violation of The TVPA)

The allegations set forth in the foregoing paragraphs of this Complaint are realleged and incorporated by reference as if fully set forth herein.

The acts against plaintiffs included, among others, the politically motivated, extrajudicial killing of Tapfuma Chiminya Tachiona, Metthew Pfebve, and David Stevens in violation of the international law of human rights and the TVPA.

On information and belief, approximately three dozen other class members were likewise murdered as a result of politically motivated, extrajudicial killings instigated and authorized by defendants in violation of the international law of human rights and the TVPA.

These murders were all perpetrated by members or agents of ZANU-PF acting under the direction, command, control, and encouragement of defendant Mugabe.

These murders were all perpetrated by members or agents of ZANU-PF acting under color of state law and authority with complicity from the police and the armed forces, and direct and outspoken support from the President of Zimbabwe.

In addition to violating the TVPA and being actionable in U.S. court under the ATCA and the TVPA, these politically motivated and extrajudicial murders violate the international standards of human rights, as set forth in, inter alia and without limitation, the 1949 Geneva Conventions, Convention Against Torture and Other Cruel, Inhuman, or Degrading Treatment or Punishment, United Nations Charter, Universal Declaration of Human Rights, and the International Covenant on Civil and Political Rights.

As a result of the brutal attacks and extrajudicial murders perpetrated at the behest of defendant Mugabe and defendant ZANU-PF, plaintiffs Tapfuma Chiminya, Metthew Pfebve, and David Stevens together with each additional member of the class suffered wrongful death and egregious pain and suffering, as well as conscious mental suffering, fear, and terror at the impending loss of life, knowledge that they were being hunted and killed because of their political beliefs, and loss of the enjoyment of life, and each of their estates is entitled to recover compensatory damages to be proved at trial, but in an amount in excess of $2,000,000 each.

Defendants' acts were deliberate, willful, intentional, wanton, malicious, and oppressive and should be punished by an award of punitive damages in the amount of at least $5,000,000 for each plaintiff and each additional member of the class.

SECOND CLAIM FOR RELIEF
(Torture)
The allegations set forth in the foregoing paragraphs of this Complaint are realleged and incorporated by reference as if fully set forth herein.

The acts against plaintiffs included a systematic attempt to inflict both mental and physical torture on plaintiffs in violation of the international law of human rights and the TVPA.

While in the direct physical control of ZANU-PF mobs, agents, or officials, plaintiffs were subjected to extensive physical and mental abuse, were beaten savagely with pipes, sticks, stones, and spears, and were taunted and abused expressly because of their suspected political beliefs.

On information and belief, Plaintiff Metthew Pfebve was physically tortured and beaten before being killed, in contravention of the international law of human rights and the TVPA.

On information and belief, Plaintiff David Stevens was physically tortured and beaten before being killed, including through the forced consumption of diesel oil, in contravention of the international law of human rights and the TVPA.

Additional plaintiff members of the class, potentially including Mr. Paul Chaziya and Mr. Revas Chimudze and other, unnamed plaintiff class members who were held and tortured at the Kamutsenzere Primary School, were similarly physically tortured in violation of the international law of human rights and the TVPA.

In addition, defendants' actions repeatedly inflicted threats of imminent death or of severe physical pain and suffering onto plaintiffs and additional unnamed class members, and thereby simultaneously and immediately inflicted mental torture solely because of the plaintiffs' and class members' suspected political beliefs, in direct contravention of the international law of human rights and the TVPA.

In addition to violating U.S. law in the form of the TVPA, and being actionable in U.S. court under the ATCA and the TVPA, these politically-motivated acts of inflicting physical and mental torture violate the international law of human rights, as reflected in, inter alia and without limitation, the 1949 Geneva Conventions, Convention Against Torture and Other Cruel, Inhuman, or Degrading Treatment or Punishment, United Nations Charter, Universal Declaration of Human Rights, and the International Covenant on Civil and Political Rights.

Plaintiffs Metthew Pfebve, David Stevens and each additional unnamed member of the class suffered mental and physical torture because of their political beliefs and/or race, and each of these plaintiffs or their estates is entitled to recover compensatory damages to be proved at trial, but in an amount in excess of $1,000,000 each.

241

Defendants' acts were deliberate, willful, intentional, wanton, malicious, and oppressive and should be punished by an award of punitive damages in the amount of at least $5,000,000 for each plaintiff and each additional member of the class.

THIRD CLAIM FOR RELIEF
(Use of terror and violence to violate freedom of thought, political opinion, and freedom to exercise the political franchise)

The allegations set forth in the foregoing paragraphs of this Complaint are realleged and incorporated by reference as if fully set forth herein.

The acts against plaintiffs and other, unnamed class members constituted a systematic campaign that was orchestrated and designed by defendants to physically terrorize, brutalize, kill, torture and suppress by any means necessary the political opposition of the MDC.

These actions violated the fundamental, universal, and non-derogable international norms of human rights guaranteeing freedom of thought, political opinion, and freedom to exercise the political franchise, as reflected in, inter alia and without limitation, the 1949 Geneva Conventions, Convention Against Torture and Other Cruel, Inhuman, or Degrading Treatment or Punishment, United Nations Charter, Universal Declaration of Human Rights, and the International Covenant on Civil and Political Rights, and are therefore actionable in this Court under the ATCA.

Named plaintiffs and each additional unnamed member of the class suffered terror and violence intended to violate their freedom of thought, political opinion, and freedom to exercise the political franchise, and each of these plaintiffs or their estates is entitled to recover compensatory damages to be proved at trial, but in an amount in excess of $1,000,000 each.

Defendants' acts were deliberate, willful, intentional, wanton, malicious, and oppressive and should be punished by an award of punitive damages in the amount of at least $5,000,000 for each plaintiff and each additional member of the class.

FOURTH CLAIM FOR RELIEF
(Use of terror and violence to violate freedom of association)

The allegations set forth in the foregoing paragraphs of this Complaint are realleged and incorporated by reference as if fully set forth herein.

The acts against plaintiffs and other, unnamed class members constituted a systematic campaign that was orchestrated and designed by defendants to physically terrorize, brutalize, kill, torture and suppress by any means necessary the political opposition of the MDC.

These actions violated the fundamental, universal, and non-derogable international norm of human rights guaranteeing freedom of association, as reflected in, inter alia and without limitation, the 1949 Geneva Conventions, Convention Against Torture and Other Cruel, Inhuman, or Degrading Treatment or Punishment, United Nations Charter, Universal Declaration of Human Rights, and the International Covenant on Civil and Political Rights, and are therefore actionable in this Court under the ATCA.

Named plaintiffs and each additional unnamed member of the class suffered terror and violence intended to violate their freedom of political association, and each of these plaintiffs or their estates is entitled to recover compensatory damages to be proved at trial, but in an amount in excess of $1,000,000 each.

Defendants' acts were deliberate, willful, intentional, wanton, malicious, and oppressive and should be punished by an award of punitive damages in the amount of at least $5,000,000 for each plaintiff and each additional member of the class.

FIFTH CLAIM FOR RELIEF
(Cruel, Inhuman, and Degrading Treatment)
The allegations set forth in the foregoing paragraphs of this Complaint are realleged and incorporated by reference as if fully set forth herein.

The acts against plaintiffs and other, unnamed class members constituted a systematic campaign that was orchestrated and designed by defendants to physically terrorize, brutalize, kill, torture and suppress by any means necessary the political opposition of the MDC, and in so doing sought to subject plaintiffs and other unnamed class members to cruel, inhuman and degrading treatment.

Examples of the cruel, inhuman, and degrading treatment against plaintiffs and other unnamed class members includes the stoning of plaintiff Ms. Efridah Pfebve's mother, aged approximately 70 years old; the brutal torture, beating and murder of Metthew Pfebve and the abandonment of his brutalized and naked body in the middle of the road; the beating and immolation deaths of Tapfuma Chiminya and Talent Mabika; the persistent, repeated, and overt death threats made against Mr. Elliot Pfebve, Ms. Evelyn Masaiti, and other MDC members and supporters in order to intimidate them against showing political opposition to ZANU-PF; and the torture and beating of David Stevens.

These actions violated fundamental, universal, and non-derogable international norms of human rights, as reflected in, inter alia and without limitation, the 1949 Geneva Conventions, Convention Against Torture and Other Cruel, Inhuman, or Degrading Treatment or Punishment, United Nations Charter, Universal Declaration of Human Rights, and the International Covenant on Civil and Political Rights, and are therefore actionable in this Court under the ATCA.

Named plaintiffs and each additional unnamed member of the class suffered cruel, inhuman, and degrading treatment, and each of these plaintiffs or their estates is entitled to recover compensatory damages to be proved at trial, but in an amount in excess of $1,000,000 each.

Defendants' acts were deliberate, willful, intentional, wanton, malicious, and oppressive and should be punished by an award of punitive damages in the amount of at least $5,000,000 for each plaintiff and each additional member of the class.

<u>SIXTH CLAIM FOR RELIEF</u>

(Racially discriminatory violence and extrajudicial killing)

The allegations set forth in the foregoing paragraphs of this Complaint are realleged and incorporated by reference as if fully set forth herein.

The acts against plaintiffs and other, unnamed class members constituted a systematic campaign that was orchestrated and designed by defendants to suppress by any means necessary the political opposition of the MDC and also to enable forcible and permanent occupations of over 1,500 privately-owned commercial farms.

These efforts resulted in a coordinated attempt to terrorize, intimidate and extrajudicially murder farmers based exclusively on their white race, in direct violation of the fundamental, universal, and non-derogable international norm of human rights prohibiting all forms of racial discrimination and violence, as reflected in, inter alia and without limitation, the 1949 Geneva Conventions, Convention Against Torture and Other Cruel, Inhuman, or Degrading Treatment or Punishment, United Nations Charter, Universal Declaration of Human Rights, and the International Covenant on Civil and Political Rights, and the International Convention On the Elimination of All Forms Of Racial Discrimination.

Defendants' authorization of race-based violence and murder are therefore actionable in this Court under the ATCA and the TVPA.

Named plaintiffs and each additional unnamed member of the class suffered terror and violence based on racial discrimination, and each of these plaintiffs or their estates is entitled to recover compensatory damages to be proved at trial, but in an amount in excess of $1,000,000 each.

Defendants' acts were deliberate, willful, intentional, wanton, malicious, and oppressive and should be punished by an award of punitive damages in the amount of at least $5,000,000 for each plaintiff and each additional member of the class.

SEVENTH CLAIM FOR RELIEF

(Use of terror and violence to illegally expropriate property without payment of just compensation)

The allegations set forth in the foregoing paragraphs of this Complaint are realleged and incorporated by reference as if fully set forth herein.

The acts against plaintiffs and other, unnamed class members constituted a systematic campaign that was orchestrated and designed by defendants to suppress by any means necessary the political opposition of the MDC and also to enable forcible and permanent occupations of more than 1,600 privately-owned commercial farms.

The acts orchestrated and taken by defendants to enable the forcible and permanent occupation of over 1,600 commercial farms without payment of just compensation was taken in direct contravention of the Zimbabwean Constitution and the rulings of the Zimbabwean High Court, and therefore do not constitute a legitimate act of state. These actions were rather the unilateral decision by defendants, acting under color of state authority, to illegally steal and appropriate the private property of Zimbabwean citizens, in violation of fundamental international human rights laws.

These actions violated the fundamental, universal, and non-derogable international norm of human rights protecting the right to property and requiring payment of just compensation for appropriated property, as reflected in, inter alia and without limitation, the 1949 Geneva Conventions, United Nations Charter, Universal Declaration of Human Rights, and the International Covenant on Civil and Political Rights, and are therefore actionable in this Court under the ATCA.

Named plaintiffs and each additional unnamed member of the class suffered terror and violence intended to deprive them of their right to property or to just compensation for the appropriation of their property, and each of these plaintiffs or their estates is entitled to recover compensatory damages to be proved at trial, but in an amount equal to the fair market value of the property taken from them measured as of the date of the taking or according to original investment cost or other just measure, in excess of $1,000,000 each.

Defendants' acts were deliberate, willful, intentional, wanton, malicious, and oppressive and should be punished by an award of punitive damages in the amount of at least $5,000,000 for each plaintiff and each additional member of the class.

PRAYER FOR RELIEF

WHEREFORE, plaintiffs pray for judgment against the defendant as follows:

(a)   For compensatory damages in amounts to be proved at trial;

(b)   For punitive and exemplary damages in amounts to be proved at trial;

(c)   For injunctive relief, to wit, that defendant Mugabe be enjoined from ordering, directing, or orchestrating violence, land occupations, extrajudicial killings and all other forms of physical intimidation alleged in this Complaint;

(d)   For reasonable attorney's fees and costs of suit;

(e)   For such other and further relief as the Court may deem just and proper.

A jury trial is demanded on all issues.

Respectfully submitted,

9 MDC Roll of honour

Where are they now? We remember them. We mourn them. We salute them.

Below is a list of all the brave men and women who have been killed in political violence in Zimbabwe since April 2000. This is not a comprehensive list and does not include the thousands who have been raped, tortured and lost their homes and all their belongings. Nor does it include the thousands that lost their lives during Gukurahundi. They have not died in vain.

Edwin Gomo. (MDC) Bindura. 26th Mar 2000

2. **Robert Musoni.** Mazowe West. 26th Mar 2000

3. **Doreen Marufu.** (MDC) Mazowe. 2nd Apr 2000

5. **Tichaona Chiminya.** (MDC) Buhera North. 14th Apr 2000

6. **David Stevens.** (MDC) Commercial Farmer. Murehwa.15th Apr 2000.

7. **Talent Mabika.** (MDC) Buhera North.15th Apr 2000.

8. **Martin Olds.** Commercial Farmer. Bubi-Umguza. 18th Apr 2000.

9. **Julius Andoche.** Farm Foreman. Murehwa South.20th Apr 2000

10. **Peter Kareza.** (MDC) Shamva. 23rd Apr 2000

11. **Mr. Banda.** (MDC) Shamva. 24th Apr 2000.

12. **Nicholas Chaitama.** (MDC) Kariba. 25th Apr 2000

13. **Luckson Kanyurira.** (MDC) Kariba. 25th Apr 2000.

14. **Matthew Pfebve.** (MDC) Mount Darwin. 30th Apr 2000.

15. **Laben Chiwara.** Harare. 7th May 2000.

16. **Allan Dunn.** Commercial Farmer. Seke. 7th May 2000.

17.. **John Weeks.** Commercial Farmer. Seke. 14th May 2000.

18.. **Takundwa Chipunza.** (MDC) Budiriro, Harare. 16th May 2000.

19.. **Joseph Mandeya.** (MDC) Mutasa. 17th May 2000.

20.. **Mationa Mushaya.** (United Party) Mutoko. 17th May 2000.
21. **Onias Mushaya.** (United Party) Mutoko. 17th May 2000.
22. **Kufandaedza Musekiwa.** Marondera West.27th May 2000.
23. **Thadeus Rukini.** (MDC) Masvingo. 29th May 2000.
24.. **Tony Oates.** Commercial Farmer. Zvimba North. 31st May 2000.
25. **Leo Jeke.** Masvingo.10th June 2000.
26. **Fainos Zhou.** (MDC) Mberengwa. 10th June 2000.
27. **Mr. Chinyere.** (MDC) 19th June 2000.
28. **Constantine Mafemeruke.** Kariba. 19th June 2000.
29. **Patrick Nabanyama.** (MDC) Bulawayo. Abducted, presumed dead. 19th June 2000.
30. **Zeke Chigagura.** (MDC) Gokwe East. 20th June 2000.
31. **Tichaona Tadyanemhandu.** (MDC) Hurungwe. 20th June 2000.
32. **Wonder Manhango.** (MDC) Gokwe North. 23rd June 2000.
33. **Matyatya.** (MDC) Gweru. 27th June 2000.
34. **Mandishona Mutyanda.** (MDC) Kwekwe. 29th June 2000.
35. **Nhamo Gwase.** (MDC) Murehwa South. June 2000.
36. **Willem Botha.** Commercial Farmer. Seke. 23rd July 2000.
37. **Itayi Maguwu.** (MDC) Harare. 27th July 2000.
38. **Samson Mbewe.** Farm Worker. Goromonzi. 9th Aug. 2000.
39. **Obert Guvi.** Hurungwe West. 14th Sept 2000.
40. **Lemani Chapurunga.** Marondera West.19th Nov 2000.
41. **Rimon Size.** Marondera West. 19th Nov 2000.
42. **Henry Elsworth.** (Commercial Farmer) Kwekwe. 12th Dec 2000.
43. **Howard Kareza.** (MDC) Shamva. 13th Dec 2000.
44. **Ropafadzo Manyame.** (MDC) Bikita. 16th Jan 2001.
45. **Peter Wayner** (Fr.) Masvingo. 22nd Feb 2001.
46. **Gloria Olds.** (Commercial Farmer) Bubi-Umguza. 4th Mar 2001.
47. **Eswat Chihumbiri.** Muzarabani. 23rd Mar 2001
48. **Ndonga Mupesa.** (MDC) Muzarabani. 30th Mar 2001
49. **Robson Chirima.** (MDC) MuzarabaniMar 2001
50. **Peter Mataruse.** (MDC) Muzarabani.Mar 2001
51. **Richard Chikwenya.** (MDC) Buhera North. 1st May 2001
53. **Misheck Mwanza.** (MDC) Zvimba North. 4th May 2001.

54. **Winnie Nyambare**. Guruve. 18th May 2001.
55. **Zondani Dumukani**. (Farm worker) Harare. 9th June 2001.
56. **James Nyika**. (MDC) Hatfield, Harare. 3rd July 2001.
57. **John Chakwenya**. Epworth, Harare. 2nd July 2001.
58. **John Manomera**. (MDC) Hatfield, Harare. 3rd July 2001.
59. **Peter Mandindishi**. Bindura. 22nd July 2001.
60. **Gilson Gwenzi**. (MDC) Mwenezi. 27th July 2001.
61. **Thomas Katema**. Harare. 2nd Aug 2001.
62. **Robert Cobbet**. (Commercial Farmer) Kwekwe. 6th Aug 2001.
63. **Vusumuzi Mukweli**. (MDC) Gokwe South. 9th Sept 2001.
64. **Alexio Nyamadzawo**. Wedza. 15th Sept 2001.
65. **Fanuel Madzvimbo**. Wedza. 16th Sept 2001.
66. **Osbon Ziweni**. (MDC) Masvingo. 18th Sept 2001.
67. **Felix Zava**. (MDC) Headmaster. Chikomba. Sept 2001.
68. **Hilary Matema**. Guruve South. 15th Oct 2001.
69. **Mhondiwa Chitemerere**. (MDC) Murehwa South. 30th Oct 2001.
70. **Ravengai Sikhucha**. (MDC) Mberengwa East. 10th Nov 2001.
71. **Johannes Sikele**. (Resettled farmer) Masvingo. 11th Nov 2001.
72. **Kufa Rukara**. (MDC) Silobela, Gokwe North. 19th Nov 2001.
73. **Lameck Chemvura**. (UZ Student) Manicaland. 24th Nov 2001.
74. **Michael Mugodoki**. (Farm Guard) Chikomba. 6th Dec 2001.
75. **Augustus Chacha**. (MDC) Gokwe. 9th Dec 2001.
76. **Titus Nheya**. (MDC) Karoi. 20th Dec 2001.
78. **Milton Chambati** (MDC) Magunge. 20th Dec 2001.
79. **Trymore Midzi**. (MDC) Bindura. 23rd Dec 2001.
80. **Rambisai Nyika** (MDC) Gokwe South. 24th Dec 2001.
81. **Moffat Soka Chiwaura** (MDC) Bindura. 29th Dec 2001.
82. **Shepherd Tigere**. (MDC) Gokwe South. 31st Dec 2001.
83. **Laban Chiweta**. (MDC) Bindura. Dec 2001.
84. **Amos Mapingure**. Bikita East. 9th Jan 2002
85. **Kenneth Matope**. (MDC) Guruve. 13th Jan 2002
86. **Simwanja Mijoni**. Kwekwe. 15th Jan 2002
87. **Kuziva Sanyamahwe**. (MDC) Murehwa South. 18th Jan 2002.
88. **Muchenje Mpofu** (MDC) Mberengwa East. 19th Jan 2002.
89. **Richard Chatunga**. (MDC) Bikita East. 20th Jan 2002.
90. **2 unnamed farm guards**. Mwenezi. 23rd Jan 2002

91. **Solomon Nemaire.** (MDC) Makoni. 23rd Jan 2002.
92. **Mthokozisi Ncube.** (MDC) Bulawayo. 26th Jan 2002.
93. **Fungisai Mutemaringa** (MDC) Murehwa. 27th Jan 2002
94. **Halaza Sibindi.** (MDC) Tsholotsho. 30th Jan 2002.
95. **Jameson Sicwe.** (MDC) Lupane. 30th Jan 2002.
96. **Joseph Sibindi.** (MDC) Bulawayo. Jan 2002.
97. **James Sibanda** (MDC) Nkayi. Feb 2002
98. **Newman Bhebe** (MDC) Nkayi. Feb 2002
99. **Tichaona Katsamudanga.** (MDC). 4th Feb 2002.
100. **Shepherd Ngundu** (MDC) Mount Darwin. 5th Feb 2002
101. **Khape Khumalo** (MDC) Mhondoro. 6th Feb 2002.
102. **Henry Moyo** (MDC) Masvingo. 7th Feb 2002
103. **Munyaradzi** (Surname unknown) Marondera East. 14th Feb 2002
104. **Tubadamo Mukakarei** (MDC) Masvingo. 14th Feb 2002
105. **Takatukwa Mupawaenda** Zvimba South. 16th Feb 2002
106. **Takesure Nhitsa** (MDC) Rushinga. 20th Feb 2002
107. **Unnamed Makokoba.** Bulawayo. 26th Feb 2002
108. **Lawrence Kuvheya** (MDC) Chikomba. Mar 2002
109. **Edwin Romio** (MDC Polling agent) Mutoko. Mar 2002
110. **Nqobizita Dube** (MDC) Nkulumane Bulawayo. 1st Mar 2002
111. **Charles Sibanda** (MDC) Zhombe. 2nd Mar 2002
112. **Peter Jeftha** Harare South. 3rd Mar 2002
113. **Noah Gwidzima** (ZANU (PF)) Makoni North. 4th Mar 2002
114. **Tafirenyika Gwaze** (MDC Polling Agent) Mutoko. 12th Mar 2002
115. **Funny Mahuni** Kwekwe. 13th Mar 2002
116. **Darlington Vikaveka** (MDC) Marondera East. 15th Mar 2002
117. **Unnamed** (MDC) Chipinge. 16th Mar 2002
118. **Unnamed** (MDC) Chipinge. 16th Mar 2002
119. **Unnamed** (MDC) Chipinge. 16th Mar 2002
120. **Sambani Ncube** (MDC) Hwange. 17th Mar

10 BCK TO ZIMBABWE AFTER 9 YEARS, DECEMBER 2011

Introduction:

I left Zimbabwe on July 31 2002 and ever since I have been in Europe, occasionally travelling to other countries to give lectures on the Zimbabwe situation. During my 9 year absence from Zimbabwe, many things have happened. The economy has been plunged into a deep dark hole, spiralling out of control forcing the government to print a trillion dollar note yet not enough to buy a loaf of bread. The politics have become bloody and entrenched, for a while it seemed nothing will come out of Zimbabwe.

Watching from the terraces is not my philosophical attitude to issues of concern. I have a history of confronting authority or perhaps perceived to be positively confrontational. Yet this time I was caught over 10 thousand miles away from home political activities not that I wasn't politically participating but in Africa there is different between public domain and community domain. Public domain is good for audit trail but it's the community spirit that makes a difference, brushing shoulders with your community leaders, sweating it out in the spiralling dust of barren Africa. Being away from such traditional blending meant that each time a political incident happened I have to bite my fingers hard, sometimes causing self inflicting blisters.

At a point a man has to take a decision, I have been campaigning world over for peace, democracy and freedom of expression in my country Zimbabwe. I decided I was going back to Zimbabwe against all odds. The probability of me being arrested for drummed up charges or worse still being murdered was a reality rather than a risk. My parents have always been abducted in every election and tortured for merely being parents of a Movement for Democratic Change (MDC) leading activist, my brothers have been maimed and tortured and worse still my elder brother Matthew was murdered. Yet finally when the call came to serve my country I made a decision to go back home against all odds.

Preparations:

While I have been planning for the possible trip for a while, it was only on the 29 October 2011 that I finally made a decision. The decision was not whether to go but when? Both these decisions were done on the same day. To many people this sound weird but having been a Zimbabwean politician, decisions of death and life have to be made swiftly and sometimes brutally in the eyes of family members. Were my family aware of my decision? No. Were the party structures aware? No. Was the top leadership of MDC including the Prime Minister aware? Yes. Was there safety concession? No. Was I likely to be murdered? Yes. Were there any contingencies put in place to avoid that? I decline to comment.

I only told my family a week after purchasing the ticket, many were concerned but that's not new, hence the reason not to involve them in the final decision in the first place. There were probably founded reasons for fearing for my life;

1. I had written a book, "Zimbabwe my home my frustration: Articles of defiance", I had sent 5 copies of my book a month in advance via Amazon, but a day before my departure, the books have not arrived, that's a cool one and half months later. The book's theme is a reflection of Zimbabwe's political and economic woes, the brutality of Mugabe's regime unmasked and an audit of horrendous human rights abuse, including systematic murders and rape by government agencies is clearly documented.
2. I was a plaintiff in a Mugabe law suit in USA Federal courts for human rights abuse. The case made headlines from October 2000 to 2006.
3. I was one of the founding members of the MDC, the main opposition party in Zimbabwe and contested as MP against one of the brutal architecture of ZANU (PF) militia violence in Zimbabwe Border Gezi.

4. I have been giving international lectures on Zimbabwe and the regime brutality.

Perhaps the most fear came from my company where I work, a few months before I had sold 17 signed copies of my books to colleagues that included management and directors. Their fear was real and I remember my line manager invited me for a drink to discuss the issue. He expresses his concern about my safety if I was to go back to Zimbabwe against the background of instability then. He sought assurance that I was going to be safe, unfortunately in Africa let alone in Zimbabwe, such assurance is none existent. Looking into his pale face pensively, I told him that I was prepared for any eventuality and that I was prepared both in soul and in the body to be with my people, whatever the risks involved.

He gulped another mouthful of local lager, with fallows on his face of mixed feeling. "So you have up your mind to die, is it?" He exclaimed. People who die for a cause don't like death nor do they choose to die, but through conviction they are sentenced to death against their will. Their heroic acts only will be realised once they depart from this earth, having saved millions of people against murderous dictators. It proved to be a chilling revelation, even I was surprised with how I seemed daring to die for a country of 12 million people so that they may live in peace and prosperity, but there was no guarantee that my death would immediately bring peace and tranquillity. Yes, it has to be done, inwardly I was convinced. My hand still holding a pint of Fosters lager was sweating as if it has succumbed to fear, but never the less I couldn't explain why.

On bound Flight, December 7, 2011
06:35, 7th of December 2011, departed at the Heathrow Airport aboard a KLM flight via Amsterdam to Harare. The flight KL1000 was on time and we all boarders the plane off to Amsterdam. London to Amsterdam journey was very short; I had a copy of my book in one hand and a glass of wine in another as if I had already started to celebrate my death.

The KLM connecting flight to Nairobi was very efficient; we didn't have to wait long before it took off. This was an Airbus KL565. Looking at the screen flight information, for the first time the direction made sense, I was bound for Zimbabwe. I was scheduled to arrive at Harare Airport at 01:25 AM on Wednesday the 8th December 2011. I sat near a lady from Canada with a baby, bound for Nairobi on holiday. Instinctively we started talking about how far the journey was, the speed of the plane and finally about Africa. I showed her my book about Zimbabwe, she glanced at the topic, "Zimbabwe my home my frustration: Articles of defiance", she wanted to know more about the contents of the book and after explaining to her my historical background that led to writing the book, she was shocked. The next question did not come as a surprise, "so you are going there now"? Yes I answered. "Is it safe for you?", I explained that safety was a relative word in Zimbabwe, there was nothing called safety assurance in Zimbabwean context, you simply watch your back 24/7. The journey was long and suddenly the anxiety of what to expect in Zimbabwe after 9 years of absence. I knew my parents were still alive as I have talked to them the previous day and so were some of my siblings.

We arrived at Nairobi Airport around 20:40 PM, making my way to the waiting area for a Zimbabwe bound plane; I could smell Africa, that aroma scent of humanity. Africa is the mother of all mankind, so this feeling wasn't misplaced either. Suddenly faces became familiar, that's my people I surged. At the gate, were many passengers going to Harare and Lusaka as the Kenyan Airways was going to Harare via Lusaka. I learned later that all planes going to Harare go via Lusaka for fuelling; they could not take chances because of economic meltdown which at one point forced the country to run dry, no food, no water and worse still no fuel. As I sat down I came face to face with Africa, a continent still laid back in processes. Suddenly somebody appeared from a "staff only" corridor and everybody heaved towards him as if he held the keys to heaven, at first I had no idea why. People were anxious to know when will be the next plane to Zimbabwe. I looked at my ticket, Nairobi to Harare 21:50, I got confused because to me I was convinced that these people should have schedules at hand. I asked one male passenger who was also going to Zimbabwe as to how long he had been waiting, "since 6 AM" he answered, that's more than 14 hours ago, I asked "yes" he answered. Everybody was grumbling and emotions were running high as this official had no idea when the plane to Harare will be available. That was shocking!!

Suddenly all attention shifted to this man, who was drinking from a 750 ml Jack Daniels (JD) strong stuff. He was shouting accusing the Mugabe government of mismanaging the economy to the extent of forcing the Air Zimbabwe broke. He kept on shouting even though the wife tried to silence him, warning him of the consequence at the airport if he continued with attacking the government. The man cared less to the amusement of us all. He talked about liberation struggle aims and objectives and how all has been hijacked by corrupt politicians. Each time he swallowed a mouthful of the bitter stuff, it would be followed by a venomous attack on Mugabe; this is my friend inwardly I exclaimed. Air Zimbabwe then was stranded in London after failing to pay landing fees, the creditors had impounded it. The airline was broken, another one was impounded in South Africa for none payment of services, it had become unreliable and unviable. The Mugabe regime had driven the once prosperous country into one of the poorest. Air Zimbabwe was one of the best run airline before Mugabe government trashed it, it had a slogan, "Air Zimbabwe, a tradition of caring", indeed it was all you needed from a first class airline. Every Zimbabwean had the right to be bitter about it, now we had to beg other airlines in endless connections.

Finally at 22:30, we had a flight to Harare via Lusaka. In Lusaka it was a short in-stay for fuel and off we went Harare.

Zimbabwe Airport arrival:

I arrived at the Harare International airport at about 03:30 local time in the morning. I had been in touch with my relatives who were going to welcome me so I knew they were waiting and so were my MDC supporters. As I walked towards immigration I smiled broadly, welcome home Elliot, I applauded myself. I knew anything could have happened but I cared less, I couldn't wait to breathe Zimbabwean fresh air again. I wasn't sure whether after 9 years I was going to recognize my relatives and my supporters, 9 years it's a long time away from home. The reality was unfolding, I was home at last.

I passed the immigration without a hitch, one down I exclaimed, the next was at the bagging and customs exit area. I managed to get one baggage and missed one. What could have happened to it, could it be that security officers had confiscated it, for what I asked myself, there was nothing of any security concerns I noted. This is Zimbabwe I reminded myself and patiently I waited, everybody was gone except myself and another lady holding also one baggage and missing one. Suddenly those who were waiting for me became restless, being a politician and having been in trouble before their fears were justified. There was a commotion as they demanded my where about, eventually a security officer came to look for me and passed over the news about the tempers flaring outside. I told her that I was safe and let her tell them that nothing will happen to me in my country but that I was waiting for my suitcase. Eventually I realised the suitcase that the other woman was holding was actually mine, with my name tag. What this meant was that she lost all her 2 suitcases; I began walking towards the customs. They were polite and helpful and within a short time I was out to unite with my dear relatives, friends and supporters.

There were only traces of resemblance to what I left of them, a new generation has come and gone.

A tour of Harare and Chitungwiza:

I stayed in Chitungwiza, the nearest town from Harare of about a million people for the night with my cousin. I had lost the directions and worse still the previous day I travelled when it was still pitch black, tower lights don't operate anymore so the roads are dangerously dark. Early in the morning the sun was already scorching hot, the terrain had changed the houses and so were the town landmarks. I got a car for the entire duration courtesy of my cousin and started a tour of the city to familiarise myself with my lost bearings. The boys I left have now grown into men and the small girls were now mothers, how crazy human race evolve very fast.

I drove to Harare about 30 km away, the roads looked long forgotten with pot holes and over growth competing for a space with cars. This was one of the major road, well constructed by Gulliver but now left derelict due years of failing maintenance. I drove zigzagging along the way obviously showing armature tendencies. The trees along the roads all have been cut by the new settlers, the once sprawling farming land has now been reduced to the huts of pole and daga with cattle overgrazing and unattended. It was like a dream yet real; I have read so much about the destruction but never came near to it that far. I made sure that I stopped along the way to take a glimpse of the view.

It wasn't far when we arrived at a road block. I have heard of how the police had become corrupt, I wondered how they would react if I gave them a British Driving Licence. I have been warned that all hell will come loose, then you have to bribe yourself out of the situation, I was not going to advance corruption I assured myself that is exactly what I have been fighting for my entire life. Suddenly we were waved down, looked at me and waved for us to continue, the first hurdle was over.

The changing Political Landscape of Zimbabwe:

I arrived at MDC HQ, I knew most of the staff was new after the NGU as many of the original MDC workers joined the government of national unity. The moment I arrived I was spotted by one MDC employee who remembered me well and soon the word spread that I had arrived. The front entrance was awash with people to have a glimpse of me and just have a talk. I was then asked to get into the MDC ground floor shop as the number of people grouping would invite the riot police who are known to be brutal to MDC party activists. I had my book in hand and it changed hands very fast and each time with a nod of approval, I was in a comfort zone, I never thought that I still commanded so much political support. It was an overwhelming welcome for a person who had been away for so long. These people were very young when I have left, now they have grown big and powerful yet they still had an important place in their hearts for the cause that I have been fighting.

The Harvest House which houses the MDC Executive including the President Morgan Tsvangirai and the Secretary General Tendai Biti has not escaped the denudation that came with the economic meltdown. You could tell that the party was trying hard to restore it to its original glory but this was still far off the mark. It had survived battering tear gas and battering from the government's overzealous security agencies. I then was taken inside the building being introduced by Tapera Macheka, Director of protocol in the President's office. I spent the entire working day very much engaged; I didn't even feel hungry until later on that day. Suddenly I have regained my political glory, the news was everywhere that I was in town.

Later that day it was time to socialize and mingle, what better way than to go Mereki, in one of the suburbs, Warren Park D. This is a massive barbeque market where almost the entire class of people meets. They talk, eat and drink with less care for the outside world. Apart from the locals who frequently patronize the place, they were Chinese and whites of European origin. They all mixed and enjoyed BBQ under tropical weather. With my personal guides we joined in and made good use of the time and place. The last time I had had a similar event was in 2001 after escaping an ambush by Mugabe's militia at Chiveso village in my constituency Bindura. Scores of my supporters were injured, some later died of their injuries and some were arrested for surviving the attack. Scores of cars were damaged and burnt, I was with Morgan Tsvangirai the MDC President and now the Prime Minster of GNU. Those flash memories almost messed up my appetite, nevertheless I dived into the succulent organic beef roast, for the first time in 9 years. It was mouth watering and it went very well with a traditional brew.

A few days that followed I was to be politically engaged but I chose to first visit my elderly parents about 200 km from Harare in MT Darwin. I stopped in Bindura my former constituency, had a meeting with the structures and had a tour of the town. This is where my political career started and history was repeating itself again, Bindura here I come. I had an overwhelming welcome, it was bewildering and humbling. One after another they spoke of how I pioneered the party in the province and how I inspired them. I didn't know that I still inspired many people to fight for their rights. It was like flipping pages of misery as they narrated those who were murdered by the Mugabe regime and those who succumbed to injuries. Suddenly I felt a cocktail of anger and bravado, if there was a time that I needed my people, this was the time. "No don't go, we need you here, we want you to be our MP. You are the lion of the region". For a time I looked at Tonga Jack the District chairman, whom I served in 2000, when he had his tummy slit by ZANU (PF) militia. I had to rush him to Hospital holding the severed stomach, he survived, now he was there, reminding me of that incident. He was now as strong as an ox but still in the trenches, I smiled and nodded. The book's theme was set on Bindura and I am not going to repeat what it feels like to be a resident of Bindura and a politician of the opposition, both means death.

Nyakatondo Village, connecting with my roots:

Back in MT Darwin, after bumps and swerving, we finally reached our rural home. The roads looked as if they never existed before, each meander was like begging for attention yet nobody cared. The government which ran out of money 3 years ago, when the wheels of the economy came off, didn't care. The last time they tried to fix the economy in 2008, they printed a $100 billion note and then a $1 trillion note before giving up completely, forcing a GNU.

I had a massive welcome from the village; I have never seen so many people at our home before except when there was a rally. The women ululated, old and young, the old limping with walking sticks to have a glimpse of me. I had countless hugs. In the midst of these good times I noticed my mother with scars and stooping yet she defied it all and smiled broadly. I asked her whether everything was ok and I was told that since she was abducted in 2008 by Mugabe's militia and tortured, she had not fully recovered. Equally so was my father, struggling to walk, had it gone so badly I exclaimed. How can a government do that to old people like them, they are harmless and all they need was to enjoy the few years left of them. It was painfully unbelievable, I felt like declaring a war, to such barbaric acts. Mugabe has to be stopped at all cost, his human rights abuse has gone too far. I remembered their abduction incident vividly as it was widely reported in both local and international press. Amnesty International had to intervene.

Later on the reality of the brutality became clear as more and more cases were put to my attention. Some women claim that they were raped by mobs of militia in front of cheering crowds and some had contracted the deadly AIDS in the process. People are raped in the name of the government, worse still the perpetrators are known and reports were made to the police yet the police didn't make any arrests instead declaring the incidents political. Reading on the internet is one thing, having face to face with victims brings inner emotions. The reality was striking.

I had 2 days at the village, revisiting my old memories. The faces had transformed, a new generation had come and yet Mugabe was still the president. So many people had died, either due to avoidable illness, lack of health facilities or murdered by the regime. A visit to my local shop showed the extent of the state of the economy, it looked derelict yet still operating. I enjoyed the comfort of my people, it was feasting every day and merry making. I travelled widely, each time moving with an army of party supporters both for my protection and a show of support. I was to come back for Christmas, meanwhile I had to go to Harare the capital city to continue my political engagements.

Prime Minister Morgan Tsvangirai Invites:

Back to Harare I received an invite from the Prime Minister to attend his book launch ceremony at the Book Café in Harare. Here I met a diplomatic community, cabinet ministers and MPs. Here was a chance to engage with these high ranking officials whom I had met or talked to more than 9 years ago. I was shocked that many of them remembered me very well, including the Prime Minister of course who had met me several times outside the country. An inaugural speech by Nelson Chamisa the minister of Information Technology was captivating, then a speech by the Prime Minister Morgan Tsvangirai caped it up in his book "At the deep end".

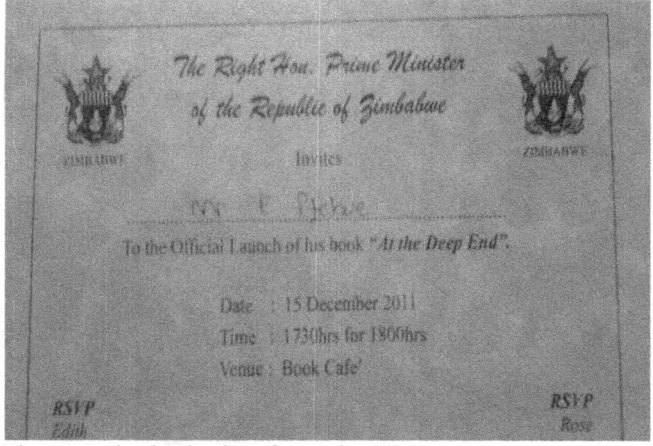

Figure 1: An invitation from the PM

Then it was time to drink and socialise. I met a lot of my friends who were now Cabinet Ministers that included Gift Chimanikire now deputy minister of Mines; Pauline Mpariwa, Labour and social welfare; Lucia Mativenga, Public service, Tapiwa Mashakada, Economic Planning; Tendai Biti, Minister of Finance among others. I had the chance to chat to the whole MDC cabinet and many more. It was a worthwhile trip to Zimbabwe, good timing I thought.

MDC Award:

I was contacted by the Organizing department that I had an award waiting at the office, I had no idea what the award was. I went to Harvest House, where I was presented with an award signed by President of the party who is also the Prime Minister of Zimbabwe. It's humbling, it conferred on me the status of the founder and pioneer of MDC political leadership, and this was kept secret during my entire journey. Surprises are sweet but when they exceed a surprise they are jaw breakers, it was just that. See the certificate below;

Figure 2: An MDC awarded to me on the 16th of December dated the 15th of December 2011

I was to be invited to yet another occasion, this time it was the Prime Minister's Christmas party held at the Old Hararians in Milton Park. This was a party of all parties to thank the PM's staff for a hard working year. The Holiday Inn Hotel was providing food and refreshments. Music was by the popular local musician, Suluman Chimbetu. For a moment I thought what a befitting party, this was an office that had turned the fortunes of Zimbabweans around since the GNU. At the time he took over as PM, the economy had collapsed with inflation over 1000% and now the inflation had come down to a single digit due to the introduction of the US dollar as the legal tender. Thanks to Tendai Biti, the Minister of Finance whose intervention served Zimbabweans from starvation.

Figure 3: The worthless Zimbabwe currency, a legal tender note of ZW$20 billion.

I saw a Zimbabwe, of my dream, people were happy all in harmony. One might have been easily mistaken that Zimbabwe is a peaceful and democratic state but wait a moment, it was because ZANU (PF) wasn't there. This was an MDC entirely party, it only reinforced that MDC if given the chance would restore Zimbabwe to its lost glory.

My stay was swift and enjoyable, I could have wanted to stay longer but I have to leave since I had work to be done back in the UK.

Despite multitudes of challenges Zimbabwe has made a remarkable improvement in the area of mobile technology as the penetration has shocked even the government its self, coverage in rural areas is wide and clear. Now with the state of the art communication before the elections, Mugabe will find it difficult this time to cheat and murder people as they always had done in the past. People will simply alert each other and take corrective action.

London bound again, I will be back!!!.

11 References:

1. ABC Evening News, Headlines, Rhodesia Protected Villages, 1 June 1976

2. BBC News, Commonwealth criticises Zimbabwe, 2 May 2000, Online, http://news.bbc.co.uk/1/hi/world/africa/733863.stm

3. The Daily News, Pfebve alleges CIO broke into his Office, 5 September 2001.

4. The Daily News, Judge orders release of three MDC supporters, Wednesday 10 October 2001.

5. The Financial Gazette, Executive profile: Computer Africa MD, Elliot Pfebve, 9 July 1998.

6. The Financial Gazette, But Bwana, how far is Bindura from Harare?, Masipula Sithole's Public Eye, 26 July 2001

7. The Financial Gazette, ZANU(PF) hails win, MDC says loss no big deal, 2 August 2001.

8. Newsweek, Africa; Taking on the Big Man, In New York five Zimbabweans sue Mugabe for millions. Win or lose, they have sent a strong message, 11 December 2000.

12 INDEX

www.ingramcontent.com/pod-product-compliance
Lightning Source LLC
Chambersburg PA
CBHW062131280526
45788CB00001B/126